T0330593

Routledge Revivals

THE FACTORY SYSTEM ILLUSTRATED

THE FACTORY SYSTEM ILLUSTRATED

IN A SERIES OF LETTERS
TO
THE RIGHT HON. LORD ASHLEY

BY
WILLIAM DODD

TOGETHER WITH
A NARRATIVE OF THE
EXPERIENCE AND SUFFERINGS OF WILLIAM DODD
A FACTORY CRIPPLE, WRITTEN BY HIMSELF

A NEW EDITION
WITH AN INTRODUCTION BY
W. H. CHALONER

First published in 1842 by Frank Cass and Company Limited

This edition first published in 2018 by Routledge
2 Park Square, Milton Park, Abingdon, Oxon, OX14 4RN
and by Routledge
52 Vanderbilt Avenue, New York, NY 10017, USA

Routledge is an imprint of the Taylor & Francis Group, an informa business

© 1842 by Taylor and Francis

All rights reserved. No part of this book may be reprinted or reproduced or utilised in any form or by any electronic, mechanical, or other means, now known or hereafter invented, including photocopying and recording, or in any information storage or retrieval system, without permission in writing from the publishers.

Publisher's Note
The publisher has gone to great lengths to ensure the quality of this reprint but points out that some imperfections in the original copies may be apparent.

Disclaimer
The publisher has made every effort to trace copyright holders and welcomes correspondence from those they have been unable to contact.
A Library of Congress record exists under ISBN: 80008958

ISBN 13: 978-0-367-17784-3 (hbk)
ISBN 13: 978-0-429-05770-0 (ebk)

THE FACTORY SYSTEM
ILLUSTRATED

TOGETHER WITH

A NARRATIVE OF THE EXPERIENCE AND SUFFERINGS OF WILLIAM DODD

THE FACTORY SYSTEM ILLUSTRATED

IN A SERIES OF LETTERS

TO

THE RIGHT HON. LORD ASHLEY

BY

WILLIAM DODD

TOGETHER WITH

A NARRATIVE OF THE
EXPERIENCE AND SUFFERINGS OF WILLIAM DODD
A FACTORY CRIPPLE, WRITTEN BY HIMSELF

A NEW EDITION

WITH AN INTRODUCTION BY
W. H. CHALONER

REPRINTS OF ECONOMIC CLASSICS

Augustus M. Kelley, Bookseller
New York, 1968

Published by

FRANK CASS AND COMPANY LIMITED

67 Great Russell Street, London WC1

New introduction © 1967

Published in the U.S.A. by A. M. Kelley,
24 East 22nd Street, New York, U.S.A.

The Factory System Illustrated

First edition	1842
Second edition	1842
New edition	1968

A Narrative of the Experience and Sufferings

First edition	1841
Second edition	1841
New edition	1968

Library of Congress Catalog Card No. 67–28260

Printed in Great Britain

Introduction to the New Edition
by
W. H. Chaloner

Edwin Hodder, Shaftesbury's official biographer, stated that his subject was "very rarely deceived in those whom he selected to be his helpers".* Unfortunately this statement is immediately followed in Hodder's narrative by an account of William Dodd, who in 1841 had published a 46-page pamphlet entitled *A Narrative of the Experience and Sufferings of William Dodd, a factory cripple, written by himself*, which later in that year went into a second edition. According to his own account Dodd was born on 18th June 1804, and from at least 1819 up to the early part of 1837 was employed, latterly as a warehouseman and packer, by Isaac and William Wilson, Quaker woollen manufacturers in the ancient Lake District textile centre of Kendal.† It is interesting to note that Dodd appears never to have been employed in the cotton industry. Lord Ashley (he succeeded to the earldom of Shaftesbury only in 1851) took up Dodd, and in his diary for 3rd December 1841 wrote "My poor cripple Dodd is a jewel, his talent and skill are

---

* *The Life and Work of the seventh Earl of Shaftesbury*, vol. I, 1886, p. 383.

† Wm. Parsons and Wm. White, *Directory and Gazetteer of the Counties of Cumberland and Westmorland*, 1829, p. 665. The Wilsons' factory was in Stramongate, Kendal.

unequalled; he sends me invaluable evidence".*
Dodd's letters to him "infuse[d] both information and
terror."†

Encouraged by this exalted patronage Dodd went
on a tour of the factory districts of the North and
Midlands, sending frequent letters to Ashley en route.
These were published in 1842 as *The Factory System
Illustrated: in a series of Letters to the Rt. Hon. Lord
Ashley, M.P.*(264 pp.), which soon went into a second
edition.

These publications and the controversies to which
they gave rise illustrate clearly the danger of accept-
ing at face value statements made in the course of the
bitter social and economic agitations which enlivened
the 1830's and 1840's. Little or nothing is known of
Dodd, apart from the information he himself gave in
his publications, and statements made in the House
of Commons by John Bright and Lord Ashley in the
debate of 15th March 1844 on the Hours of Labour in
Factories Bill.‡ In this debate Bright attacked not
Ashley's good faith, but his lack of wisdom in the
choice of informants on factory conditions:

'I do not charge the noble Lord with being
actuated by feelings of malice in his conduct
towards the manufacturers of this country, but I
do believe him to have been, and to be now, grossly
imposed upon by the persons upon whose information he relies. I can tell the noble Lord that he will
never obtain credit for the statements he makes;

---

* *Ibid.*, p. 384.
† *Ibid.*, p. 384 (23rd December 1841).
‡ *Hansard's Parliamentary Debates*, 3rd series, vol. 73, 1844,
cols. 1149–58. Hodder's account of this debate is a severely trun-
cated and dishonest one, *op. cit.*, vol. II, 1888, pp. 27–29.

unless he can obtain them from more honest characters than those he has hitherto employed. I know that one of these individuals has published many statements respecting the manufactories of the north, some of which are wholly false, and most of which, I believe, are grossly and malignantly exaggerated. I have in my hand two of these publications; one is "The Adventures of William Dodd the Factory Cripple" and the other is entitled "The Factory System", and consists of letters addressed to the noble Lord,—both books have gone forth to the public under the sanction of the noble Lord. I do not wish to go into the particulars of the character of this man, for it is not necessary to my case, but I can demonstrate, that his books and statements are wholly unworthy of credit. Dodd states that from the hardships he endured in a factory, he was "done up" at the age of thirty-two, whereas I can prove that he was treated with uniform kindness, which he repaid by gross immorality of conduct, and for which he was at length discharged from his employment. I have in my possession letters written by this individual, in which he states that the noble Lord and his party had used him as long as they could get any thing out of him. He said also, that the noble Lord had given him dinners at his own house, and that when he applied for a small balance due to him, the noble Lord had written him an angry letter, recounting the dinners he had eaten at his table. He had also stated that the noble Lord had shown him to his visitors as a cripple, as a specimen of what the factories were doing for the population employed in them. I do not wish to dwell upon this point, but I am free to tell the noble Lord, that unless he employs agents more respectable his statements and his professions of benevolence will ever be viewed with suspicion by the manufacturers of the north and I may add, that others who are thus employed, are in no degree more respectable or more creditable than Dodd.'*

Ashley was naturally upset by Bright's strictures,† but the Quaker pressed the attack home:

'I tell the noble Lord quite plainly, that I have letters in my hand, which will prove all that I have stated. I will hand them to the noble Lord with pleasure. I will go further, and tell the noble Lord, that the individual who wrote the letters I hold in my hand, offered, for a sum of money [£35], to sell a friend of mine a large number of other letters, which that friend of mine was, as I think, too fastidious to lay hold of. I tell the noble Lord not to trust these men. I have always thought that the noble Lord was honest in his convictions. I have always said so, both in public and in private; but I repeat that the instruments that he has worked with are not worthy of him or his cause.'‡

The letters referred to were addressed by Dodd to the master cotton spinners Edmund and Henry Ashworth of Turton, by Bolton, Lancs.,§ and the following extracts were printed in the columns of *Hansard*:

---

* *Ibid.*, cols. 1149–50.

† *Ibid.*, cols. 1151–52.

‡ *Ibid.*, cols. 1152–53.

§ For the Ashworth brothers, see the *Dictionary of National Biography*, W. Cooke Taylor, *Notes of a Tour in the Manufacturing Districts of Lancashire*, 2nd ed. (1842), A. W. Silver, *Manchester Men and Indian Cotton*, 1847–1872 (1966), pp. 18–19.

William Dodd to Messrs. H. and E. Ashworth of Turton, by Bolton, September 26, 1842:

'You are, Gentlemen, from personal observation, acquainted with my unhappy situation, you are also, I have no doubt, aware that my case has been laid hold of by Lord Ashley and his party in furtherance of their views and objects; that I have been held up to public view by these phil-anthropists(?) as an object of charity, and as an instance of the cruelty of the manufacturers, and you will be surprised when I say that after all this fuss, I have been extremely ill-used by them. I have no blame to attach to Lord Ashley, except being misled, and induced to act contrary to his promises, by a man of the name of Benjamin Jowett, the man of all work for the ten hours' Bill party, and he is also the author of a pamphlet called "The Conspiracy", in which work your name and that of Mr. Greg of Ashton, is prominently set forth. This man Jowett is not the friend of the working classes, and he deserves to be shewn in his true colours.* He has injured me to a great extent. I should most willingly undertake to show the factory operatives and the public, that he and his party are not to be relied on; and was I to state the facts I am in possession of, it would, in my opinion, disperse the junta of which he is the organ; but this exposure

---

* Benjamin Jowett (1788–1859), father of the Oxford scholar. Jowett senior, an Evangelical furrier of Bermondsey, later became a printer in Bolt Court, Fleet Street, London, and was employed by Lord Ashley to collect statistics in the cause of factory reform. (E. Abbott and L. Campbell, *Life and Letters of Benjamin Jowett, M.A.*, vol. I, 1897, pp. 12–17; J. T. Ward, *The Factory Movement*, 1830–1855, 1962, p. 167 and passim.).

would destroy my present source of living, and my
future prospects, by setting all my friends against
me, and without I was protected by some other
parties, it would involve me in inevitable ruin."

*William Dodd to Messrs. H. and E. Ashworth of
Turton by Bolton, October 1, 1842:*

"The manner in which I was taken hold of to
serve party purposes, the work I have been
employed upon, the insignificant wages I have
received, the hopes and expectations which have
been held out to me, and now (when they have got
all out of me they can) the manner in which I have
been cast off, even by Lord Ashley himself, without
assigning any reason, and refusing to listen to my
claims, all this would form a pamphlet as large as
that of Jowett's, which I enclose.

I could then expose this Jowett, who has taken
so much pains, as you will see by the inclosed
pamphlet, to cast a stigma on your firm and others.
In order that you may know what sort of a man
this is, I will tell you the orders I received from him
previous to visiting your place last year. 'You
must go to Turton and get all the information you
can concerning the works of Messrs. Ashworth,
they are show mills. The Ashworths are deep,
cunning fellows, and you must take particular care
not to come in contact with them, or their people.'
Thus you see, I was to stroll about in the immediate
vicinity of your mills, and get in the company of
any stray person I might see, and by treating them
with beer or by any other means, get all the
information I required—if the person was one that
you had cast off, so much the better.

"My name having acquired a notoriety in consequence of the manner in which my case had been held up to the public, I have had an offer to write articles on the Factory System, for a low weekly paper; I have already wrote one as a trial, but it is much against my feelings, only it supplies me with a dinner when, otherwise, I might probably be obliged to go without.

William Dodd to Messrs. H. and E. Ashworth of Turton by Bolton, November 2, 1842:

"You will perhaps be surprised to hear, that in my necessity, I wrote to Lord Ashley, stating my circumstances, and requesting the remittance of a small balance due to me for services rendered, and received a very angry letter, saying that I had 'no claim upon them', that my employment was 'a mere matter of charity', that I had received so much money, and even recounted the dinners I had received at his lordship's table, and told me the condition I was in at the time he took notice of me, and other matters equally galling. It is very clear that the party has all along considered me only as a tool, and that having made all the use they can of me, I may now go about my business. I am sorry that I am not in a situation in life as would enable me to speak my mind freely; was I in a good business and entirely independent of the party, I could "a tale unfold", but this, circumstanced as I now am, would be my ruin.

Ashley gave the following account of his connection with Dodd:

"It is perfectly true that I was acquainted with

Dodd, and it is perfectly true also that he called on
me in London. I received a letter from him in
which he stated that he had been injured while
working in a factory. He afterwards called on me,
and certainly I never saw a more wretched object.
He had lost his hand, and I may say had almost
lost his shape. He hardly looked indeed like a
human being. I certainly assisted him, and as far
as refreshments went he had them, not with me, but
I told him that if he chose to come when the
servants dined he might have some dinner with
them. He afterwards went down into the manufacturing districts, and from there he wrote me
some letters; but I assure the hon. Gentleman that
I never except once quoted a single fact from any
one of his communications. Certain facts regarding
him have since come to my knowledge, and I am
certainly inclined now to think that he was
unworthy [of] my kindness.*

For Bright's attitude to factory reform and the
welfare of the workers employed by his firm, the
student should consult J. T. Mills, *John Bright and
the Quakers* (1935) vol. II, pp. 171–99, which forms a
useful corrective to the distortions and wild allega-
tions of Oastler, Ferrand, etc., and later writers. The
William Dodd case and the debate of March 15th
1844 are mentioned on page 178. Mills comments:
"Lord Shaftesbury's biographer, Mr. Bready
[*Lord Shaftesbury and Social-Industrial Progress*,
1926], and his statement is echoed by Mr. and Mrs.
Hammond [*Lord Shaftesbury*, Pelican ed. 1939],
asserts that the sense of the House compelled

---

* *Ibid.*, cols. 1154–55.

Bright to an apology. There does not appear to be any reliable evidence for this statement—certainly not in *Hansard*. That the country gentlemen were vociferous in support of their champion is no doubt true, but it is equally true that an apology was not forthcoming, and in Bright's opinion was not demanded: 'I had a row on Friday night with Lord Ashley', wrote Bright to McLaren. 'I got the better of him by universal admission of the House.' This impression is confirmed by Cobden, who writes with reference to Bright's onslaught upon Ashley: 'It was a perilous effort but our friend came off well.'

Little further is at present known about Dodd. In the opinion of one who is at present engaged on a study of the Ashworths and their firm, Ashley came out badly from the whole affair and also from his extended interviews with Henry Ashworth when visiting Turton in October 1844.*

Dodd appears to have emigrated to the U.S.A. about 1843, and there in 1847 he published at Boston a pseudonymous work, by "an Englishman", entitled *The Laboring Classes of England, especially those engaged in agriculture and manufactures*, to which was appended a poem by Caroline E. S. Norton, 'A Voice from the Factories'. In this book Dodd revealed that Ashley had paid him 45*s.* a week and coach hire while on tour visiting the manufacturing districts, and 20*s.* a week while resident in London.

April 1967   W.H.C.

---

* For Ashley's Northern progress of 1844, see Hodder, *op. cit.*, vol. II, pp. 71–75. I am indebted for this information to Mr. Rhodes Boyson of London.

THE

FACTORY SYSTEM

ILLUSTRATED;

IN A SERIES OF LETTERS

TO

THE RIGHT HON. LORD ASHLEY,

M.P., ETC. ETC.

BY WILLIAM DODD,

A FACTORY CRIPPLE.

"Thou shalt not oppress an hired servant that is poor and needy, whether he be of thy brethren, or of the strangers that are in thy land, within thy gates."—DEUT. XXIV., 14.

LONDON:

JOHN MURRAY, ALBEMARLE STREET.

1842.

PREFACE.

MANY defects will doubtless be found in this volume by the intelligent reader, both as regards the matter, and also the general arrangement of the subject; but when it is considered under what great disadvantages I have written—having had no other education but what I was able to acquire after my day's work in the factories was done—I humbly hope that my little Work will not be looked upon with too severe an eye.

My situation has been, in many respects, peculiar. Five and twenty years of my short life I have spent as an operative in the Factories. I am not aware that any one else who has published upon the Factory System can make a similar assertion. But I have

not only toiled, but have been a sufferer from protracted mill-labour to a painful extent.   I am not
only a decided cripple, but I have had to submit to
amputation four inches below the elbow of my right
arm, in consequence, not of accident — but of disease
of the bone, brought on entirely by unremitting and
exhausting labour.   My experience, therefore, of the
Factory System has been dear-bought experience.   I
can speak feelingly.   I have, at the same time, endeavoured to speak temperately, and to avoid, to the
uttermost, every unguarded expression; every expression which it would not become an humble operative
like myself to use; and I can add with truth, that
I am not conscious of one unkindly or resentful feeling towards any human being.

It is possible that some of the statements which
I have felt it my duty to make in this volume, may
be deemed too highly coloured; it may be thought
that they are in a greater or less degree exaggerated.
I can only say, that I shall not hesitate (if required)
to call upon any individual or party whatever, and
give such further explanations as may be in my

power; for I shall deem it to be my duty to satisfy every such querist as to the truth of my statements.

In addition to the experience I have had in factories, I made a Tour through the West Riding of Yorkshire, Lancashire, Cheshire, and Derbyshire, in the latter part of the year 1841, and had then ample opportunities of seeing and conversing with all classes likely to afford me any information on the subject of factory life; particularly clergymen, and dissenting ministers of various denominations, manufacturers, surgeons, inspectors, overlookers, workmen, &c. &c. I had also opportunities of studying the habits and manners of the working classes, in their factories, cottages, places of amusement, public-houses, and other haunts; and also of investigating the various causes of decrepitude, mutilation, or death—whether arising from long hours of labour, or accidents by machinery.

The facts distributed through this volume have been carefully inquired into on the spot, and in most cases taken from the parties themselves, and corroborated by others not interested in the matter. They were transmitted by me, in a rough form, to the Nobleman to whom these letters are now addressed, in whose possession the originals remain.

It had been my intention that a few plates, representing factory cripples, should accompany these letters; and they had accordingly been announced to appear. On more mature consideration, however, and acting under the advice of friends, I have thought it best to deviate from that intention.

With these introductory remarks, I humbly submit this volume to a generous public.

WILLIAM DODD.

39, *James-street, Manchester-square,*
May, 1842.

CONTENTS.

viii CONTENTS.

LETTERS,

E T C.

" When fallen man from Paradise was driven
Forth to a world of labour, death, and care;
Still, of his native Eden, bounteous Heaven
Resolved one brief memorial to spare,
And gave his offspring an imperfect share
Of that lost happiness, amid decay;
Making their first approach to life seem fair,
And giving, for the Eden past away,
Childhood, the weary life's long happy holyday."
A Voice from the Factories, p. 11.

LETTER I.

Leeds, September 25, 1841.

MY LORD:

Agreeably to an arrangement I had made, with the
intention of gratifying a long cherished wish,—that of
once more visiting my two sisters in the North, whom
I had not seen for many years, and who are now nearly
the only relations I have left,—and also for the purpose of making a short tour through the factory districts, I left London on the 23rd instant.

On reaching Birmingham, I called upon the Rev.
GEORGE STRINGER BULL, incumbent of St. Matthew's, who received me with his usual affability and

kindness. And when I had informed him of my intended tour, he gave me his advice as to the plan I should adopt, and also furnished me with letters of introduction to many of his friends in Yorkshire, who, he thought, might be of service in assisting me in my inquiries; and, on my taking leave of him, he wished me every success in my undertaking. On the following day I left Birmingham for Leeds, intending to make my first stay there. As I drew near the town, and as the tall chimneys of the factories became, one by one, visible through the dense clouds of smoke which are constantly hanging over it, my feelings were of a most conflicting nature. The knowledge that I was once more in the vicinity of factories similar to those in which I had spent so many painful years of my existence, called up from the oblivion in which I had fancied they were buried, many bitter recollections of the past. A thousand reflections flashed through my mind, and I seemed to live over, in a few minutes, the whole course of my factory life. Again, as I passed along the streets in the omnibus that conveyed me from the railway-station, and saw the many marks by which a manufacturing town may always be known, viz., the wretched, stunted, decrepid, and, frequently, the mutilated appearance of the broken-down labourers, who are generally to be seen in the dirty, disagreeable streets; the swarms of meanly-clad women and children, and the dingy, smoky, wretched-looking dwellings of the poor; all this forcibly reminded me of the time when I had been a resident in a similar place.

Having procured myself a comfortable lodging, and got some refreshment, I took a walk through the town, the general appearance of which, in the eyes of a stranger, is disagreeable in the extreme. You in vain look for a square, a street, or a row of buildings, at all like what you see in towns which are not depending chiefly on factory pursuits. This is not to be wondered at, when we take into consideration the immense number of factories in the neighbourhood, each vomiting forth clouds of smoke, which collect in dense masses, and poison the surrounding atmosphere, and from which are continually falling particles of dirt and soot. At one time, when the air seemed a little clear, I counted the factory chimneys in sight to nearly one hundred, and this is but a portion of the whole number in Leeds and its vicinity. The amount of coal consumed in these factories, must be some hundreds of tons daily. Hence we need not wonder at the gloomy appearance of the town.

Although I was not surprised at finding Leeds in the condition above described, as it was what I was led to expect, from the fact of its being the chief seat of the woollen and flax manufactures in Yorkshire; yet I was not prepared for, and could not have believed that such misery existed, as I found this morning in some of the narrow streets and lanes of this wealthy town. I there found families crowded together in cellars and attics from fifteen to twenty feet square, more like animals of an inferior race than human beings, having very little to support their wretched existence. These dwellings were ill fur

nished, and many had no other sort of bed than
chaff, straw, or shavings; while some had neither
blankets nor sheets, the only covering to their beds
being an old cloak or coat, together with their other
wearing apparel, which, at nights, is promiscuously
thrown over all.   I asked the question, How is all
this? Have the manufactures of the town been all
along a losing speculation? Have men of wealth embarked their capital in the trade, and kept gradually
losing it, till they have reduced themselves and their
dependents to the miserable condition which I see?
What is the cause of all this misery? In answer to
my questions on this subject, I was informed by
several respectable tradesmen, at different times, and
unknown to each other, that so far from wealthy individuals having embarked their capital in the trade,
nearly all the mill-owners (who are the richest class
of· men here, some of them possessing upwards of a
million sterling) had risen from a very humble origin.
As a proof that such is the case, I was told that, out
of a population of upwards of 150,000 individuals,
not half a dozen names could be found of men who
have not been brought up to some trade or profession; consequently, Leeds is strictly a manufacturing
town.   To what cause it owes its present misery, it
will be my endeavour to find out.

  With respect to the manufactures being a good
or a bad speculation for the town, I was further told,
that for the last fifty years they had been a source
of wealth to the inhabitants,—that riches had continued to flow in almost without intermission.   " And

even now," said those with whom I conversed, " our markets are plentifully supplied, as you may see, with every article we want; our warehouses and shops are filled with every thing that can make a people happy, and yet, amidst all this plenty, we are literally starving. Our trade is monopolized by a few hands, which are every year becoming fewer and fewer; and as the smaller firms give way beneath the pressure, the work-people are thrown out of employment, and thus increase the number of famishing poor, and swell the already-glutted market of labour. At the same time, our manufacturers (take them as a body) possess the means of relieving effectually every case of distress in the town. But do they so? No; there are honourable exceptions, undoubtedly, but too many of them live sumptuously, and act as if all was prosperity and happiness; and having kicked down the ladder by which they rose to their high station, they now look on the misery by which they are surrounded (and which is in no small measure of their own producing) with indifference and neglect."

With this state of things I was deeply affected, and was satisfied in my own mind that the ALMIGHTY never intended that such should be the case.

My Lord, it is my intention to remain here a few days, and to investigate, as far as my humble abilities will allow, every circumstance which is at all calculated to throw any light upon the all-important question of the factory system. Hoping your Lordship will bear in mind that it is an unschooled factory cripple who is thus committing his thoughts to paper, and be so kind as to overlook all imperfections in this and any further letter I may write to your Lordship,

I am, with much respect,
Your Lordship's much obliged
and very humble servant,

To the Lord Ashley, M. P.,   WILLIAM DODD.
&c. &c. &c.

L E T T E R II.

Leeds, September 27, 1841.

MY LORD:

Having been informed that a committee was sitting for the purpose of enumerating the cases of distress in Leeds, I thought it might assist me in my inquiries to find out the cause of that distress. Accordingly, I made application (in company with Mr. CRABTREE, whom I accidentally met with) at the committee-room, in a public-house in Briggate, and the landlord very civilly allowed me to inspect the books; but I soon saw clearly that the object of the committee was quite different from the one I had in view, and that their endeavours were only to serve a party purpose. I had already found many cases in Leeds of factory cripples of which they had not taken any notice; cases, perhaps, as bad as any they had on their books; and, as I think, that *all cases* of distress ought to be investigated, I shall, in these letters, lay before your Lordship such cases as I may happen to meet with in my tour.

I called upon several gentlemen this morning, to

whom I had letters of introduction, and was received
very kindly by all; and particularly by Mr. SAMUEL
SMITH, surgeon to the Leeds Infirmary, who entered
freely into conversation with me on the subject of
factory legislation, decrepitude, accidents, &c. He
stated that, in the capacity of surgeon to the Infirmary, he had had many cases of accidents under his
care, some of a very serious nature; and a great many
cases in which the fingers only had been injured. This
gentleman has had very extensive practice in Leeds,
and therefore his opinion on this subject, as formerly
given in evidence, and as now expressed, will have
much weight; and as it will serve to explain the cause
of much misery, I shall transmit it for your Lordship's perusal.

Speaking of early decrepitude, and after describing
the formation of *bone*, Mr. SMITH says:—"From
what I have now stated, it would readily be seen that
the Divine Author of our being never intended that
young children should be kept standing on their legs
twelve, fourteen, or sixteen hours in the day, for He is
all-wise; and if so, a proper material would have
been provided for that purpose, the same as in the
full-grown man.

"The effects produced on the bones by too long
standing, which I have particularly noticed, are the
following: There is a beautiful arch of bone formed
in the foot, on the middle of which the main bone of
the leg is planted; in walking, the heel and ball of
the great toe touch the ground: the bridge of bones
is of a wedge-like form (the same as the stones which

form the arch of a bridge); this bridge receives the weight of the body; and by its elastic spring, prevents any shock being felt in leaping, &c. The weight of the body being too long sustained in factory working, this wedge-like form is lost; the bones give way, fall in, and the elastic spring of the foot is for ever gone; the inside of the sole of the foot touches the ground, constituting that deformity which is called the splay foot. The ligaments of the ankle-joint then give way, and the ankle falls inwards or outwards, as the case may be. The ligaments of the knee-joint give way, causing what is called 'knock-knee'd;' or, where the leg is bent outwards, it constitutes that deformity called 'bow-legged.' After the ligaments have given way, then the bones also bend, but not so much in the middle as at the extremities. This bending of the bones of the lower extremities is sometimes so striking, that occasionally six or even twelve inches of height are lost, in consequence; which I prove in this manner. A man of correct proportions will, in general, be about the same height as the length of the arms when extended. I have frequently seen cases of factory deformities in which the length of the arms thus, was six inches more than the altitude of the body, and in some cases eleven inches. One of the last men I measured was under five feet high; but his arms, when extended, were five feet six inches. And this was a man who worked in a mill long hours when a child, and his master gave evidence before the last parliamentary committee, in 1816, that the health of children was

improved by working in factories, and their stature
not diminished. Deformities and diseases of the
spine are a very common consequence of working in
factories. I have never seen any instances of deformity of the arms from this cause, for a very good
reason, because these limbs have not to sustain the
weight of the body. Since I have spoken of the
effects of the factory system, I have been frequently
reminded (by those who oppose the Bill for shorten-
ing the hours of labour) of the great number of individuals who are to be seen with deformities who have
never worked in factories at all. I am very ready to
admit this fact, but these cases are of a very different
kind to those which I have alluded to; they are cases
of deformity produced by a well-known disease called
rickets, a disease which commences in infancy, and
has generally run through its course, and the deformities completed, before the age at which children
are sent into a factory. I have seen deformities produced in individuals of seventeen and eighteen years
of age, who, up to that period, had been well-formed,
perfectly straight, and even muscular. A short time
ago, I saw a fine lad of seventeen years of age, whose
ankles and knees had become deformed in consequence
of working only three months in a factory; and to
show the frequency of this, he informed me that his
two partners with whom he worked were both more
deformed than himself. Let those who oppose my
opinions show me examples of this kind produced by
natural disease at this period of life. I know of no
individuals in whom these kinds of deformities are

common, except factory children and chimney-sweepers."—*This Extract is from a Work on Mills and Factories, page* 39; *published by* R. INCHBOLD, *Leeds.*

"In passing through the town, I noticed a striking illustration of the effects of the factory system, in a poor deformed man about thirty years of age. Knowing it instantly to be a factory case, I inquired of the man what had caused his deformity? He said, it was standing too long at the factory. I desired him to call upon me in the afternoon. But for this system, he would have been a man of fine person and proportions; he would have stood six feet high, for his arms when extended were upwards of five feet eleven inches, although he only stands five feet high. In addition to his deformity, he has lost the forefinger of the left hand, from the knuckle-joint; and the mid-finger is rendered useless, by an accident at the mill. Now, what advantage has this poor man gained for all these sacrifices? For thirteen and fourteen hours' work in the day, for six years, the whole of his earnings did not amount to 20*l.*, for he had only 1*s.* 3*d.* per week. I inquired of him, 'Have you a pension?' 'O yes,' he said, 'he had 2*s.* a week allowed.' This I thought kind; but, on inquiry as to who allowed this weekly stipend, I found that, unknowingly, part of it came out of *my own pocket*, for it was his parish pay."—*From the same Work, page* 41.

My Lord, I find there are a number of factory cripples in Leeds, but they are extremely shy, and do not like to have their cases known ; preferring rather to brood over their sorrows in secret, than to be brought before the public. I took some cases, on condition that they should not be made known ; but as I am under no such promise with respect to the following case, and as the miserable object may be seen any day in the streets, and will gladly corroborate my statement, I shall give it as nearly in the cripple's own words as I can :

" MICHAEL HOPKINS lives in Galloway's-yard, West-street. He was born at Skircoat, near Halifax. *His mother was left a widow, with a family of thirteen children ;* and their united earnings procured them food. He was sent to the mill of HENRY LODGE, esq., at Lower Willow-hall, near Halifax, *at the age of six years,* and received no wages for twelve months, excepting a penny or two occasionally, as the overlooker thought fit. At the age of seven, he had 1*s.* 6*d.* weekly, with an advance of 2½*d.* per week yearly for the succeeding period. At the age of fourteen years, he had 3*s.* per week. *He commenced work before five o'clock in the morning, and continued at work till eight o'clock at night, without stopping for breakfast or drinking* (tea), *and had only three-quarters of an hour for dinner ! If more, it was always worked up at night !* AND, DURING THE WHOLE TIME OF WORKING HOURS, THEY WERE NEVER ALLOWED TO SIT, EVEN FOR FIVE MINUTES ! WITHOUT RECEIVING A KICK, OR A BLOW, OR SUCH LIKE ! They were, to use his own words, ' SORELY BEATEN,' AND WERE PUT ON EACH OTHER'S BACKS TO BE

FLOGGED! He stood this treatment seven years:
he was then very ill, but continued to work at the
mill till he was sixteen or seventeen—not exactly sure
which of those two years he left. [He was then done
up, and cast off as waste lumber.] At thirteen he
was ill several months, *and was hugged* [carried]
*by his elder brother to and from work. And had
then to* STAND *all the while at his work, from five in
the morning to eight in the evening!* At one period,
he was twelve months, and never out of bed—all
from over-work! He was in Leeds Infirmary some
time; and he believes, that if he had stopped longer
there, he would have been well, *but he was obliged to
return to his work.*

" He is now fifty-two or fifty-three years old—not
certain which. He gets gradually worse and more
helpless, and cannot move a yard without something
to catch hold of. His height, as he walks, varies
considerably, on account of the jumping action which
he is forced to use; but, on an average, he does not
exceed thirty-six inches! He was perfectly straight
before he went to the mill. Had he the proper use
and shape of his limbs, he would be, at least, six feet
high. He spans, from the tip of his right hand to the
tip of his left hand, when his arms are expanded,
seventy-four inches; he measures round the chest
thirty-six and a half inches, round the waist thirty-
three and a half inches. Nature evidently designed
him for a strong athletic man. His right ankle and
knee are both enlarged, and out of joint.

" I think no one, who does not see him, can have

an adequate idea of the effort required when he moves ever so short a distance ; and, as to going up stairs, the sight is almost insufferable—*he actually screws himself up, with both feet and hands engaged to the extent of his powers, in order to preserve his equilibrium; and, withal, you are continually expecting him to roll to the bottom.* He obtains a very poor and a very precarious living by selling blacking, &c. He carries his wares in his basket, which also serves him for a stick, in resting or walking.

"*He receives no weekly pension from any one* excepting from Mrs. SUMMERS, who allows him a penny, and sometimes twopence a week. *He never received a farthing from the parish, and says, He* CANNOT *get anything.*"

The above account was furnished by a gentleman who kindly waited upon him for the purpose of getting it. My Lord, what a disgrace it is to this Christian country, and to the town of Leeds in particular, that cripples like this poor man, after having done all they can for the manufacturers, should be under the necessity of obtaining a precarious subsistence in the manner above described !

I am, &c.

LETTER III.

Leeds, September 28, 1841.

MY LORD:

I have this day been in various directions about the town, and I have seen much misery. In the morning I met about twenty men sweeping the streets, and on inquiry found they were mostly men who had served a legal time to some trade, such as croppers, flax-dressers, and others connected with the manufactures. They generally affirm that the introduction of machinery is the chief cause of their misery; they are employed by the parish at 1*s.* per day, and in consequence of the great number of applications, they are only allowed to work two and three days a-week, as the case may require.

From them I went to the outside of the town, near Water-lane, where I saw a number of men breaking stones for the roads, and others standing with their hands in their pockets looking on. I was very much surprised to see the immense quantity of stones these men had broken; there was a heap containing many thousand cart-loads, and the incessant rap, rap, rap, of the numerous hammers, gave tokens of its being likely to be increased to a much greater extent. They are generally men who have been thrown out of employment by the introduction of machinery, according to their own account, and are now employed, like those sweeping streets, at 1*s.* per day.

These men say, that when they were employed in their own work, they could earn from 5*s.* to 7*s.* per

day, and could then maintain their families in comfort; but now they are under the necessity of sending
their wives and children to the factories, to assist in
supporting them.

I have also had an interview with some woollen-
cloth-dressers, commonly called croppers; these men
were formerly in the habit of earning from 36s. to
40s. per week by hand, and were obliged to serve a
term of five or seven years to the trade. In 1814,
there were 1733 croppers in Leeds, all in full employment; and now, since the introduction of machinery, the whole of the cloth manufactured in this
town is dressed by a comparatively small number,
chiefly boys, at from 5s. to 8s. (some working for
8s. per week have a wife and two children), and a
few men at from 10s. to 14s. per week. The old
croppers have turned themselves to any thing they
can get to do; some acting as bailiffs, water-carriers,
scavengers, or selling oranges, cakes, tapes and laces,
gingerbread, blacking, &c. &c.

A great many of the machine-makers are now leaving this town for want of employment; they are
chiefly engaged to go to different parts of the Continent at good wages. Nearly twenty of them stopped
at the house where I am lodging, and they seemed
glad of an opportunity of getting away.

In my walks I saw the great new flax mill of
Messrs. MARSHALL, in Water-lane, said to cover upwards of two acres of ground. It is one story high,
and lighted from the top by dome lights; one great
improvement in this mill is the plan adopted of

16

placing the main shafts by which the machinery is propelled, in the cellar or room under the floor in which the machinery is working. The straps pass through the floor, and are all boxed off, as I was informed, thereby greatly lessening the risk of accidents. This is creditable to the firm. I also witnessed the liberation of the work-people from their old mill, about 1500 in number, as I was informed: the proportion of males to females appeared to be about one to ten. The females were chiefly young women and girls, generally pale and sickly-looking creatures.

My reflections on viewing the mills of Messrs. MARSHALL were of a very conflicting nature ; I saw the many hundreds of persons to whom they furnished employment, and consequently daily bread; and, viewing them in this light, unconnected with any thing of an opposite nature, they appeared to me a great good. But when I took into consideration that the 1500 persons employed therein were but a small proportion of that vast number which would have been employed, had it not been for these places, I could not look upon them in any other light than as a great monopoly of the worst description; having a direct tendency to enrich a few individuals at the expense of thousands. The result proves this to be correct; for while, on the one hand, we see the poor workmen, who in former times were able to maintain themselves and families in comfort, breaking stones for the roads, for the meanest trifle, in order to eke out a miserable existence ; we find, on the other hand, three or four men possessing a sum (as I am informed) of nearly two millions sterling. Is this as it ought to be?

I also visited Mr. BENNYON's flax mill, and having been told that it would not be possible to get admittance into it, I went over to a public-house opposite, seating myself in a room over against the entrance to the mill, and saw the people discharged for dinner. One young woman, about eighteen or twenty years of age, came into the room where I was sitting, to get her dinner, which an elderly person had brought. They called for a glass of ale, which the young person drank. The elderly person urged her to get her dinner, but she could not eat it; so, after resting herself till the bell rang for them again, she wrapped up the dinner without tasting a *single bit*, got a second glass of ale, and went to her work. While she sat, I asked her if she was unwell? She said, "No; this is nothing uncommon: I have no appetite for eating." This brought to my mind what I had myself experienced in former years. She was pale and sickly-looking; spoke and breathed with difficulty, and did not seem to enjoy life at all. She said, "Nothing but poverty would make them bear what they did." I suggested the idea of her getting a situation as a domestic servant: she quickly asked me, if I had ever known a factory girl get employed in such a situation? I told her that I had met with one or two instances of the kind. She shook her head, seemed to feel her situation very acutely, and went to work; leaving an impression on my mind that she would soon have finished all she had to do in this world. Her wages were about one penny per hour.

Last evening, I had some conversation with one of Messrs. MARSHALL's overlookers, who had been employed by the firm from twelve years of age : he is now thirty-seven. He says, that previous to the introduction of machinery, he could earn, as a flax-dresser, 6s. to 7s. per day; that his wages as an overlooker are 24s. per week ; and, although he considers himself fortunate in having obtained his present employment, yet *his loss* from the introduction of machinery, he considers at least 400l. to 500l. Out of his present wages of 24s., he generally gives to his unfortunate fellow-labourers, who have been totally deprived of work thereby, about 3s. per week, in various ways. He considers himself a worn-out man ; does not expect to see the age of forty-three ; and is afraid some part of his life will have to be spent in the workhouse. He is very much stuffed with dust, &c., from the flax. He has nearly lost all appetite for his ordinary food, and is obliged to humour and pamper himself, by getting any little tit-bit he may take a fancy to; this he finds very expensive. He has a difficulty of breathing, cough, and symptoms of an asthma. This person says that his wages are as high as any that are given to overlookers, and that many of them are working for 14s. and 16s. per week. He did not like to have it known that he had said anything to me, being afraid it would get to his master's ears, and then he would lose his place.

I am, &c.

LETTER IV.

Leeds, September 29, 1841.

My Lord:

I beg to draw your Lordship's attention to an evil
in the system, which I think might be greatly miti-
gated; that is, the great number of accidents which
occur in the factories. I have already seen and conversed with many poor people here, who have suffered
severely from this cause; and although it might occupy too much of your Lordship's time, and be a
tedious thing to read over all the cases which I have
met with, yet I think the two following are deserving
of notice, and may be considered a fair specimen of
the whole.

T—— M——, a young man, was in the act of
oiling some part of the machinery he was attending,
and the teeth of a pair of wheels caught hold of the
oil-can. In an instant the can was taken in, and
crushed to pieces; and he, being unable to take his
finger out of the handle of the can in time, his hand
also was taken in between the wheels. The result
was, that it was dreadfully crushed, and that the injury extended from the tip of his long finger to the
middle of his fore-arm. It was thought for some
time that amputation of the arm would be necessary;
but, by the skill and care of the surgeon, it was
saved, with the loss of the long or middle finger.
He was under the care of the surgeon for several
months, and all this time he was supported by his
friends, without any assistance from his masters. He

has never since been able to resume his work, and is at present getting a scanty living by doing little odd jobs as a porter. His hand presents a sad appearance, much the same as my sister's, which I have before described to your Lordship, and which was crushed in a nearly similar manner.

The other case, is that of MARY BUCKTROUT, a fine girl of fourteen years of age. She was working in the card-room of Mr. HOLDSWORTH's flax mill, and met with an accident while taking out some waste flax from the machinery, by order of the overlooker; " who," she says, " threatened to fine her 6*d.* a time, if she did not keep her machine clean." She has lost by this, and a preceding accident, the *right arm*, a little below the elbow, and the *thumb of her left hand.* Her master has given her 1*l.*, which is all she has had; and the father of the girl, who is a poor working man with five children, has been obliged to support her since. She had been working two years in the same mill. She is a remarkably interesting girl, and is at present in St. John's School, under the care and superintendence of Dr. HOOK, the vicar of Leeds, receiving such instruction as may enable her to undertake the management of an infant school. I was extremely pleased to hear her read, and see her write. The manner in which she holds her pen is rather curious; for this purpose she has a contrivance made of leather, somewhat similar to the two forefingers of a left-hand glove; these are fixed together, in close connection with a small leathern tube, for holding the pen, which, by means of this tube, is made to lie on the *upper* side of her two fore-fingers, and is moved up and down, in the act of writing, by the first and second joints of the said finger. I desired her to copy part of the 23rd Psalm for me, which I inclose, as a specimen of her hand-writing, for your Lordship's inspection. In this school there is also a governess, who has lost one arm by an accident in a factory.

On the subject of accidents, Mr. SAMUEL SMITH says: " Little children, whose intellects are not suffi-ciently advanced to enable them to form a proper estimate of the dangers by which they are sur-rounded, show their tempers, have their quarrels, and push each other about, when almost in imme-diate contact with the most dreadful kinds of ma-chinery; accidents of a very shocking description often occur from this cause; in addition to this, the young children are allowed to clean the machinery, actually while it is in motion; and consequently the fingers, hands, and arms, are frequently destroyed in a mo-ment. I have seen the whole of the arm, from the tip of the fingers to above the elbow, chopped into mince-meat, the cog-wheels cutting through the skin, muscles, and, in some places, through the bone, every half-inch: I have seen the arm torn off by the shoulder-joint, and sent in a basket after the patient to the Infirmary. On several occasions I have seen every limb in the body broken: in one instance, every limb but one was broken; there was considerable in-jury to the head; the pelvis was split up so as to expose the viscera of the belly. The worst part of

the case is to relate: the poor boy was alive, aye, and
sensible too ; but, happily for him, and for those who
witnessed them, his sufferings were speedily terminated by the friendly hand of death.   With respect
to the number of accidents, our institution annually
admits about 5000 patients : I do not know the
number admitted in the Dispensary, it is however
considerable.   Mr. SHARPE, the house surgeon of
the Infirmary, has made a calculation that thirty-five
per cent. of the whole number are accidents ; while,
in the public institutions of an agricultural district,
the accidents will not average above seven or ten per
cent.   Are such evils as these to exist year after
year, and no attempt to be made to remedy them?
Are a certain number of lives and limbs of our children to be annually sacrificed to this modern English
Juggernaut, in order that a few, very few, individuals
may obtain a large amount of that, the love of which
has been emphatically said to be, the root of all
evil?"—*Mills and Factories, page* 42.

Mr. ROBERT BAKER, superintendent of factories
in Leeds, with whom I have had some conversation
on this and other subjects, gives a similar opinion.
This gentleman thinks with me, that the manufacturers ought to be compelled to box off, or guard their
machinery, in such a way as would prevent in a great
measure these, *often fatal* occurrences.

Mr. BAKER says, "The Factories' Regulation Act,
at present in force, not having provided any remedy
for this important object [the boxing-off of machinery,]
and aware in a great measure of the extent and nature

of the accidents which have occurred, I have for some time taken upon myself to recommend precautionary measures with certain kinds of machinery; and even have entered in some of the time-books of the mill-owners, that, if any accidents did occur from machinery which had come under my notice, evidently very dangerous, the mill-owners would be held personally responsible for the consequences.

"*By this means much machinery has of late been rendered more secure than formerly.* But that a great deal remains to be done, the following table, taken from the Records of the Leeds General Infirmary for the year 1840, of mill-accidents happening within the townships of Leeds, Holbeck, and Hunslet, and admitted therein, will show.

" The cases described as ' in patients ' are to be considered as of the first class, *i.e.* requiring the sufferer to be confined to bed. Those of the ' out patients ' have been only of minor importance, but yet requiring surgical treatment.

In Patients.

Males 23 ; females 10 : total 33.

Of which

Were Admitted.		Years of Age.	Were Admitted.		Years of Age.	
1	at	8	5	at	14	
2	,,	9	4	,,	16	
3	,,	10	5	,,	17	and upwards.
1	,,	12	1	,,	18	
7	,,	13	4	,,	21	

OUT PATIENTS.

Males 161 ; females 67 : total 228.

Of which

Were Admitted.		Years of Age.	Were Admitted.		Years of Age.
4	at	9	17	at	15 ⎤
5	,,	10	22	,,	16 ⎥
12	,,	11	21	,,	17 ⎥
11	,,	12	16	,,	18 ⎬ and upwards.
24	,,	13	11	,,	19 ⎥
20	,,	14	4	,,	20 ⎥
	,,		61	,,	21 ⎦

		Requiring Amputation.	Deaths.
For compound dislocation of foot .	1	1	0
For compound fracture of shoulder .	1	1	1
Serious injuries to the arm . . .	9	1	0
,, ,, hand . . .	5	1	0
,, ,, thumb . . .	2	1	0
,, ,, fingers . .	15	6	0
Total cases [admitted]	33	11	1

For injuries to the arm	17
,, hand	39
,, thumb	14
,, fingers	158
Total out patients	228
Total in ditto	33
Total cases	261

"Thus it appears that in 1840 there were on the average about five accidents a-week, showing a very large amount of human misfortune, resulting from the want of precautionary measures with regard to the machinery at which the people are employed. How MUCH GREATER THE ACTUAL AMOUNT IS CANNOT BE ASCERTAINED, FOR IT MUST BE REMEMBERED THAT THIS IS A RETURN FROM ONLY ONE PUBLIC INSTITUTION, WHERE THERE ARE SEVERAL OPEN FOR THE RECEPTION OF LIKE ACCIDENTS, INDEPENDENTLY OF THE PRIVATE HOUSES TO WHICH MANY OF THE SUFFERERS APPLY!"

Mr. BAKER also remarks: "A part of a dress coming in contact with one of the revolving shafts, will become instantly lapped, and either strangle the person so seized, or, by forcible impulsion through a space too narrow to admit so large a body, produce instantaneous death. I have known one or two accidents of this nature, in which females have been torn to atoms by their clothes catching in revolving shafts."*

Hoping your Lordship will excuse all imperfections,
I remain, &c.

---

* Such accidents have often happened ;—in a single number of the *Bolton Chronicle*, published in December last, three fatal accidents by machinery were recorded. By one a lad, aged sixteen, was "torn literally limb from limb;" by another, a girl about fourteen years of age, had "her head smashed to atoms, both her legs torn from her body, and nearly every bone broken piece-meal." This last accident was caused by an upright revolving shaft, which caught her clothes and whirled her round and round. The shaft might have been boxed-off for 5s.

LETTER V.

Leeds, September 30, 1841.

My Lord:

I have now to mention to your Lordship a subject of very great importance in the factory system, viz., the condition of the women and children employed therein. This subject is important, for many reasons, the chief of which are, the very great proportion of women and children employed in the factories of this country, and the fact of their not having been intended by the Creator for such like employments. That there is a great proportion of women and children in these sinks of iniquity, no one acquainted with the factory system will deny. That women and children were never intended by nature to work in such places, is equally clear, to any one who has studied the organization of the human frame. These truths admitted, it will be my painful task to describe their condition, as I have found it here.

In Leeds and its neighbourhood, many thousands of women and children are employed in the various departments and processes of the flax and woollen mills; all of whom are subject to the pernicious effects of the pestilential atmosphere they are obliged to breathe from morning to night; and which bring on a number of diseases, which often prove fatal. They are also liable to be crippled and rendered miserable for life, by standing at their machines such long hours, or by accidents from machinery, which, as we have seen, are common. And last, not least, they are continually exposed to a species of temptation, and vice; which they are but very rarely able to resist.

A great number of these women and children live at a distance of two and three miles from their work; this distance they are obliged to travel night and morning in the summer season; and generally crowd together in cellars, and attics, near their work, in the winter. They go home only once a-week during that season. Their wages for this employment are about one penny per hour, for women who are well acquainted with their business; and one halfpenny per hour for children. There may be a few cases where they earn more than this; but there are also a great many, where they are not able to realize so much. The women seem very anxious to leave, but cannot tell how to get away, as very few people will employ females in any other line, who have been brought up in the factories.

Many of the women, both married and single, work in a far advanced state of pregnancy; the consequence of which is sometimes fatal to the infant or its mother. This is a painful subject to touch upon, but it is also necessary that it should be known. I shall, therefore, without any apology, lay before your Lordship the opinion of Mr. SAMUEL SMITH, who has had much practice in this line. This gentleman says:

" I allude to a very important, although a delicate point, and there may perhaps be those who will think the subject had better not be noticed; but the question is important, the interests of humanity are at stake, and I will not, as a professional man, compro-

mise my public duty by an affectation of false delicacy.
It is well known that a great change takes place in the
external form of the female at about fourteen or fifteen
years of age. At that period the hips grow larger
and broader, giving that flowing outline to the female
form at this part which so peculiarly distinguishes it
from that of the male, and which, although a beauty
in the female, would be considered deformity in the
male. This alteration in the female form up to that
period, is a wise provision of nature, by which the
bones of the pelvis are developed; but from which
no advantage is derived until the most critical period
of the life of a female—I mean, the time of child-
bearing. The superior part of the pelvis is formed
of an oval ring of bone, which, in standing, has to
sustain the weight of the body. This ring of bone
is increased in its diameter, when the development of
the pelvis takes place, so much as to be sufficiently
large to allow the head of the child to pass through
it. By long continued standing in factories, the diameter of this ring of bone becomes diminished; it
falls in in such a manner, by the pressure of the back-
bone behind, and the thigh-bones at the sides, that
instead of being an oval aperture, it forms a triangular
one, through which, in many instances, the child cannot pass during labour without the use of instruments;
and, in others, it is necessary to destroy the life of the
child to accomplish the delivery. I have had much
practical experience in this particular branch of the
profession at an early period of my practice; perhaps
as much as most men in the country, because I was

then much engaged in that department amongst the
poor. I have been occasionally driven to the dreadful
alternative of destroying the life of the child in the
womb, as the only means by which the more valuable
life of the mother could be saved : a few weeks ago,
I ascertained that in every instance in which this was
done, saving in one individual, the females had spent
that period of their lives when the pelvis is developed,
and several years after, in a factory. I had thought
that the fact of the effects produced on the female
pelvis by too long continued factory working, was an
original observation of my own ; but upon reáding the
evidence given before Parliament in 1819, I find the
same observation had been made by an old friend and
fellow-student of mine, Dr. JONES of Chester. I
would recommend that gentleman's evidence to be read
by every medical man who wishes for information as
to the effects produced by too long continued labour
in factories."—*Mills and Factories, p.* 41 *and* 42.

In about three or four weeks after the birth of the
child, the mother returns to her work in the factory,
the child being put to nurse in the daytime, with some
old woman or girl. These old women generally take
charge of two or three such children, at the rate of
about 6*d.* each per day. The child, from the want
of its natural nourishment, soon begins to languish,
and, if death does not step in to relieve it from
its misery, it becomes a weak, sickly, delicate child.
The payment of its nursing is a great drawback from
the earnings of the mother. It is very clear that it
would be much better for herself and child, to remain

at home, if she be married, and the husband capable of supporting his family. But stern necessity often compels them to these things, which they would gladly avoid.

Respecting the single females in this situation, I cannot say much; it is very deplorable to witness so many young women in such places, surrounded as they are continually by temptations of every description; and we too frequently see they give way to them. From the *Leeds Intelligencer*, printed a few days ago, I extract the following paragraph on this subject:

"*The Factory System.*—It must be apparent to every one residing in a manufacturing district, that the indiscriminate mixing of the sexes in our factories is a most prolific source of demoralization and pauperism. In almost every case of application for illegitimate children that has come before the magistrates here, or at Huddersfield, the mother had been working in a factory; and, in order to that application, it was necessary that she should have received relief from the parish, thereby making herself a pauper. It is high time that some legislative enactment was in force to put a check to this growing and debasing evil."

This paragraph will give your Lordship some idea of the extent of this evil. It does not, however, inform us of all the consequences resulting from it to the poor young women themselves. In a great many cases we find them driven to the dreadful alternative of choosing between a workhouse and the streets, and very often we see them preferring the latter.

As for the children, especially those under age, *i.e.* those between the ages of nine and thirteen, and who are specially protected by the law, I think they have a good and faithful friend in the factory superintendent of Leeds; who seems to pay great attention to the duties of his office.

I have found the people in Leeds very much afraid of speaking to strangers on the subject of factory life; many of them having lost their situations in consequence of giving information before the Committees of both Houses of Parliament, and also for allowing the people to see the machinery, &c. This last offence is a very great one, in the eyes of some of the manufacturers; at which, indeed, I do not wonder, when I consider how injurious are many of the processes adopted in many of these establishments, and especially in the *flax mills.* I conversed a little yesterday with an overlooker, who had lost his situation for letting a man see through a room. Finding that the mills of Leeds were uniformly difficult of access, I invited this overlooker to take dinner with me to-day. He promised to come; but has not fulfilled his engagement. I suppose that (although out of employment) he is afraid of being a marked man.

In taking my walks through Holbeck and Hunslet, I saw several mills stopped and the bailiffs in. I was told that twelve small flax manufacturers had failed within a very short time, and that, like the fishes in the sea, the large ones were swallowing up all the others.

I intimated to the bailiff at one mill, that I wished to inspect the lots of machinery prepared for sale, and

was admitted to view.   By this means I got a tolerable insight into the machinery employed in flax mills.
I also contrived to get access to a house directly over
against one large new mill, from which place I had a
good view into the spinning rooms.   In these rooms
I saw a great number of hot-water frames, or frames
in which every thread passes through hot water; the
finer the threads to be spun, the hotter the water
required.   The steam arising from the hot water
forms such a cloud, that the windows are obliged to
be kept open, even in winter, to let it out.   Each
frame, the ceiling, the walls, and windows (seven of
which were open in one room), were all covered with
steam, and water which is constantly trickling down.
In such a place as I have attempted to describe, the
women work twelve hours a-day.   It is scarcely necessary to add, that they look pale and unhealthy, I
had almost said, unearthly; which would perhaps
have been the more fitting term.   Their wages are
about 6s. a week for full time.   They have no
dust to contend with in these rooms, their great
enemy is steam.   Their clothes, of course, are constantly wet, partly with steam, and party with spray.
Those who have no steam around them, viz., the
carders, &c., have the dust to trouble them; which is
enough, at times, almost to choke them.   Those who
work in flax mills, suffer greatly from colds, coughs,
rheumatism, asthma, and a variety of pulmonary complaints.

  This morning I called upon Dr. Hook, the vicar
of Leeds, a staunch friend of the factory people.   I

also waited upon the Rev. GEORGE HILLS, and the
Rev. J. TODD, both young clergymen, who will, I
have no doubt, with the example of their vicar, and
the assistance of Mr. BAKER, the superintendent of
factories, do much good in the cause.

The proportion of male and female labourers is different in the different mills. In some mills, there is
one male for about four females ; in others, one male
for seven or eight females. There is no doubt that
the mills and factories here are hot-beds of vice and
wickedness. I have seen 1200 or 1300 hands libe-
rated, and their discourse is equally bad with what I
have heard elsewhere.

In walking through the streets to-day, I met many
cripples, and entered into conversation with some of
them ; but they mostly endeavoured to evade the
questions I asked. A few, however, seeing that I
was myself a cripple, did give me an account of their
sufferings, of which the following is a specimen :

" G—— B——, went to work at twelve years of
age, a fine strong lad. He worked in three different
flax mills ; in all, about six years, and was then obliged
to give over, as he was unable to work any longer.
His hours of labour were from five o'clock in the
morning, till nine o'clock at night : the sum total of
his earnings was about 50l., for which he was rendered a miserable cripple for life."

His legs are very much deformed, both his knees
are turned in; his body has every appearance of having
been intended for that of a stout man.

The flax-dressers are suffering severely from the

introduction of machinery. I have spoken to several who are in work, and they tell me that their earnings are considerably less than what they were a few years ago.

My Lord, I intend to leave Leeds for Bradford this evening, from which place your Lordship may expect to hear from me shortly; and in the meantime believe me,

My Lord, &c.

Note.—That the condition of the workers in flax mills may be better understood, the reader is referred to the Appendix (A.), for some important extracts from the Reports of Mr. DRINKWATER, and Mr. STUART, who were appointed Factory Commissioners in 1833. Many of the worst abuses then disclosed, the factory inspectors have not the slightest power to prevent: they can only remonstrate.

LETTER VI.

Bradford, October 2, 1841.

MY LORD:

Since I arrived here, I have visited some of the worsted mills, and weaving establishments of this town; and in this letter my object will be to draw your Lordship's attention to the general state of the factories of Bradford. The condition of the workpeople in the worsted mills here, is, generally speaking, bad. Their hours of labour are the usual factory hours, which are decidedly injurious, and much immorality and ignorance prevail; but the material upon which the hands are employed, is less pernicious to health than flax or cotton, and, except in the wool-combing department, they are not required to work in such high temperatures. However, I find that there are many things in these mills which require the interference of the Legislature.

In the worsted mills of Bradford, as in the flax mills of Leeds, the preponderance of females is excessive. Immense numbers of women and children are employed in the factories here; chiefly the wives and daughters of woolcombers, and poor hand-loom weavers.

In a work recently published, entitled "The History of Bradford, by JOHN JAMES," it is stated, that " *five-sixths* of the persons employed in the factories of this town and neighbourhood are *females*."

One reason of there being so many females employed in the factories here, is, that the husbands and the fathers cannot, as they used to do, support them at home; and another unquestionably is, that the females can be induced to work for considerably lower wages. I occasionally entered into conversation with these men (the woolcombers and hand-loom weavers), and was informed of the sad effects that machinery had made in their trades, throwing a great many out of employment, and reducing the wages of those who had still a little work to do by hand. Your Lordship will please to bear in mind, that they cannot comb all sorts of wool by machinery, and I am inclined to think it would be better for the *consumer*, if they could not comb any; for it is evident to any person who knows anything of machinery, that the staple or fibres of the wool must be greatly injured thereby. The men, boys, and girls, employed to attend the *machines* for combing wool, are very sickly-looking, emaciated beings. This work is calculated to ruin the strongest constitution in seven or eight years. The men who have lost their work in consequence of the introduction of machinery, naturally thinking that "half a loaf is better than no bread," offered to do the little that was left to be done by hand, for less wages; and the manufacturers, seeing the labour-market glutted, concluded they could have their work done at their own price. Hence, I found woolcombers in Bradford working the same sort of wool for 10*d.* per lb., for which, in 1838, they were receiving 1*s.* 8*d.* per lb. Many of these woolcombers work at home, and in order to make up the deficiency in the family income, the wife, and children of very tender age, are compelled to take up a pair of combs; and thus, by turning off a greater quantity, keep up their income as well as they can. This gluts the market of labour still more. I have conversed with a man who had formerly been able to maintain his family in comfort by his own unassisted labours; and now, although he has the assistance of his wife, who works a pair of combs, standing from morning till night at the pad post, he is scarcely able to keep a home to put his head in. The wages of the woolcombers, generally, are not more than two-thirds, and in most cases only one-half, of what they were *three years*

BRADFORD. 37

ago, and great numbers have nothing at all to do. For this they blame machinery, as the chief cause of their sufferings, and such it undoubtedly is.

The condition of many of the female factory labourers here is anything but enviable. A great number of them live at a distance of two and three miles from their work, and have to walk this distance every morning and night, in addition to twelve hours' work in the mills. I saw, last evening, scores of young women and girls on their way home, with their little tin cans in their hands, in which they had taken their milk or tea; some of them scarcely able to move one foot before another. As I looked at their pitiable condition, I was forcibly reminded of the sufferings of *my early days* when going home from work, and of the many times I had to sit me down, and rest by the road-side. These young women have to travel a distance of from thirty to forty miles weekly, besides working sixty-eight or seventy hours in the mills. Their earnings are from 4*s.* to 8*s.* per week; out of which many of them have to pay for nursing one or two children, and some have also a husband to maintain. Many of them work these hours in an advanced state of pregnancy, and until they are obliged to give it up: some, who live near the mill, go to work till the last *month*, *day*, and I have conversed with two who stayed till the last *hour* of their time. The infants are put to nurse in the same way as at Leeds, which I mentioned in a former letter.

I took breakfast this morning with a gentleman who had been a teacher in a Sunday-school for several

years. He described the manner in which the
children under his care sank gradually, from the time
they entered the factories, in nearly the following
words :—

" I was introduced to the Sunday-school by that
indefatigable friend of the factory children, the Rev.
G. S. BULL. When I first entered that school, it
was composed of perhaps from seventy to eighty
scholars and teachers ; and, when I left it, I should
suppose there were about 400,—so rapidly do Sunday-
schools increase the number of their scholars in such
densely populated manufacturing towns as this of
ours. We had many scholars of from eight or nine
to thirteen or fourteen years of age, who worked in
the factories during the week. When I first became
acquainted with them, their appearance to me was
healthy and strong, and as fresh and blooming as
the flowers in May; and continued so for a short
time. But this did not continue long; for, in the
short space of three years, I saw many of them sink
into the grave ; the factory system having worn out
their very vitals. The long hours they had to stand
on their feet, the nauseous smells arising from the
employment they were engaged in, and the confinement from six o'clock in the morning until half-past
seven at night, with but very little intermission for
meals or rest, was the cause, and, in my opinion, the
only cause of their sinking into a premature grave.
I have attended many of these poor creatures in their
sickness, and witnessed their dying moments, and I
unhesitatingly affirm, that although their disease

might be properly called consumption, yet the factory labour was the real cause. I have seen, when the system was beginning to take hold upon them, they could scarcely drag themselves along the street. I remember one poor girl of the name of ELIZABETH HEAD the last time she ventured to the school; she was not able of herself to return, and had to be supported home by two faithful companions.

"I am glad to say that the death-bed scenes I have been called to witness, while I was superintendent of that school, afforded me proofs that many of that class were religiously inclined, and might have made good members of society, if they had not been connected with the factories. One poor girl, whom I knew, was brought up from an early age in a factory in this town, bore a good character, and worked hard for a long time : she had no mother, and her father was in an asylum. She worked and toiled until her physical strength was gone, and when she could bear up no longer, she was provided with an asylum, at the expense of a Christian public, in the Leeds Infirmary. In this place she lingered on sixteen weeks, and then was turned out. But where has she to flee to? Has her master provided for her after she is worn out? O! no; but, from the Infirmary she is sent to Halifax Workhouse, there to linger out her miserable existence, until death, welcome death, puts an end to all her sufferings."

Many accidents have occurred with the woolcombers' washing-rollers. These are large iron rollers, about ten or twelve inches in diameter, and three or four feet long, working close together, so as to press out the water from the wool, after it has been washed. Great care is requisite in persons working at these rollers, in order to prevent the fingers being taken in with the wool, in which case they would be crushed as flat as a sheet of paper. A person of the name of SAMUEL LISTER, got his hand in a pair of these rollers in Mr. HOLMES' mill, and, as a matter of course, he was obliged to submit to amputation of the hand.

A young woman of the name of SPENCER, had her hand crushed in a similar way; amputation in this latter case was *not* resorted to, and she died.

Another young woman met with a similar accident, some time ago, in Mr. JERRISON's mill, by which she had *both* hands, and *part of the fore-arm* crushed; amputation of *both arms* was the consequence. She eventually recovered, and I believe is still living upon a small income arising from a subscription entered into for her, by the inhabitants of Bradford.

Many more cases might be mentioned, but these will serve to show the danger to be apprehended from these rollers, and the care requisite in persons attending them. There are also many accidents from other parts of the machinery.

Only three days ago, a little girl, named EMMA GREENWOOD, met with an accident in Mr. SUTT-CLIFFE's mill, Willow-hall, in this neighbourhood, whereby *all the fingers* of her left hand were more or less severely injured. She was taken to the Infirmary, where it was feared two of her fingers would have to be amputated.

My Lord, I hope to be able on Monday to forward an account of the worsted mills of Messrs. WOOD and WALKER of this town, which, I find, are admirably conducted.

I am, &c.

LETTER VII.

Bradford, October 4, 1841.

MY LORD:

I shall now briefly endeavour to describe what I saw of the factories of Messrs. WOOD and WALKER. By the kindness of Mr. WALKER, one of the partners in the firm, I was permitted to view their mills; and their schoolmaster, Mr. BALME, evidently took a pleasure in showing me everything worthy of notice. In the first place we went over their works, and I remarked that the work-people generally looked more healthy than factory people usually do; this is accounted for by the regulations of the establishment being of a more mild and generous kind than those to be found in most factories. Their hours of labour, even when times are brisk, are not more than eleven per day: they come during the winter at half-past six o'clock in the morning; breakfast at forty minutes past seven (twenty minutes); dine at twelve (fifty minutes); tea at five (twenty minutes); they leave the mill at seven o'clock in the evening. In the summer, they begin at six o'clock in the morn-

ing, have thirty minutes for breakfast, the same for
tea, and an hour for dinner : while most, if not all the
rest of the factories work twelve hours, unless indeed
they happen to be prevented by the depressed state
of trade.   No part of the time allowed for meals is
occupied in cleaning machinery (as is too commonly
the case), but the whole of the meal-time is at the
disposal of the work-people.   A surgeon liberally
paid is provided by the firm, for the purpose of inspecting the hands daily ; this gentleman goes over
the works, and if he notices any one looking ill, he
makes inquiry as to the cause, and should it be
anything requiring rest or medicine, they are ordered
home immediately : or should any of the work-
people find themselves unwell, they apply to the
surgeon, and obtain timely advice and assistance.
During the time they may be off work, their wages
are sent to them, the same as if they had been at
work.   Those work-people who live at a distance,
and who are obliged to bring their food with them,
have a warm comfortable room provided for them to
sit in, and their victuals are made warm and comfortable, as if they had been at home : this arrangement is attended with very little cost, while it
enables every one to have warm, clean, and comfortable meals.   I was very much pleased with this
room and its furniture, which I shall endeavour to
describe to your Lordship.

    The *room for meals* is a large one on the ground-
floor, kept for this and no other purpose.   It is
capable of holding 500 children and young persons.

It is provided with good strong tables and forms, and kept very clean and orderly. Adjoining this room is a smaller one, used for the sole purpose of warming the provisions of the work-people; it is well fitted up, with a steam-apparatus, troughs, shelves, &c. The children and others, who live at a distance, bring their breakfast, dinner, and tea, when they come to work, in tin cans (which are all numbered), and place them on the particular shelf allotted to the room in which they work. A man (and sometimes also a woman) looks after this room, and gets every can made warm, by means of the steam-apparatus, and all placed on their respective tables in proper time. It gave me great pleasure to inspect the arrangements of these well-regulated rooms. These preparations being over, imagine, my Lord, yourself in the room, waiting the coming of the children.

Mr. BALME, the schoolmaster, kindly accompanied me a few minutes before half-past seven o'clock in the morning, and we took our station at the lower end of the room, directly opposite the entrance, and awaited the coming of the children. This, I was told, is part of the schoolmaster's duty, and his presence preserves silence and order during meal hours. When, exactly at the half-hour, the engine stopped, and the children, to the number of about 400, began to come into breakfast. All the tin cans, containing their tea or coffee, have been placed on the tables ready, and all have taken their seats; the boys on one side of the room, and the girls on the other, and unfolded their little portions of bread and butter; but no one begins to eat. How is this? I turned to the schoolmaster for an explanation. He had got his watch in his hand, and at the expiration of five minutes from the time the engine stopped (which time is allowed for them all to get seated), he made a signal. At this signal they all rose, and sang a beautiful verse as *grace before meat :* this surprised and pleased me much; I could scarcely believe I was among factory workers. The grace being ended, they began to eat their breakfast, the schoolmaster still remaining in his place. Some of the boys had soon done their breakfast, and seemed to manifest a little impatience to get out to play; these boys kept their eyes steadfastly fixed upon the schoolmaster. At exactly ten minutes from the time of commencing breakfast, he gave the word " go ;" immediately the boys and younger girls departed, not in a hurry-scurry sort of way, but quietly, two or three together; while the young women remained to spend their remaining quarter of an hour in knitting or sewing. Now, my Lord, look into the play-ground; see their merry little faces, and active limbs, striving who can be most happy. How very different is all this from what I experienced!

I think I hear your Lordship ask the question, How does it happen that these children are so active and playful, and the generality of factory children so jaded and tired? It is because these children enjoy many privileges, of which ninety-nine out of every hundred factory children know nothing. In every room

in which the children work, there are at least half a
dozen spare hands, who relieve the others by turns,
and the children are not only allowed but *provided
with seats.* The seats are placed along both sides of
the rooms, in addition to which every frame attended
by any young person has stools attached to it, by
means of a joint, which allows them to be placed
under the frame when not wanted. The seats which
are at the sides of the room, are for the use of the
spare hands ; those attached to the frames are for
the children at work. The plan of having seats was
originally suggested by Mr. RICHARD OASTLER, the
friend of the factory children ; and as a compliment
to that gentleman they are called " Oastlers." I
have been several times in these rooms, and invariably found some of the children sitting, and all
seemed happy and cheerful. The children have no
harsh treatment to endure from their overlookers,
who seem to be an intelligent set of men, and endowed with a large share of the Christian spirit of
their masters. Should one of these overlookers *dare
to strike at a child,* he would be dismissed from the
place. It is considered in Bradford a great favour to
get children into the mills of Messrs. WOOD and
WALKER, and the children themselves are duly
sensible of the advantages they enjoy.

The *school-room* is a large new building, erected
near the mills, for the use of the children. The
firm provide, at considerable expense, a schoolmaster
and a schoolmistress, who are brother and sister ;
also books, slates, maps, pens, ink, &c. The

children under thirteen years of age, to the number
of between 300 and 400, are divided into sections,
each attending school at least two hours per day.
The boys learn reading, writing, arithmetic, geography, and singing; and the girls learn knitting
and sewing, in addition to the above. Adjoining the
school-room is the washing-room, which is provided
with a number of large basins and clean towels, and
water is laid on, and can be had by turning a tap. A
quarter of an hour suffices to enable a division to
clean for school. With a more cleanly, healthy-
looking set of factory children I have nowhere met.

It is but justice to state, that this school and its
arrangements were originally planned, and superintended, by that indefatigable friend of the factory
labourers, the Rev. G. S. BULL; and that it was
opened for the children, previously to the introduction of the Factories' Regulation Act.

When the children arrive at the age of thirteen
years, they are then permitted to work full time, and
on leaving the school they are presented with a
handsome Bible, with the following inscription on
the inside of the cover :—

" *This copy of God's Holy Word was given to*
      on attaining the thirteenth
year of her age, as a reward for good conduct during
three years' attendance at Messrs. WOOD *and* WAL-
KER'S *Factory School.*

" *May you ever ' read, mark, learn, and inwardly*
digest;' may you ' embrace and ever hold fast the

blessed promises of everlasting life,' contained in this *Sacred Book*.

" *May it be your guide through life, and your sup-port in the hour of death*.

" M. BALME, *schoolmaster to*
Messrs. Wood and Walker.

" *Bradford*, 184 ."

The young women (chiefly reelers) in this esta-blishment are of a superior cast. This arises in part from the care which has been taken of them, when they were children; and from the rules respecting their government now they are grown up, which rules are strictly enforced. The principal of these are, that *no married female shall be allowed to work in these mills;* and that any "single female" being known to *conduct herself improperly, must instantly quit her employment*. The hours of labour also, not being so long as at most places, allow them more time to learn domestic habits, and improve their minds. They enjoy also a great advantage in having warm, comfortable meals on the premises, if they should require it. Their appearance is clean and decent, and they seem to take a pride in keeping themselves so. They are not obliged, like the fe-males in cotton factories, to work half naked, in hot rooms. In short, if they were not in the mills, they might very easily be mistaken for respectable do-mestic servants. On inquiry, I found that most of them had been brought up in this establish-ment, and may be said to know very little of the vice and wickedness generally prevailing in other factories.

There are not many men employed in the spinning departments of this establishment; but of wool sorters and combers there are a great number, who enjoy good wages and regular work; occasionally they may be put on short time; this, however, I think occurs but seldom. Altogether this concern, which is the largest worsted spinning establishment in the *world*, is conducted in a manner which does great credit to the firm, and affords a striking proof of what may be done by those manufacturers *who feel disposed to improve the condition of their work-people.*

When I had satisfied my curiosity, I repaired to the counting-house, to thank Mr. WALKER for the kindness shown to me, in allowing me to inspect their works. He expressed himself pleased at having an opportunity of granting me the favour, and to some of my remarks said, " that although they did all they could to make their work-people comfortable, yet they were well aware their system was not what it ought to be. They were anxious to reduce their hours of labour to *ten* per day, if the other manufacturers would but do the same. This," he said, " would be of the utmost advantage to the work-people and manufacturers, and, until that took place, he did not see what other improvements could be made. If the Legislature did not pass a law to restrict the hours of labour, he was of opinion that the *conscientious part of the manufacturers* would be under the necessity of withdrawing from the trade altogether."

I have seen several cases of decrepitude and mutilation, which I must reserve for another letter.

I am, &c.

LETTER VIII.

Bradford, October 4, 1841.

My Lord:

I now come to the subject of the cripples made by over-exertion and long hours of labour in this town, who, I find, are very numerous. In passing through the streets, I met many who would, in all probability, have been stout, able-bodied men, had they never known the factories; but who are now, although in the prime of life, unable to earn a living in any way whatever. I invited several of them to take tea with me at my lodgings, and visited others at their own homes; and I now beg to lay before your Lordship the history of a few of them, in nearly their own words.

I had the pleasure of taking tea last evening with two brothers, R. and J. H——, both factory cripples, and both presenting to the eye of an observer, a sad spectacle of factory suffering. One of them is married, and has two children; and it was at his house we met to take tea. We sat down to our repast in mutual good humour (Mr. and Mrs. H——, his brother, and myself), four poor abject cripples; three made so by the factories, and the fourth (Mrs. H——), being obliged to use a crutch, in consequence of a white swelling on

her knee, which she had had for many years. I do
not remember to have spent a more pleasant evening,
in the whole course of my existence, than I did on
this occasion, with these simple, kind-hearted people.
The history told me by these young men of their
sufferings, is very much the same in both cases; I
shall, therefore, content myself with relating that of
the elder brother, which is as follows: " R. H——
went to work at PEARSON and WHITEHEAD's worsted
mill, at Laister Dyke, at six years of age. He had two
miles to go morning and night, winter and summer,
and was obliged to be there at six o'clock in the morning, and stop till eight o'clock at night ; with only
half-an-hour for meals and rest during the day. He
was frequently strapped, boxed, and pulled by the
ears. He blames the long hours and night-work for
his lameness. He worked for Mr. GARNETT about
eighteen months *at night*, and was obliged to leave, in
consequence of ill-health caused by night-work. He
was off work three months. When he got well he
went to the mill again nine or ten weeks ; but he was
in such pain that he could not do his work, and was
obliged to be taken away from it : he was then about
sixteen years old. He was working in the factories
altogether about ten years ; sometimes sixteen, seventeen, and eighteen hours per day, for which he received
in all about 100*l.*, and is now a confirmed cripple. The
right knee is *turned in about nine inches,* and the left
knee turned *out* to the same extent. He was perfectly
straight on entering the factories." He stands about
five feet high, and has every appearance of having

been intended for a well-proportioned man. He is rather hard of hearing, caused by the continual noise of the mills. He has learned to comb wool, but can earn but little. His wife is a power-loom weaver, and worked so long in a state of pregnancy with her last child, that it was born within an hour of her leaving work. She went to work again as soon as she got well; and directly the child, which was a healthy one, began to dwindle away. She was then obliged to give up her work to save the child's life, and a finer little fellow I scarcely ever saw.

The brother's story is very similar, except that he worked on till seventeen years of age, before he was done up. He is very hard of hearing, and is at present combing wool for a livelihood. Neither of them have anything allowed from their masters, either in sickness or since. They have received several slight wounds, and experienced some narrow escapes from death by machinery. They can read and write a little; the elder brother is studying arithmetic, this diverts his mind from his sad condition.

"WILLIAM HIRST, near the 'Neptune Inn,' Bradford, entered the worsted mill of Mr. ROE, in Union-street, at the age of nine years. He was then quite straight in his limbs, and a strong hardy lad. He worked a month for nothing, and then had 2s. 6d. per week, for which he had to work fifteen hours per day, till the Factory Act came into force. He was advanced about 6d. per year till he got 5s. per week. His wages then remained stationary till he was twenty years of age;

after which time he was appointed assistant - overlooker at 8s. per week. He continued in that situation till he was twenty-three years of age. He
was then unable to work, and was cast off without
a penny; a complete cripple, his legs being similar
to R. H——'s, as described above. He worked part
of the time for Mr. HOLMES, of Baildon, four miles
from Bradford, and his successors, Messrs. TREES and
Co. In fourteen years he earned about 183l., and by
this labour was rendered, at the age of twenty-three
years, unable to get his own living. He has no friends
to assist him, and was thinking of going to the
workhouse when I saw him. Nature had evidently
intended this cripple for a strong man. He has a
broad, well-formed back and shoulders; stands, when
resting on a stick, four feet eight inches high, and is
very much deformed in his legs : he would apparently have stood five feet six or seven, if he had not
worked in the factories. He can read and write a
little.

I cannot describe to your Lordship my feelings, as
I sat in my lodgings listening to the heart-rending
tales of the many cripples who came to see me; or
when I met them in the streets, creeping out of sight
of the passers-by.

BENJAMIN GOMERSAL, of Bowling-lane, Bradford, thus described his own case sometime ago :

" I am about twenty-five years old,   I have been a
piecer at Mr. COUSEN's worsted mill, I have worked
nowhere else. I commenced working in a worsted
mill at nine years of age. Our hours of labour were

from six in the morning to seven, half-past seven, and
eight at night, with *thirty minutes off at noon for
dinner. We had no time for breakfast or drinking.*
I found it very hard and laborious employment. I
had 2*s*. per week at first. We have to stoop, to
bend our bodies and our legs. I was a healthy
and strong boy, when I first went to the mill. When
I was about eight years old, I could walk from
Leeds to Bradford (ten miles) without any pain or
difficulty, and with little fatigue ; *now I cannot stand
without crutches ! I cannot walk at all !* Perhaps
I might creep up stairs. I go up stairs backwards-
way every night ! I found my limbs begin to fail,
after I had been working about a year. It came on
with great pain in my legs and knees. I was very
much fatigued towards the end of the day. The
overlooker beat me up to my work ! *I have been
beaten till I was black and blue in my face !* and
have had my ears torn ! Once I was very ill with it.
*He beat me then, because I mixed a few empty bob-
bins, not having any place to put them in separate. We were beaten most at the latter end of
the day, when we grew tired and fatigued.* The
highest wages I ever had in the factory, were
5*s*. 6*d*. per week. My mother is dead; my father was obliged to send me to the mill, in order
to keep me. In a morning I was very 'stark' indeed. I had to attend at the mill after my limbs
began to fail. I could not then do as well as I
could before. *I had one shilling a-week taken off my
wages.* I had lost several inches in height. I had

frequently to stand thirteen and fourteen hours a-day, *and to be continually engaged.* I was perfectly straight before I entered on this labour !

"Other boys were deformed in the same way. A good many boys suffered in their health, in consequence of the severity of their work. I had a brother who became deformed, but he recovered after he left the mill. I had no opportunity of attending any night school. I cannot write. I can read a little, but very poorly. I now help my sister to knit heels to weave with. When I stand, I have very much pain. It came on when I was working long hours. They did not shorten my hours when I became lame and deformed, I worked the same hours ! I never worked shorter hours than the rest ! Sometimes I was bad, and was forced to go home. *My master never sent the doctor to me ! He makes me no allowance now !* The doctors say, they can do me no good. *I am quite sure this pain, and grievous deformity, came from my long hours of labour.* My father, and all my friends, believe so too. *It is the opinion of all the medical men who have seen me.* I am sure that ten hours' actual labour in a mill is enough for a strong boy. I cannot work in the mill now. The children conceive it to be a very great mischief, to be kept so long at labour; and I believe their parents would be very glad if it was not so."

" JERVIS HARTLEY went to work at the worsted mill of JOHN RAND and SON, at an early age; he does not exactly remember how old he was, but thinks about seven. He had 1s. per week for one

year, for which he had to work from six in the morning until eight o'clock at night; with half-an-hour
for meat and rest. He then went to work at Mr.
FAWCETT's, where he was very badly treated. He
had 2s. per week, and was raised 6d. a-year, but he
never had more than 5s. 6d. per week. He continued
to work at Mr. FAWCETT's mill, until he was thirteen
years of age ; he then worked for BANKART and BEN-
SON, till he was seventeen years of age, when he was
completely done up, and rendered unable to do anything. He was a long time in the Infirmary, where he
underwent several operations, and was afterwards an
out-patient, and all this time supported by his parent.
He had no assistance whatever from his masters.
Poor HARTLEY, who is now thirty-four years of
age, feelingly describes the situation of his mind,
while labouring under these sufferings. His limbs
were so painful, that he could scarcely get from home
to work; he had no appetite for his victuals; could
not sleep at night; was ill-treated by day; and was
completely tired of his life. He says that he had
often wished he had been born a horse, a cow, or a
dog, or anything but what he is. His sight and
hearing are both impaired; his legs are miserably deformed; his right knee turned in, and his left out,
like the preceding cases. He is now picking up a
scanty subsistence by woolcombing, and can only
work an hour at a time."

A great many cases of a similar description might
be laid before your Lordship, but they are so nearly
alike, in every respect, that it might be considered tire-

some, and occupy too much of your Lordship's valuable
time.   In the instances above-mentioned, the deformities are nearly alike, viz., the right knee turned *in*, and
the left knee turned *out*, to the same extent. There are,
however, a great many cripples who have both knees
turned *in*, as in my own case ; and I have met one
man, of the name of CHARLES BAINBRIDGE, whose
knees are both turned outwards so far, that a child
of five or six years of age, may run between them,
when he is standing in his usual position.   This will
give your Lordship a tolerable idea of what worsted
spinning, with long hours of labour, is capable of
doing.

My Lord, I intend to leave this place to-night, for
Rochdale, from whence your Lordship may expect to
hear again from,   Your Lordship's, &c.

LETTER IX.

Rochdale, October 6, 1841.
MY LORD:

I arrived here on Monday evening, and took an
early opportunity of calling upon the Rev. JAMES
TAYLOR, a dissenting minister, to whom I communicated the object of my visit. He received me
very kindly, and after some general conversation
accompanied me to the residence of a working man.
This man called an especial meeting of some of the
old hands working in the cotton factories, with whom

I spent several hours, as they expressed themselves pleased at having an opportunity of conversing with me on the subject of wages, machinery, &c. From these men I learned that a great number of spinners had been thrown out of employment, a few days before, in consequence of the introduction of *self-acting mules*, and other kinds of "improved" machinery. That the wages were getting less and less, year after year, and that the masters were getting so high-minded, and the work-people so humbled, that they scarcely durst speak, or object to any measure, however arbitrary, that might be introduced into the factories. That the women were working in the mills till the latest stage of pregnancy; and that one had been assisted home from her work three days before my arrival, while in the pains of labour, and had been delivered of a child within a few hours after she got home. That on such occasions the women generally returned to their work in three or four weeks, the infants being put out to nurse with old women, or girls, and occasionally carried to the mother in the factories to be suckled.

This I thought a sad account, and therefore I determined to spend a couple of days in Rochdale, for the purpose of testing the accuracy of their statements, by comparing them with what I might learn from other quarters.

This morning I met with some of the spinners who had been thrown out of employment by the introduction of self-acting spinning-mules, whose tale fully corroborated what I had heard on the pre-

ceding night ; and I further learnt, that the manufacturers were striving with each other, who could
introduce the best machines for spinning cotton yarn,
with the least possible expense. I was told that
three new patent machines for spinning, invented by
different men, and of different construction, were each
undergoing a trial in the factories of this town and
neighbourhood.

The wages for spinning are very much reduced of
late years. In 1817, a machine for spinning cotton
yarn, called a throstle, with twelve dozen spindles,
would spin one hank (containing 840 yards of cotton
thread) per spindle, per day, which was considered a
fair day's work. In 1841, the same sort of machine,
worked by the same number of hands, and in which
are fifteen, sixteen, and, in some instances, eighteen
dozen spindles, will spin four hanks per spindle, per
day, of the same description of yarn. Now let us
see how this will affect the market of labour. We
have, in 1817, a machine with 144 spindles, producing
144 hanks per day : in 1841, a similar machine
with 204 spindles, producing 816 hanks in the same
time. The wages for attending those machines in
1817, were 10s. 6d. per week, or 1s. 9d. per day :
in 1841, the wages are 8s. 6d. per week, or 1s. 5d.
per day. So that we see a person spinning at present *five* or *six times* as much as he did in 1817, and
for 4d. a day less.

I met to-day with a mule spinner, who has to mind
a pair of double-deckers, or two wheels coupled together, containing 1440 spindles. He does not ex-

pect to be able to work beyond forty years of age.
I also met with an intelligent man, who had been
connected with the cotton factories for many years,
particularly the warping department. He stated to
me, that the wages were greatly reduced since he
could remember. In 1817, for a certain quantity of
work he got 3*d.* : in 1841, for the same quantity and
kind of work, he got *five-eighths of a penny.*

The weaving department is equally depressed. I
saw one poor man (a sad cripple), who is attending a
pair of power-looms, in which he weaves *six webs,*
three in each loom. This would have been the work
of three men by hand, and would, a few years ago, have
enabled them to earn about 20*s.* per week each ; this
poor man is doing the whole, for 9*s.* per week.

On my road home I met with a poor hand-loom
weaver, drying his web of flannels on the road-side,
and he informed me that he was earning about 6*s.*
per week, and, about twenty years ago, he was able
to earn 1*l.* 2*s.* 6*d.* with as much ease. Flannel
sells nearly as high as before. He looked the picture
of misery.

The distress prevailing here, though not so great
as at some places, is deserving of notice. Many
families, I found, had no bed or bedding worthy of
the name to lie upon, and were crowded together like
animals of an inferior race, and subsisting on a mere
trifle, scarcely sufficient to keep soul and body together ; some on as little as 2*d.* a-day.

There are many cases of cripples here from long
hours, and accidents ; the following cases I had from

the lips of the parties themselves, and they are all that I am allowed to make known.

The first is a rare instance of the generosity of the manufacturers. It is one of those bright spots which occasionally shine out, in the dark and gloomy horizon of the factory system.

"A fine boy of the name of J—— S——, went to work in Messrs. COLLINS and ASHWORTH'S cotton mill, at thirteen years of age, as a card-room tenter; and in sweeping up behind the frame, he got his arm in, under the strap of the carding engine. He was carried round several times, and was very much injured in the head, arms, and legs; the *right arm* was amputated, and he recovered. He was off work two months. His masters allowed him 4s. 6d. per week, and as soon as he was able to do anything, he was taken on again, and his wages were raised to 6s. per week. What makes this case the more honourable to the firm is, that the poor boy had only worked four days for them when the accident occurred. Would that every manufacturer acted in this manner!"

The next case is of an opposite description.

"THOMAS, JAMES, and ABRAHAM LORD, three brothers, were bound apprentice to CHARLES RUDD, cotton manufacturer, in the township of Weardale and Wardale, in the parish of Rochdale. At the time they were bound, THOMAS was twelve, JAMES eleven, and ABRAHAM nine years of age. Their indentures expressed that they were to learn the business of manufacturing cotton goods. They continued with their master about seven years, when he failed in business, but still kept possession of their indentures ; and sent all three to work in his brother-in-law's *woollen mill.* In this mill they continued to work for about twelve months ; their original master, CHARLES RUDD, still reaping the benefit of their labour. About that time JAMES met with an accident, in the ' teasor,' or, as it is commonly called, the ' devil,' whereby he lost his left arm a little below the elbow. The master, thinking he would be of little service after his loss, gave up the indentures, and turned all three adrift without a shilling ; refusing to pay the surgeon, or to give up part of their clothes in his possession. The surgeon remains unpaid up to the present time, and has frequently asked JAMES LORD for the money. The young men having no friends to stand up for them, were obliged to submit, and leave the premises." It is high time, my Lord, that such unfeeling work should be investigated, and put a stop to.

I have not been able to ascertain the condition of the children in this neighbourhood ; but have reason to believe it is much the same, as at the cotton factories in other places.

I intend to leave this place for Bolton-le-Moors to-morrow ;

And am, &c.

" For them the fervid summer only brings
A double curse of stifling withering heat;
For them no flowers spring up, no wild bird sings,
No moss-grown walks refresh their weary fcct ;—·
No river's murmuring sound ; no wood-walk, sweet
With many a flower the learned slight and pass;
Nor meadow with pale cowslips thickly set
Amid the soft leaves of its tufted grass,—
Lure them a childish stock of treasures to amass."
A Voice from the Factories, p. 16.

LETTER X.

Bolton-le-Moors, October 8, 1841.

MY LORD :

On my arrival here, I waited upon several gentlemen, and workmen, who, I had been told, would be
likely to assist me in my inquiries. By these persons I was received very kindly, and to them I am
chiefly indebted for the information I have gained.
Availing myself of their proffered assistance, I commenced an investigation of every thing which I
thought might tend to throw any light upon the
object I had in view.   Under their direction, I
visited the factories, the cottages, cellars, taverns,
and other places likely to afford me an insight into
the manners and customs of the manufacturers,
and their work-people ; and have conversed with
men of all grades in society, who have freely given
me their opinions as to the cause of the prevailing
distress in this town and neighbourhood.   I now lay
before your Lordship the result of my inquiries, so
far as I have been able to proceed, and to-morrow

will (if spared) resume the subject in another letter.
—The condition of the women and children employed in the factories, first attracted my attention;
which I find is equally as bad here as at those places
I have previously visited. The education of the
children, it would seem, does not occupy much of
the care of the manufacturers, for out of forty factories in this place, I have not heard of a single
instance of a school having been erected on the premises; the education clause in the Factories' Regulation Act, appears little better than a dead letter.

I find there are a great many women employed
in winding and reeling, and in power-loom weaving,
in these cotton factories; working, in every respect,
under the same distressing circumstances as the
generality of factory labourers. I was very much hurt
to see the mothers in a morning, at the first sound of
the factory bell, running with their infants in their
arms, wrapped in a piece of old blanket or rug, to
the house of the person who is to take charge of them
for the day; and then hurrying off to the factory,
in order to get in before the gates were closed, as
they very well know, that if they are half a minute
too late, a fine of 2*d.* or 3*d.* will be entered against
them : which fine it will take them as many hours'
work to redeem, and often more. It is not surprising that many of the infants die from utter
neglect, and not having that nourishment and care,
which none can supply so well as their natural parents. Some prefer having their infants carried to
the factory at stated periods to be suckled, but very

few of the manufacturers will permit this, as they think it hinders work.

"A—— R——, a married woman, (employed in Messrs. H—— and B——'s cotton factory,) when pregnant of her fifth child, a short time ago, worked till dinner-time one day, and was brought to bed of a fine boy before the following morning. She went to work again about the nineteenth day, the child being as usual put out to nurse. In a little while the infant, not having proper nourishment, began to be poorly, and the mother was obliged to give up her work. However, it was too late; the child died. The mother again went to work, and is still working in the factory, earning about 7s. per week. Her husband is a *big piecer*, and earning but 9s. per week.

"C—— F——, a cotton-spinner in Mr. O——'s factory, had three *piecers*, about a fortnight ago, two of whom were married women. These two women had both infants, which were brought to the factory at regular periods to be suckled."

It is not necessary to multiply cases, the above will show the condition in which the women in this neighbourhood are obliged to work; while, in a great many instances, the husbands are kept idle at home. It is quite pitiable to see these poor men taking care of the house and children, and busily engaged in washing, baking, nursing, and preparing the humble repast for the wife, who is wearing her life away by toiling in the factory.

While I stayed in this place, I had an opportunity

of inspecting a wadding-hole, or, in other words, a place for the manufacture of every description of waste and damaged cotton, the refuse of other mills; this waste is in these factories worked up into counterpanes, coverlids, &c. These wadding-holes seem to be the connecting link between the woollen and cotton manufactures; every process being nearly the same as in the woollen. It requires some nerve in an inexperienced person to enter one of these places; accordingly, we find few persons willing to undertake a tour through one : even those persons whose duty it is to inspect them, look shy at entering. I was told by a person who had been two years an over-looker in this factory, that *in all that time he had not had a single visit from either surgeon or inspector.* When the person who conducted me through the factory opened the door, a scene presented itself which surprised even me, who had been accustomed to the factories from infancy. I can compare it to nothing more appropriately, than a heavy fall of snow; the machines, and the people working them, were indistinctly seen; and when we got near them, they had more the appearance of apparitions, than anything earthly. They were mostly covered with dust, and loose particles of cotton, which, from the nature of the material, and the great speed of the machinery, must always be the case. They generally wear a handkerchief over their mouths, in order to keep out the dust and cotton; this does not, by any means, improve their appearance. In short, no one would work in these places,

but from the most dire necessity. If I had an
enemy whom I wished to punish severely, I would
condemn him to ten years' imprisonment, and labour, in a *wadding-hole;* and I am persuaded but
few would live out their term of years.   I saw in
this factory women spinning with heavy machines,
doing men's work, which would in the end be sure
to ruin their constitutions, especially with the long
hours which they are obliged to work.   The wages
of these people are lower than what is obtained in
the better description of cotton-mills.   On leaving
this place, it required some time to recover myself
sufficiently to enable me to breathe freely, and divest
myself of all the cotton which had settled on my
clothes.

From the wadding-hole, I was conducted to a *fine*
factory, or one spinning, and weaving, the finest description of cotton goods.   On application being
made for admittance to this factory, I was given to
understand it was a great favour ; but, in consideration of my conductor being a friend of the manager,
I was allowed (after being kept a short time at the
door) to enter.   It was a cold, showery day, and we
had been more than once compelled to shelter from
the rain on our journey ; but, on entering the factory,
we were made sensible of a great change.   The
thermometer in the spinning rooms ranged from
seventy-three to seventy-eight degrees ; these were
fine rooms, be it remembered, where the greatest degree of heat for spinning is required.   I have found a
great variation in the temperature of a room between

morning and night, as also between the beginning
and latter end of a week ; evidently from their cool-
ing considerably in the night, and at the week's end.
As might be expected, I found the work-people in
the spinning rooms, working with scarcely any clothes
on. The men, generally, had only a thin pair of trousers, and shirt ; no shoes or stockings, waistcoat, or
any other articles of dress. The young women and
girls (who were mixed indiscriminately with the men),
had each on a pair of stays, a short petticoat of light
material, generally cotton, and a pinafore, or, as they
call them, " aprons," which come over their shoulders,
with no shoes or stockings, cap, or any other article
of dress.

The machinery in this place was kept very clean,
but not generally guarded, as it ought to be, in order
to protect the work-people from accidents. The dust
and loose cotton are not so troublesome in fine factories as in those spinning yarn of an inferior quality,
but the sense of heat is overpowering in the extreme.
I had not been long in these rooms, before I felt the
perspiration pouring down my face profusely, though
I was only a looker-on ; how the *work-people* are
able to bear it, day after day, and year after year, I
cannot imagine. It is no wonder that they are generally pale, sickly-looking, swarthy, diminutive people;
and greatly inclined to asthma and consumption.
Nor can it surprise us in the least, that, working
under such circumstances, and associated together in
this manner for such a length of time, their morals
should be of a lower order than usual ; especially

when we take into consideration the state of ignorance in which these people pass their lives. Their
opportunities of learning what is useful are very few,
and they are so tired and exhausted by the long hours
of labour, that there is little inclination to study.
Again, I regret to be compelled, in justice to the
work-people, to state, that the example set them by
their masters, in many instances, has not a tendency
to raise, but rather to lower and debase their moral
character.

To the credit of the manufacturers of Bolton it
may be said, that wages are kept as high there as at
any place I have visited ; the work-people are all
paid by four o'clock on the Saturday evening, and,
with very few exceptions, they are paid *separately*,
and in the *current coin* of the realm.

On looking over their list of prices for mule-spinning, dated May 23rd, 1840, agreed to by masters
and men, I find there is a premium held out to the
manufacturers to introduce machines working a high
number of spindles ; and the double-decking or coupling of the smaller ones.   And this will account for
the mania at present existing among the manufacturers, to couple their machines, and do with fewer
hands ; often, half the number, or even less than
that.   For instance, the list now before me is calculated for all descriptions of yarn spun on mules of
324 spindles.   But, do mark this :—if the same sort
of yarn is spun on mules of 408 spindles, $10\frac{1}{2}$ per
cent. will be deducted from the prices paid to the
person spinning on mules of 324 spindles.   If on

mules of 516 spindles, 20 per cent. will be deducted. If on mules of 732 spindles, 30 per cent.; and, in some descriptions of yarn, $32\frac{1}{2}$ per cent. will be deducted. If on mules of 804 spindles, 33 to $35\frac{1}{2}$ per cent. will be deducted; or, more than one-third of the price paid to a person working a mule of 324 spindles. It must be borne in mind, that the number of spindles above-mentioned refers to one mule only; and that, till within a year or two, each spinner had to mind a pair of mules with 300 spindles each; which was then thought to be as high a number as could be worked by one man. Latterly, however, for the reasons above stated, the spinners have had to work two, and three pairs of these mules, decked, or (as the term implies) coupled together. These double-deckers contain from 1500 to 2680 spindles. The only *check* upon the inducement held out to manufacturers to enlarge their wheels, is an exception mentioned in their list of prices, to this effect, that " double-decked mules of all sizes [are] to be subject to 5 per cent. less discount than single mules—on all numbers," or all descriptions of yarn.

This double-decking throws out a great number of hands, and ruins the constitution of those employed in working them. Is it then surprising that we find spinners hanging about the streets idle, serving the wallers, bricklayers, and paviors; or doing anything they can get, however contrary to their former life and habits? and hear of others dying in declines, asthma, &c., at a very early period of life? But to make this a little more plain to your Lordship, let us

take an account of the number of spindles working
in Bolton, in 1835 and 1841 ; also the number of
hands required to work these spindles, at these different periods. I find, on looking over a document
containing information carefully collected on the spot,
that in 1835 there were 30 cotton factories at work
in Bolton, in which were 601,226 spindles ; giving
employment to 798 spinners, and 2527 piecers. In
1841, of 40 factories, 38 were working, in which
were 751,555 spindles, employing 737 spinners, and
2,457 piecers.

Now, by a simple rule in arithmetic, we shall find,
that if the increase of spinners and piecers had kept
pace with the increase of spindles, instead of dimi-
nishing, there would have been employed in 1841,
997 spinners and 3158 piecers ; which is more by
260 spinners, and 701 piecers, than are employed.
Consequently, we may fairly conclude, that 961 persons have been thrown out, or deprived of employment, by increasing the labour of those retained ;
and that the persons thus thrown out, tend to glut
the market, and lower the wages of labour, which,
indeed, we find is always the case.

In illustration of the above, I may mention that
I was credibly informed, that in Mr. ROTHWELL's
factory, three pairs of 400 spindle-mules, containing
in all 2400 spindles, were decked together. These
mules, in separate pairs, employed 3 men and 9
piecers ; as they are now decked, or coupled together, they employ 1 man and 7 piecers : thus throwing out 2 men, and 2 piecers, by double (or, more

correctly speaking, *treble* decking) these machines; but with a tremendous addition of labour to the only remaining adult, and causing 8 persons to do the work of 12.

Since writing the above, I have been informed that one pair has been uncoupled, or taken away from this machine, in consequence of the master being unable to get men willing to work them: it appears that several have tried, and have been obliged to give it up. I was told by men who work these double-deckers, that *six years*, with the present hours of labour, are quite sufficient to break down the strongest constitution. The saving to the masters, from having this sort of wheels, is very considerable; in many cases, 1*l.* to 2*l.* per week for a single machine.

My Lord, I have met here with a great many cases of cripples, from long hours and accidents; and to-morrow will endeavour to inform your Lordship of a few of them.

I am, &c.

LETTER XI.

Bolton-le-Moors, October 9, 1841.

My Lord:

I now sit down to communicate to your Lordship a few cases of the cripples I have met with here. The first is what may be called a compound case, as the poor fellow was partly indebted to long hours of labour, and partly to two accidents, for the injuries

he has received ; the other cases are all accidents :
and I humbly request your Lordship will take particular notice of the paltry and insignificant trifles
that have been given them by their employers, for
the serious injuries they have received. This, I
think, will clearly prove the necessity of something
being done by the Legislature, to protect the factory
people from the lamentable consequences resulting
from accidents like these.

When I was going through the Market-place, the
day after my arrival in Bolton, I met a cripple wad-
dling along in a strange manner.   Seeing the factory
mark upon him, I asked him a few questions, and finding him willing to answer them, I invited him to have
something to eat and drink, and he then told me his
history, as follows :

" JONATHAN ODDSON, went to work in the cotton
factory of Mr. ORMROD in Bolton, as a piecer, at
eleven years of age ; he worked two weeks for
nothing, and then had 2s. 6d. per week for about four
years, and 3s. 6d. about six months longer, when he
had his left arm broken by the machinery, and was
off work thirteen months.   He then went to Mr.
ROTHWELL'S, as a middle piecer, at 5s. per week
for two years.   Afterwards, he was employed as a
big piecer, at 7s. per week for about eighteen months,
when he again got his left arm broken and crushed
in the machinery, and was off work three years ! ! !
He was then engaged as a spinner on a 400-spindle
mule, and could earn about 10s. per week ; he was a
spinner a little more than five years, and was then

done up, past all work. His legs are very much deformed. His knees, which are both turned in, almost wrap over each other. In the act of walking, he has to move the centre of gravity from side to side, and balance himself like a rope-dancer. He has nothing to depend upon but little jobs which he gets to do for the market-people." He cannot read or write his own name, can scarcely count to twenty, does not know his age, the day of the month or year of our Lord: the long hours of labour have crippled both his body and mind. His deformity had been the means of driving him out of society, and he told me he had spent a part of his leisure time in company with a sow (kept by his mother) and her pigs, of which he speaks with affection, but seldom mentions his relations. He knows the number of times the sow had pigs, and the number each time; and this serves him as a sort 'of almanack, to which he constantly refers in making calculations, of ever so trifling a nature; in short, he seems very little removed from the condition of the pigs themselves.

Your Lordship will see that I am relating things as they occur to my mind, rather than in the actual order in which they first became known to me. I had not been an hour in Bolton, before an accident occurred, to a boy of the name of SAMUEL SKELTON, of a very distressing nature, almost under my own eye. This took place in the cotton factory of Messrs. GREGSON and LEEMING, on Thursday the 7th instant. I visited this youth, and sitting by his bed-

side, I took the following particulars from his weeping
mother : She told me that, "having a large family,
she had been under the necessity of sending him
to the cotton factory belonging to Mr. W. GARNETT
TAYLOR, at nine years of age, where he worked only
a short time before he got his *right arm* entangled in
the machinery, and so dreadfully crushed and torn, as
to render amputation *above the elbow* necessary.   In
consequence of this accident, he was off work *three
years*, during which time he had no assistance from
his master !   About three months ago he was again
employed in the card-room of a cotton factory, belonging to the firm of Messrs. GREGSON and LEEM-
ING, and on Thursday last, his left hand was caught
by the machinery.   By this accident he has lost the
two middle fingers, and it is thought the little finger
will have to be taken off; his hand also is very
much torn.   If he gets well, he will only have the
forefinger and thumb on his left hand, and having
previously lost his right arm, he will have to depend
on some one for a living the remainder of his days."
I was told that SAMUEL SKELTON's masters had
done nothing for him ; but I hope some public-
spirited individual will take the case in hand, and
try to get them to assist him in some way.   His
father is a striker at an iron-foundry, and gets 15s. a-
week, when fully employed.   He has a wife and eight
children ; one at service, one earning 5s. per week, and
another 2s. 6d. : this is the whole income of a family
consisting of nine persons.   My Lord, I am sorry to
say, that a great part of the machinery in cotton

factories is not guarded as it ought to be, and wants looking after.

Yesterday, a young man, standing about five feet eight or nine inches, and straight as a wand, came to me from a village about three miles distant. He is about twenty-three years of age. He had met with an accident which had deprived him of *both arms;* one wrenched out of the *socket at the shoulder*, and the other torn off about three inches below. This being a sad case, I will give your Lordship his history, in his own words.

" I commenced working in a cotton factory at eight years of age, and continued to follow the same occupation until I met with an awful accident, by which I lost *both arms*. This accident happened in the following manner : I was then about nineteen years of age, and working in a mill belonging to Mr. JOHN RYLAND, in the parish of Ainsworth. On the 3rd of January, 1838, I was assisting to couple a strap, and standing on a trestle about three feet six inches high, holding the strap to prevent it rubbing on the shaft ; the shaft was polished, and went at the speed of about 185 revolutions per minute. Whilst I was holding the strap, it gave a twitch, and in an instant my whole body was coiled round the shaft ; and in this manner I was carried round for the space of a minute. When the engine was stopped, I was suspended *by the flesh of my right arm*, the other was completely torn from my body. I recovered, and am now depending on my parents for support : my father is a poor working man, and I am the *eldest of eight children.* This accident has caused great privation in our family. It is now four years since it happened, and since then I have received from my master, at different times, *between* 30s. *and* 40s. I am not able to do anything for myself, and am obliged to have a brother to wait on me."

Had he sustained these injuries while fighting for his country, he might have looked forward to an asylum in Chelsea or Greenwich Hospital; but in vain we look for such asylums for the mutilated factory cripples. There are no such institutions, though we travel throughout the length and breadth of the land. The Union workhouse and the grave are the only asylums for such cases; though accidents more or less severe are of daily and almost hourly occurrence, often issuing in death, immediate, or lingering.

My Lord, it is unnecessary to comment further upon this case, it speaks for itself. A finer young man we seldom meet with. Your Lordship may more easily imagine, than I can describe, my feelings on this occasion; especially when he took a *pen in his teeth and showed me how beautifully he could write.* A specimen of his writing I inclose for your Lordship's inspection. This accident shows the necessity of boxing-off the *horizontal,* as well as the upright shafts.

" JOSEPH TAYLOR went to work in Mr. GARNETT TAYLOR's mill at eleven years of age, as a scavenger. He had nothing for his work the first fortnight, but then got 1s. per week for one month, and was gradually raised at the rate of about 6d. at a time, till at the end of about five years he had 5*s.* 6*d.* per week. He continued at this mill about twelve months longer, and then went to Mr. ORMROD'S, for the same wages of 5*s.* 6*d.*, as a piecer. He left this place in about six months, and was then engaged at Messrs. AINSWORTH'S at 6*s.* per week, and had been working twelve months, when he met with an accident, by getting his left arm entangled in the feed-rollers of the carding engine; by which it was so dreadfully crushed as to render amputation necessary. The arm was taken off a little below the elbow. This was in 1840. He is now nearly nineteen years of age. Messrs. AINSWORTH have given him 10*s.* as a compensation, and this is all he has received from any quarter. He is depending on his father for a living, a poor hand-loom weaver, who has six children besides him. He worked in the factories in all about seven years and a half; and earned in all about 70*l.*" The injury resulting from the accident is irreparable, and he is cast off with 10*s.* I state the facts : the reader must draw his own conclusion.

" MARY HILL, twenty-five years of age, was working at ADAM KAY'S cotton factory in Acre-field, about seven o'clock one morning, when she had her left arm taken into the scutcher, by which serious accident she lost her hand. In a short time she got well, and was again employed in the same place, at her old wages of 6*s.* 6*d.* per week, for a few weeks ; but her master, finding she was not so serviceable as formerly, offered to keep her on, if she would take one-half, or 3*s.* 3*d.* This, she told him candidly,

she could not live upon. So she was turned off
without giving her anything; and the overlooker,
whose duty it was to discharge her, although he was
steeled in such-like work, thought this such a hard
case, that he could not find in his heart to tell her the
determination of his master, but got a carder to be
the messenger of the dismal tale. Her master was
compelled to pay 1*l*. to the surgeon; but that was
all he did pay. The spinners and other work-people
collected a few shillings for her; and with this small
sum she bought some calico prints, with which she is
now travelling the country." This account was given
me by the person who took her to the surgeon, and
was an eyewitness of the whole melancholy affair.

"HENRY CROSS was working in a card room, and,
in the act of putting a strap on, was caught by a
buckle on the strap; the tongue of the buckle got
under a ring which he had on his finger. He was
carried up to the ceiling, and being caught by a boy
was pulled down. His finger broke off at the second
joint, and thus his life was saved by the loss of his
finger."

"JOSEPH DITCHFIELD, a youth of seventeen years,
was working among the throstles in Mr. BARNES'
factory, Halshaw Moor, two miles and a half from
Bolton, on the 6th of March last; and, in the act of
putting a strap on, was caught and taken up to the
ceiling of the room. By this accident his left arm
was torn off about the elbow. He has since got well,
and his master has put him to school, and kept him
there ever since, and pays him 6*s*. per week, besides

his schooling." This is christian-like behaviour on
the part of Mr. BARNES, and as it ought to be.

" JAMES COOK, a spinner in Mr. BARNES' factory, was putting a strap on, and was caught and
squeezed between the drum and the pillar.   The flesh
and sinews of his arm were *burned* from the bone.
He has not been able to spin since.   He was off work
nine months.   His master let him live rent free, paid
his surgeon, and gave him a flock bed, and has now
put him to an easy job at 15*s.* per week."

" JOHN HARRISON, a youth of sixteen years of
age, was working in the card room of Messrs. AR-
ROWSMITH's factory, and his hand being drawn into
the wheels, he had all his fingers taken off close by
the hand, except the forefinger, which is half an inch
long."   His masters paid him his wages, and the
surgeon's bill, and gave him work when he got well.

The above three cases show that there are still a
few manufacturers willing to act honourably to their
work-people who have the misfortune to be crippled
by accident, or otherwise, in their mills.   And to any
one who knows how the manufacturers have got their
great wealth, it is matter of surprise how any of
them can find in their hearts to act dishonourably in
such cases.   It can be accounted for in no other way
than by the fact, that as " riches increase, they have
set their heart upon them."

Many are the amusing anecdotes told me of the
origin of most of the wealthy firms which we find in
the list of manufacturers ; men who now possess half
a million, and in some cases a million and upwards

sterling.   Some of them might have been seen walking about the streets of Bolton, Manchester, and
other places, from twenty to thirty years ago, with
scarcely a shoe to their foot, a coat to their backs, or
trousers that would hide their limbs; without the
means of obtaining a dinner for the day, or a lodging
for the night.   I have taken some little trouble to
analyse the firms of Bolton (in company with, and
assisted by persons who are well acquainted with these
men), and the result proves, that of forty-five individuals known in the firms, twenty-five were originally
very poor, twelve brought money more or less into
the trade, and the remaining eight are doubtful, but
my friends were inclined to think them poor.   And
again, out of 751,555 spindles at present at work in
Bolton, at the least three-fourths of that number have
been set a-going by mill-gotten money.   Another important feature in factory statistics is, the immense
sum of money paid to joint-stock, and other banks,
in the form of interest on money borrowed to raise the
many tall chimneys we see in the manufacturing districts.   Looking at the factory system in any point
of view, and bearing in mind the wealth it has been
the means of creating and bringing into this country,
any disinterested person would naturally suppose that
the people who had created this wealth would live
happily and comfortably, and that there would not
be a single case of distress and misery in all the factory districts; but how different do we find the
reality.   We see, on the one hand, a few individuals
who have accumulated great wealth by means of the

factory system; and, on the other hand, hundreds of thousands of human beings huddled together in attics and cellars, or crawling over the earth as if they did not belong to it. Maimed, mutilated, deformed, emaciated, ruined in health, their spirits broken, their mind and reasoning powers toppling from their seat, and many of them catching, like drowning men, at straws, to save themselves from what would be a happy release from their miserable situation; crying out with Job, "Wherefore is light given to him that is in misery, and life to the bitter in soul?"

Contrast this, my Lord, with what man was originally intended to be. We are told that man was made "in the image of God;" that God "saw his substance yet being imperfect," and that in "His book all our members are written;" that he was made "a little lower than the angels," and "crowned with glory and honour," and placed in this world "to have dominion over the works of His hands." If, as we are told, all our members are written in His book, what an awful reckoning will some of these manufacturers have to meet! How will they be able to account for the lives, and limbs, which they have heedlessly, if not wantonly, sacrificed?

I am, &c.

" Oh, men ! blaspheme not freedom ! Are *they* free
  Who toil until the body's strength gives way ?
  Who may not set a term for liberty ?
  Who have no time for food, or rest, or play,
  But struggle through the long unwelcome day
  Without the leisure to be good or glad ?
  Such is their service—call it what you may.
  Poor little creatures, overtasked and sad,
Your slavery hath no name,—yet is its curse as bad ! "

A Voice from the Factories, p. 20.

LETTER XII.

Bolton-le-Moors, Oct. 25, 1841.*

My Lord :

After an absence of a fortnight, I revisited Bolton,
on the 23rd instant ; and the same evening had some
conversation with many of the cotton spinners, particularly one who had that day accompanied Mr. Doherty, of Manchester, to Turton, as a deputation
from the spinners' committee to Messrs. Henry and
Edmund Ashworth.   It appeared they were de-
puted to wait upon the above gentlemen for the purpose of ascertaining how they were disposed towards
a Ten-Hours' Bill, and they seemed pleased with the
result of their mission.   I have not yet had the
pleasure of seeing Mr. Doherty, but Mr. J——
R——, the person who went with him on this occasion, tells me that Messrs. Ashworth have said

---

* For the sake of bringing the information respecting Bolton
together into one part of this volume, the above letter is placed
here, though written nearly three weeks after the preceding
one, and in consequence of a second visit paid to that town.

BOLTON-LE-MOORS.   83

they would not in any way oppose them in trying to
obtain a Ten Hours' Bill, in the next Session of Parliament; and that if the spinners wanted a Bill for
eleven hours, they would go with them for it.   He
also stated, that one of their objects was to ascertain
whether Messrs. ASHWORTH paid their spinners the
full *Bolton prices;* they having heard that *ten per
cent.* was regularly deducted.   He says, "We put
the question to Mr. ASHWORTH, the gentleman we
saw, in this form : — Do you, sir, in paying your spinners, take *ten per cent.* from the Bolton list of
prices?"   Mr. ASHWORTH immediately answered,
"We do."   This question and answer were considered of great importance to the spinners, and were
repeated to me three different times; and in order
that I might remember the question and answer
correctly, I entered them in my note-book.   It was
stated to me that this ten per cent. would produce
Messrs. ASHWORTH upwards of 2000*l.* per annum.
Again, he informed me that Messrs. ASHWORTH
had heard of my being in the factory district, and
had formed some erroneous opinions as to the object
of my journey.   This information at once decided me
to pay a visit to Turton, and lay before those mill-
owners the objects I had in view in coming into these
quarters.   The spinners agreed, that this would be
the best plan I could adopt, to remove any misappre-
hension which those gentlemen might have respecting my objects.   Accordingly, this morning, I waited
upon them, and had the following conversation with
one of the partners, I believe, Mr. EDMUND ASH-

WORTH, the magistrate. I began by saying, "I have been informed, Sir, that you were aware of my being in this neighbourhood, and had formed some erroneous opinions as to the objects of my journey; I have therefore made bold to wait upon you, for the purpose of removing those impressions, and to tell you what my objects really are."

Mr. ASHWORTH said, they certainly had heard of my being in the factory districts, and that I had come with the intention of collecting a number of extreme cases for publication, in order to make the system appear as black and frightful as possible; that he was pleased that I had come to their establishment, and that he should be glad to hear what I had in view, and if he approved of it, he would afford me every facility in viewing their works, &c.

To this I made answer that, so far from wishing to collect extreme cases only, I had come with the intention of getting such information from the manufacturers and workmen, as would enable me to lay before the public a correct account of the life led by factory people; that, as he might see, I was a factory operative myself, and that, after spending twenty-five years in the factories, I had found myself completely worn out at the age of thirty-six, and rendered unable to get a living by any ordinary means. Also, that I had published a "Narrative" of my sufferings and experience in the factories, and that the encouragement I had received on that occasion, had induced me to undertake my present task; that I was well aware of the difficulties I should have to contend with, but that I would take especial care to avoid any thing which might lead the public to suppose, or say, that I was actuated by a party spirit, or groundless prejudices; and that I particularly wished to impress upon his mind, that I was not hired for the purpose, as some writers of the system had been.

Mr. ASHWORTH said, he thought I was acting rightly, to avoid party spirit in treating on a subject of so much importance; and that he did not know that writers had been hired to give favourable views of the system.

I then told him that a certain writer had received 5l. from the manufacturers for a small pamphlet he had written; and that the said writer had afterwards come to a spinners' committee, and offered to write a second pamphlet contradicting every assertion he had made, if the spinners would give him a sovereign for his trouble; but that they not being willing to give him the money, he undertook to write an article for the newspapers on the comparative merits of Black and White Slavery, for which he got a few pots of beer from the spinners. I then told him, that one principal feature of my work would be, to describe cases of accidents from machinery, and endeavour to point out the means of preventing them; and also to inquire into the circumstances of cripples made by long hours of labour and over-exertion, and to draw the attention of the manufacturers and the public generally to the claims which these unhappy creatures had on society for a comfortable maintenance,

and to the necessity of something being done to prevent others being brought into a similar situation.

To this Mr. ASHWORTH made answer, that with
respect to accidents, they had very few in their
mills; and that they had taken care, by boxing-off
the machinery, to prevent them, as far as they were
able; and, as for cripples from long hours, he did not
know that they had any. Alluding to what I had
thrown out respecting their maintenance, "Thou
knowest," said he, "that they have always the Poor-
law to fall back upon, in case of necessity."

I then drew Mr. ASHWORTH's attention to a family I had seen and conversed with, a few days before, who were then working in the factory of Messrs.
JONES, BROTHERS and Co., of Leigh.* This family, I told him had come from Suffolk, in 1836, and
had been engaged by them (the Messrs. ASHWORTH)
for three years. I added, that the parents of this
family had informed me, that their children were all
straight and well-formed, previously to leaving Suffolk; and that in the short space of five years, their
son and two daughters had been made *cripples for
life*, the young man, who is twenty years of age,
being under the necessity of walking in *irons;* that
neither the young man himself, nor his parents, had
charged them, or his present masters, with ill-usage,
but had attributed it solely to *long hours of labour*.
Referring to what Mr. ASHWORTH had stated, re-

---

* For a further account of this case, see Letter XVII., dated
Leigh, October 22.

specting factory cripples falling back upon the Poor-law, I said it was my opinion that we deserved something better, after seeing all our prospects in life blasted, than the dietary and confinement of a work-house. Mr. ASHWORTH could not recollect the family I mentioned; but, on making inquiry of the manager, he found that what I had stated respecting the connexion of this family with Messrs. ASHWORTH's mills was perfectly correct.

We then conversed upon the subject of the long hours of factory labour, when he expressed his views, which were similar to what the firm had stated to the deputation of the Bolton spinners, when they waited upon them two days before. His views were to this effect: he said they were anxious to reduce the hours of labour, but could not see the propriety of reducing them to *ten* per day; they were favourable, however, to *eleven*. This gentleman then kindly accompanied me over the mills, schools, and the cottages of the work-people, and explained any little difficulty, and allowed me to ask any questions I thought proper of the work-people.

In the first place, I inspected their mill at Turton. You will please to bear in mind, my Lord, it was Monday morning, when we see everything in a cotton-mill to the best advantage. All was as clean, and looking as comfortable as could be expected in such a place under the present system. The machinery is generally of an improved kind, the most dangerous parts of which are well boxed-off. The thermometer stood a little above sixty-one degrees, in a room on the ground-floor ; but, being Monday morning, I was not surprised at the low temperature, and was fully aware that this ought not to be taken as the mean, or average temperature of the week. Before night, it would, in all probability, rise to nearly seventy degrees.

In this mill I saw suspended their rules of order, of which the following is a copy :—

" OBSERVE.

Waste not !—Want not !
Put everything in its proper place.
Use everything for its proper purpose.
Do everything at its proper time.

REMEMBER,

That nothing can be done well without
  Order, Promptitude, and Perseverance;
And never despise attention to small things in great
  matters.
Remember, also, that whatever man has done, man
  may do."

With the whole of these observations I perfectly agree, with the exception of the last. It is very clear to me, that this is erroneous. For instance, we will go no farther than their own business of cotton manufacturing. In this business we find men, who began without a shilling in the world, whose families are now enjoying fortunes of one, one and a half, and two millions sterling ; but can men beginning now with such slender means, acquire like fortunes, in so short a space of time ? I believe that Messrs. ASHWORTH themselves will say *no,* to this question.

And, God forbid, say I, that any men, should ever again acquire such enormous fortunes by similar means.

In this mill, and their other mill, two miles higher up, on the Blackburn-road, I found no *self-acting mules*. I was told that they had tried them some little time before, but finding they did not answer their purpose, they were laid aside. There were some double-deckers, but not so large, or containing so many spindles, as some I had met with in Bolton and Manchester. I saw some women working single wheels, nearly half naked, as is generally the case in the spinning-rooms. The work-people here, certainly, look more healthy than factory people generally. This may be accounted for in the following manner: The cottages of the work-people are generally built on high ground, adjoining the mills; they are good substantial stone buildings, roomy, well drained, well lighted, well watered, and well aired, having one door in front, and another at the back, through which a current of air can be allowed to pass. Many have a small patch of ground in front, and, I believe, all have a yard, and other conveniences behind. The rents are about 3*s.* per week. No more than one family lives in a house; which is generally well furnished. A custom prevails here, which I think it would be well to imitate elsewhere, of inspecting the cottages of the work-people once a quarter, or oftener, if found necessary; and should anything be wanting to make them comfortable (such articles as blankets, sheets, &c.), money is instantly advanced by the masters, the necessary articles procured, and the money paid back by instalments, as they can afford it. In these cottages I found a great variety of books, such as bibles, prayer-books, hymn-books, and books of miscellaneous literature, not excepting "Fielden's Curse of the Factory System;" and I could not but think how much more happy these people would be, if they had sufficient time to read them, which, I am certain, is not the case.

Another thing which greatly conduces to their health and happiness, is the absence of all public-houses (excepting two beer-shops) and pawn-shops. It is true they can go to Bolton, which is only two-and-a-half or three miles from Turton; but who, after working in the factory all the day, would do this from choice? He must like drink very much indeed, who would do that; and such a man, I am persuaded, would very soon be told to go, and remain in Bolton altogether: he would not suit Messrs. ASHWORTH. I was told they have special constables sworn in, who are provided with staffs, handcuffs, &c. These constables go round to the beer-houses at a certain hour of the night, and if any unlucky fellow is found, he is taken care of for the night, and brought before his master (who is a magistrate) in the morning. His conduct after that is narrowly watched, and he must either reform, or go about his business.

Again, the work-people living in these houses are almost all in some way related to each other; and, generally speaking, have never worked in any other factory. They do not, therefore, lose anything by moving, or shifting about. It may be necessary

here to mention, that there are a great many more
working for Messrs. ASHWORTH, who live at a distance of one to two miles from these mills. How
they are situated, I had not an opportunity of knowing; but I saw several of them, when the people were
discharged at noon, sitting in the cart-house, on
stones in the yard, and other places about the premises, getting their dinners; and I ventured to suggest to Mr. ASHWORTH the propriety of having
a comfortable room for them to sit down in, and
have reason to believe my suggestion will be attended to.

The mills are driven partly by steam, and partly
by water power; one of the water-wheels is said to
be among the largest in the kingdom. It measures
sixty-one feet in diameter, and is about twelve feet wide;
and, if I remember rightly, is about sixty horse-power :
the saving in fuel at this one mill, I was told, is about
20*l.* per week.

As I passed through the mills, I asked many questions of the work-people, some of which they declined
to answer, although their masters were not near.
The reason for refusing, they said, was, because something they had stated to former visitors had been
made public, and they were afraid of giving offence.
Among other questions, I asked two young men,
who had been brought up as agricultural labourers,
whether they found themselves better off as spinners,
or as labourers? giving them at the same time to
understand, that they might answer the question or
not, as they pleased. They hung down their heads,

and said nothing; and perceiving how the matter stood, I asked them no more questions.

In conversation with some tradespeople in Bolton, I was told that the Messrs. ASHWORTH'S men were generally good customers, and they were not afraid to trust them a little, as their work was constant, and wages sure every Saturday night; that they were paid separately, so as not to be under the necessity of going to a public-house, in lots of ten to twenty, for change ; and that they were paid in money.

Although there are a great number of females, generally single, employed in this establishment, I have reason to believe they conduct themselves in a more becoming manner than is usual in cotton factories in large towns. The absence of a great many temptations, which generally accompany factory life, and the vigilant eye of the masters, will in a great measure account for this. The women, in short, both married and single, whether working in the mills, or staying at home, seem to be as much afraid of the masters, as of their fathers and husbands. Hence the families are kept more comfortable than in most towns.

With respect to the children, I cannot say much. Your Lordship is well aware, that this firm has been fined, on more than one occasion, for employing children a greater number of hours than is allowed by law; and also of the opinion expressed by Mr. HENRY ASHWORTH, on the 7th of May, 1840, before the Select Committee on Mills and Factories, of which your Lordship was chairman, to the effect that he considered they were exonerated from all responsibility if they had a certificate from the surgeon that the child was of proper age. Also, that a friend of his, JOSIAH BARKER, of Preston, had stated by letter, that he had " no doubt that in some cases children may pass for *thirteen years of age—when the surgeon receives a fee per annum*—who are not more than *eleven years of age.*" And again, that the education of the children belongs either to the parents, or to the State, and not to the employer. I could not have thought that gentlemen of this opinion would have provided schools for the education of the children; which, however, I was pleased to find was the case.

The schools of Messrs. ASHWORTH are conducted in a manner that does the firm great credit, at a cost to them, as I was informed, of 200*l.* per annum. In these schools I met some very sharp boys, very quick at mental arithmetic; but these were not all factory boys, be it observed. The children of the village have access to the schools, although they may not be working in the factories. At one school, there is a master for the boys, and a mistress for the girls. These girls learn knitting, and sewing, as well as reading, writing, and accounts: great care is taken to teach them industrious and notable habits, and also to instil into their minds precepts of morality and religion.

The establishment of the Messrs. ASHWORTH seems, in many respects, to be conducted on a better plan than cotton factories generally are. It is, however, matter of regret, that these gentlemen, who

have done a good deal (as I readily admit) towards
making their work-people comparatively comfortable, under the long hours of labour, should not
join the working classes in endeavouring to obtain a
Ten-Hours' Bill, especially as they have proofs immediately before them, that the constitution of man
is not capable of bearing the present long hours
of labour in factories. The ten-hours' restriction,
making, with meals, a day of twelve hours, is,
in my opinion, absolutely necessary, in order that
man should once more go through life with a chance
of living out his full term of threescore years and ten ;
and not be compelled to crowd the whole term of his
existence into a few short years ; many now being done
up at twenty and twenty-five years of age.

My Lord, I have spent seven or eight hours of
this day in examining the mills, cottages, schools,
&c., belonging to this firm ; and I feel it due to the
Messrs. ASHWORTH to say, that I have experienced
great kindness from them and their overlookers,
with one of whom I took dinner, with another tea,
and on taking leave of Mr. HENRY ASHWORTH, he
gave me a few shillings to assist in defraying my expenses.   How deeply it is to be lamented, that these
gentlemen—estimable in many respects—should hitherto have been conspicuous, beyond perhaps any other
cotton firm, for determined hostility to the Ten Hours'
—or, if it had its proper appellation, the *Twelve*-Hours'
Bill ? When will they learn, in reference to this great
question of humanity, "to do justice, and love mercy?"

I am, &c.

" Oh! shall it then be said that tyrant acts
  Are those which cause our country's looms to thrive ;
  That merchant England's prosperous trade exacts
  This bitter sacrifice, ere she derive
  That profit due, for which the feeble strive ?
  Is her commercial avarice so keen,
  That in her busy multitudinous hive
  Hundreds must die like insects, scarcely seen,
While the thick-thronged survivors work where they have been ?''
          A Voice from the Factories, p. 22.

LETTER XIII.

Manchester, October 14, 1841.

My Lord:

Since I last addressed your Lordship, I have had
the pleasure of meeting both my sisters, at Chorley,
whom I had not seen for several years, and am desired to express their grateful thanks for the present
your Lordship was pleased to send for the one who
has had her hand crushed in the machinery. She
feels herself highly honoured by your Lordship's
notice of her misfortune. While I stayed at Chorley,
I had not many opportunities (in consequence of
the bad state of the weather) of observing the condition of the factory people.

I arrived here yesterday, and will endeavour to
give your Lordship a general view of Manchester and
its inhabitants, as they appeared to me in the walks
I have taken yesterday and to-day. Manchester,
like Leeds, is in every respect a manufacturing town,
and bears all the characteristic features mentioned in
a former letter on Leeds. We do, however, find

some redeeming things in Manchester, of which few manufacturing towns can boast; such as its valuable institutions, splendid buildings, immense store-houses, and occasionally a clean, respectable-looking street; but, those parts of this great town in which I felt the deepest interest, have but little to recommend them.

The impressions which Manchester, and its teeming population made upon my mind, are so similar to those which they produced upon the mind of Dr. KAY, formerly a physician here, and the author of a pamphlet on the condition of the working classes, that I shall endeavour to fortify my opinions by a few extracts from his work.

" Visiting Manchester, the metropolis of the commercial system, a stranger regards with wonder the ingenuity and comprehensive capacity which, in the short space of half a century, have here established the staple manufacture of this kingdom. He beholds with astonishment the establishments of its merchants, the masses of capital which have been accumulated by those who crowd upon its mart, and the restless spirit which has made every part of the known world the scene of their enterprise. When he turns from the great capitalists, he contemplates the fearful strength of that labouring population, which lies like a slumbering giant at their feet. He has heard of the turbulent riots of the people—of machine-breaking—of the secret and sullen organization which has suddenly lit the torch of incendiarism, or well nigh uplifted the arm of rebellion in the land.

He remembers that political desperadoes have ever loved to tempt this population to the hazards of the swindling game of revolution, and have scarcely failed. In the midst of so much affluence, however, he has disbelieved the cry of need." *

The streets and lanes, in which are the dwellings of the working classes, are generally narrow, and dirty; very little attention seems to be paid to the comfort of the people living in these crowded neighbourhoods. The dwellings of vast numbers of the poor people have been erected without any care for the health of those who were destined to live in them. In the first place, the ground has not been properly prepared, there being no sewers or drainage in many of the streets; nor has the slightest regard been paid to the warmth, ventilation, and convenience of the houses; many of them are built back to back, so that the admission of a fresh current of air through them is impossible. The rooms are so small, and the ceilings so low, that they are not capable of admitting a sufficient quantity of air to support healthy respiration.

There is no boiler, oven, wash-house, or any convenience needed by a family. The sleeping rooms are not sufficient for decency, or even morality, to say nothing of salubrity. Frequently there is only one out-office in common to several tenements, and that always partially, and often altogether open

---

* J. P. KAY, M.D., Esq., on the Moral and Physical Condition of the Working Classes employed in the Cotton Manufacture of Manchester.

and exposed.   In short, houses built not only without regard to the ordinary comforts, and the common decencies of civilized society, but even without
regard to the primary and essential requisites to life
and health.

The inhabitants of these loathsome dwellings take
but little care of their health and comfort; for in
many of the streets we find heaps of filth, and pools
of stagnant water; sufficient of themselves to breed
fevers and diseases, by the poisonous exhalations
arising from decaying vegetable matter, and other
filth which ought to be removed.   In the centre of
the town there is a mass of buildings inhabited by
the very lowest orders; these are again intersected by
narrow streets, and close courts, defiled with every
description of refuse.

Dr. KAY thus describes the houses in the crowded
parts of the town, and the manner in which a great proportion of the operatives are accommodated in them.

" The houses in such situations are uncleanly,
ill-provided with furniture; an air of discomfort, if
not of squalid and loathsome wretchedness, pervades
them; they are often dilapidated, badly drained,
damp, and the habits of their tenants are gross.
They are ill-fed, ill-clothed, and uneconomical, at
once spendthrifts and destitute; denying themselves
the comforts of life, in order that they may wallow
in the unrestrained license of animal appetite."

" Instructed in the fatal secret of subsisting on
what is barely necessary to life, the labouring classes
have ceased to entertain a laudable pride in furnish-

MANCHESTER.   99

ing their houses, and in multiplying the decent comforts which minister to happiness.

" Without distinction of age or sex, careless of all
decency, they are crowded in small and wretched apart-
ments ; the same bed receiving a succession of tenants,
until too offensive even for their unfastidious senses.

" A whole family is often accommodated on a
single bed, and sometimes a heap of filthy straw and a
covering of old sacking, hide them in one undistin-
guished heap, defaced alike by penury, want of economy, and dissolute habits."

The manners and customs of the lower orders (who
are chiefly dependent on the factories) are of a very
inferior description ; drinking and smoking being
quite common to both sexes. I was somewhat surprised at seeing the women smoke, in some parts of
Yorkshire ; there, however, it was in a smuggled,
underhand sort of way ; but here there is no necessity for disguise or concealment: in this part of Lancashire, the women enjoy their pipe and glass in
company with the men, without considering they are
lowering their dignity in the least. I am told, a very
great quantity of gin (or rather a compound bearing
the name of gin) is consumed here. I have visited
several of the gin-shops, and endeavoured to make
some calculation of the consumption of this pernicious drug; but it would not be a good criterion to go
by, as the town at present is in a very depressed
state. " Mr. BRAIDLEY, the boroughreeve, when
the town was in a flourishing condition, observed the
number of persons entering a gin-shop during eight

successive Saturday evenings, and at various periods, from seven o'clock till ten. The average result was 112 men, and 163 women, or 275 in forty minutes, which equals 412 per hour." The calculation was confined to *one* gin-shop.

Taking the above causes into account, and also the long hours they are obliged to remain in the factories, we need not be surprised at the wretched condition they are in. I visited two factories last night, about half-past seven o'clock; and, soon after, they stopped for the day. When the work-people came out, it wanted a quarter to eight o'clock. I was told the engines of both these factories had started at five o'clock in the morning, and continued working all day, with the exception of a short time at noon, while the machinery was cleaned; leaving the work-people no time for meals, which they were obliged to eat as they best could. Immediately after the liberation of the work-people, music was heard in two public-houses adjoining. I went into one of them, and was followed by about twenty or thirty young men and women, chiefly factory people. There was no dancing going on, but fiddling, singing, drinking, and smoking, were the order of the day. At the other public-house there was another kind of amusement going on; they had erected a tall pole, at the top of which was tied a leg of mutton, the pole being *well greased and soaped;* the landlord then invited the boys to climb up and get it. He thus contrived to amuse his tired customers, and fill his pockets with their hard-earned pennies.

I have now, my Lord, to introduce a passage from Dr. KAY's pamphlet, to which I desire to call your Lordship's special attention. What a state of suffering is here exhibited ! *

" These artisans are frequently subject to a disease, in which the sensibility of the stomach and bowels is morbidly excited; the alvine secretions are deranged, and the appetite impaired. Whilst this state continues, the patient loses flesh, his features are sharpened, the skin becomes pale, leaden-coloured, or of the yellow hue which is observed in those who have suffered from the influence of tropical climates.

" The strength fails, all the capacities of physical enjoyment are destroyed, and the paroxysms of corporeal suffering are aggravated by the horrors of a disordered imagination, till they lead to gloomy apprehension, to the deepest depression, and almost to despair. We cannot wonder that the wretched victim of this disease, invited by those haunts of misery and crime, the gin-shop and the tavern, as he passes to his daily labour, should endeavour to cheat his suffering of a few moments, by the false excitement procured by ardent spirits ; or that the exhausted artisan, driven by *ennui* and discomfort from his squalid home, should strive, in the delirious dreams

* This Dr. KAY is so unfortunate as to have had a namesake, who, in his capacity of Assistant Poor-law Commissioner, did his utmost to decoy the families of agricultural labourers—widows, with numerous orphans—into the manufacturing districts. I should be sorry to judge so hardly of him, as to suppose him to be the same individual.

of a continued debauch, to forget the remembrance of his reckless improvidence, of the destitution, hunger, and uninterrupted toil, which threaten to destroy the remaining energies of his enfeebled constitution."

I sat down by a spinner, about thirty years of age, and entered into conversation with him; he told me that he had scarcely power to walk, and had come in, not for the amusements, but to get a glass and a pipe to drown his care, and rest himself a little before going home. This man seemed to be at least twenty years older than he really was; and was evidently fast hastening to a premature grave. He spoke of the masters as unfeeling men, obliging the work-people to do more than they were able; and, if they dared to say a word, they were immediately told that if they would not do it, they might go about their business, and let others come who would. In consequence of the great number of hands now out of employment, the work-people are very much afraid of losing their places. And although the spinners in work have reason to complain bitterly of the long hours, the heavy wheels, and the low wages, still, the condition of those out of employment is worse; and the "improvements" in machinery are constantly throwing additional numbers out of work. It is the study of the manufacturer to get rid of adult labourers as far as he can, and to make those, with whose aid he cannot dispense, work to the uttermost of their strength, and beyond. The manufacturer's ingenuity is constantly upon the stretch, for this purpose.

In the last quotation of which I availed myself
from Dr. KAY, reference was made to a particular
disease to which the factory operatives are liable. In
the following passage, the ordinary, every-day effects
of the system are described.

" They are engaged in an employment which ab-
sorbs their attention, and unremittingly employs
their physical energies. They are drudges who
watch the movements, and assist the operations, of a
mighty material force, which toils with an energy
ever unconscious of fatigue. The persevering labour
of the operative must rival the mathematical precision,
the incessant motion, and the exhaustless power of
the machine. Hence, besides the negative results—
the total abstraction of every moral and intellectual
stimulus—the absence of variety—banishment from
the grateful air and cheering influence of light, the
physical energies are exhausted by incessant toil,
and imperfect nutrition. Having been subjected to
the prolonged labour of an animal—his physical
energies wasted—his mind in supine inaction—the
artisan has neither moral dignity, nor intellectual, nor
organic strength to resist the seductions of appetite.
His wife and children, too frequently subjected to
the same process, are unable to cheer his remaining
moments of leisure. Domestic economy is neglected,
domestic comforts are unknown. A meal of the
coarsest food is prepared with heedless haste, and
devoured with equal precipitation. Home has no
other relation to him than that of shelter—few pleasures are there—it chiefly presents to him a scene of

physical exhaustion, from which he is glad to escape, himself impotent of all the distinguishing aims of his species, he sinks into sensual sloth, or revels in more degrading licentiousness."

If we look upon their factory life, and especially that of the females, we see them surrounded by vice and wickedness in almost every form and shape, from their youth up. Debarred the lawful pleasures enjoyed by other classes of the community, they catch with avidity at those immediately within their reach, without asking themselves whether they be lawful or not, and without regarding the consequences that may result from their indulgence. And some, instead of having kind paternal masters to guide their wandering steps in the right way, are under those who too often avail themselves of the power they possess over these poor unhappy beings, of the weaker sex, to gratify their own evil and corrupt propensities, and by their conduct and example, spread an immoral contagion around them. I have heard, my Lord, statements respecting the conduct of some manufacturers, which I dare not lay before your Lordship, and would hope they are exaggerated; but the parties from whom I had the information are so respectable, as to leave but little doubt of their truth.

And if we look at the females who have been brought up in the factories, and who by some cause have been thrown out of employment; what, I would ask, is there left for them? To attempt to obtain employment as domestic servants is well known to be

quite useless, as we do not find one person in five
hundred willing to engage them in this capacity.
The reason is obvious ; for, in addition to their vulgar, ignorant, and uncouth behaviour, and want of
recommendation or character, the long hours and
unceasing toil of the factories have utterly incapa-
citated them for properly discharging the commonest
duties of domestic servants. We do not find that
even the manufacturer (who ought to bear a little
with their want of ability) will engage these girls to
do the work of his household. If the factory female
turns to any other line of life, it is mostly pre-occupied
by parties who have been regularly trained to the business ; and, consequently, she is unable to compete
with them. Should she have no friends, the workhouse is then her only alternative ; and it but too
often happens that, instead of going there, the unhappy girl gives way to what seems to her inevitable,
and commences a life of abandoned profligacy.

I cannot resist the opportunity which another passage in Dr. KAY's pamphlet affords me, of corro-
borating the opinion I have formed of the tendencies
of the factory system, in a moral and religious point
of view.

" With unfeigned regret, we are constrained to add,
that the standard of morality is exceedingly debased,
and that religious observances are neglected amongst
the operative population of Manchester. The bonds
of domestic sympathy are too generally relaxed ; and,
as a consequence, the filial and paternal duties are
uncultivated. The artisan has not time to cherish
these feelings, by the familiar and grateful arts which

are their constant food, and without which nourishment, they perish : an apathy benumbs his spirit.
Too frequently the father, enjoying perfect health and
with ample opportunities of employment, is supported
in idleness on the earnings of his oppressed children ;
and, on the other hand, when age and decrepitude
cripple the energies of the parents, their adult children abandon them to the scanty maintenance derived
from parochial relief."

That there are a few instances of good moral characters, I admit; but, when compared with the great
mass who are not so, they are as a grain of sand on
the sea-shore.   The line of life in which they have
been brought up, is diametrically opposite to the character of the life laid down in the Gospel, for our example and imitation; and it is also very different to
the life led by the domestic servants of those manufacturers, who wish to be considered religious characters.   I have known manufacturers who would call
their servants around them in their parlour, to hear
morning and evening prayers ; and, at the same time
that they were reading prayers to five or six favoured
individuals, five or six hundred of their factory people were working in the mills, having risen, if in
winter, several hours before day, and having scarcely
had sufficient time even to get their meals.

In short, the people working in factories are often
treated as if they were not the same class of beings,
ór had souls to be saved ; but as though they were
regarded in the same light as machines, and kept for
a similar purpose.   And when they have worked till
their physical powers give way, they are cast off as

useless lumber; just as a cylinder, or any other piece
of machinery, would be laid aside when worn out,
and with as little remorse.

My Lord, I must apologise for the length of this
letter, which has reached farther than I intended.

I am, &c.

> " Vain hope, alas! unable to forget
> The anxious task's long, heavy agonies,
> In broken sleep the victim labours yet!
> Waiting the boding stroke that bids him rise,
> He marks in restless fear each hour that flies;—
> Anticipates the unwelcome morning prime,—
> And murmuring feebly, with unwakened eyes,
> ' Mother! O mother! is it yet the time ? '
> Starts at the moon's pale ray, or clock's far distant chime."
>
> *A Voice from the Factories, p. 36.*

LETTER XIV.

Manchester, October 16, 1841.

MY LORD:

In selecting a situation for my place of residence,
during ny temporary stay in Manchester, I was actuated by a desire to be as much as possible among
the working classes; accordingly, I took lodgings in
the vicinity of some factories, in order that I might
have ample opportunities of becoming acquainted
with their manners and habits.   The daughter of
the people with whom I lodge, is working in one of
these factories, and it may be interesting to your
Lordship to know something of her mode of life;
which will furnish a tolerable idea of that of most of
the females employed in those establishments.   It

will be necessary to inform your Lordship, in the first place, that the bed in which I sleep, is in the front room, and consequently facing the street. Previously to retiring on the first night, I was told that I should hear a knocking at the window in the morning, and was not to be alarmed, as it was only for the purpose of calling their daughter up to work ; but that they would feel obliged if I, or the other man who slept in the same room, would answer, as the person would continue to knock till some one answered him. At about *half-past four o'clock* (mark the time), a rattling noise was heard at the window, which was answered, as agreed upon, from within. The watchman, or person who performs this duty (for which he gets 3*d*. per head, per week, from all he calls up in the mornings), then went to the next house, and so on through the streets, disturbing the whole neighbourhood, till the noise of his "infernal machine" died away in the distance. This machine was made for the purpose of making a great noise on the glass windows without breaking them, and is somewhat similar to a shepherd's crook, only longer in the handle, to enable the person using it to reach the upper windows. And now let us see to the poor girl who is thus disturbed from her rest. The person at the window might knock and rattle, till his patience was exhausted, before *she* would hear him ; but the watchful, waking mother, well knowing the consequence of being too late, is now heard at the bedside of her daughter, rousing the unwilling girl to another day of toil. At length you hear her on the floor ; the clock is striking five. Then, for the first time, the girl becomes conscious of the necessity for haste; and having slipped on her clothes, and (if she thinks there is time) washed herself, she takes a drink of cold coffee, which has been left standing in the fireplace, a mouthful of bread (if she can eat it), and having packed up her breakfast in her handkerchief, hastens to the factory. The bell rings as she leaves the threshold of her home. Five minutes more, and she is in the factory, *stripped and ready for work.* The clock strikes half-past five; the engine starts, and her day's work commences.

At half-past seven, and in some factories at eight, the engine slacks its pace (seldom stopping) for a short time, *till the hands have cleaned the machinery,* and swallowed a little food. It then goes on again, and continues at full speed till twelve o'clock, when it stops for dinner. Previously to leaving the factory, and in her dinner-hour, she has her machines to clean. The distance of the factory is about five minutes' walk from her home. I noticed every day that she came in at half-past twelve, or within a minute or two, and once she was over the half hour; the first thing she did, was to wash herself, then get her dinner (which she was seldom able to eat), and pack up her drinking for the afternoon. This done, it was time to be on her way to work again, where she remains, without one minute's relaxation, till seven o'clock; she then comes home, and throws herself into a chair exhausted. This repeated *six* days in the week (save that on Saturdays, she may get back a little earlier, say, an hour or two), can there be any wonder at

their preferring to lie in bed till dinner-time, instead
of going to church on the *seventh*?   Is this the way,
my Lord, to make " our sons grow up as the young
plants," and "our daughters to become as the polished
corners of the temple?"

This young woman looks very pale and delicate,
and has every appearance of an approaching decline.
I was asked to guess her age; I said, perhaps fifteen,
which, I thought, would be about right.   Her mother
seemed surprised, and told me she was going nineteen,
which equally astonished me.   She is a fair specimen
of a great proportion of factory girls in Manchester;
many of whom are wives, others are mothers, although not married.

"More than one-half of its inhabitants," says
Dr. KAY, " are either so destitute, or so degraded,
as to require the assistance of public charity, in
bringing their offspring into the world.   The children
thus adopted by the public are often neglected by the
parents.   The early age at which girls are admitted
into the factories, prevents their acquiring much
knowledge of domestic economy; and even supposing them to have had accidental opportunities
of making this acquisition, *the extent to which
women are employed in the mills, does not, even after
marriage, permit the general application of its principles*.   The infant is the victim of the system;
it has not lived long, ere it is abandoned to the care
of a hireling or neighbour, whilst its mother pursues
her accustomed toil.   Sometimes a little girl has the
charge of the child, or even of two or three collected

from neighbouring houses. Thus abandoned to one whose sympathies are not interested in its welfare, or whose time is too often occupied in household drudgery, the child is ill-fed, dirty, ill-clothed, exposed to cold and neglect ; and, in consequence, more than one-half of the offspring of the poor (as may be proved by the Bills of Mortality of the town) die before they have completed their fifth year. The strongest survive; but the same causes which destroy the weakest, impair the vigour of the more robust; and hence the children of our manufacturing population are proverbially pale and sallow."

Many of them have to endure great hardship in bringing their offspring into the world, and in rearing them afterwards ; a great many infants are still-born, or die soon after birth. Those children who live, are subjected to the same treatment as the children at Leeds, Bolton, and other towns mentioned in my former letters.

The ex-registrar of Birmingham, Mr. PAER, I am told, instituted a comparison between the mortality of that town and Manchester, a year or two ago. There is, doubtless, much that is wrong going on in Birmingham in reference to the maternal care of children; but Mr. PAER, notwithstanding, could state that, *in the same aggregate of deaths, the number in Birmingham, under sixteen years of age, did not exceed those in Manchester under* THREE YEARS !

I have several times watched the hands discharged from the factories at dinner-time, and at night, and —factory cripple as I am — have been surprised (as every one indeed must be, who witnesses these things with attention) at the squalid, and wretched appearance of the work-people generally. How different (thought I, on those occasions) are the inhabitants of Manchester now, to what they were fifty or sixty years ago! In the history of this town we read that, in 1777, a subscription was entered into, to raise a regiment of Volunteers, to be employed against the rebels in America. This fine body of men was called the Seventy-second, or Manchester Regiment; and their gallant conduct on the rock of Gibraltar, when it was attacked by the Spaniards, and defended by General ELIOT, obtained for them lasting renown. On their return to England, they were received in Manchester with enthusiasm, and their colours were deposited with much ceremony in the Collegiate Church, from whence they were removed to the College, where they still remain as trophies of the gallantry of the regiment, and of the patriotic ardour of the town.

Contrast, the above, my Lord, with a statement made to me by a very respectable surgeon, with whom I dined in this neighbourhood. This gentleman had been one of the surgeons engaged to examine men for the Militia, a few years ago; and out of 200 men examined, *only four* could be said to be *well-formed men*, and these four stated, in answer to questions from the surgeon, that they *had never worked in a factory*. This fact is not at all surprising to those who know how the poor men have to work, and how they live and lodge. A factory la-

bourer can be very easily known-as he is going along
the streets; some of his joints are almost sure to be
wrong. Either the knees are in, the ankles swelled,
one shoulder lower than the other, or he is round-
shouldered, pigeon-breasted, or in some other way
deformed. From the observations I have made (and
I have had opportunities of making many), I would
unhesitatingly assert, that if factory people were to
continue to work in the same way as they have for
the last fifty years; and if they were not to inter-
marry with any other kind of labourers, but live entirely among themselves; they would, in two or three
generations, become a race of pigmies and cripples,
and almost lose all traces of the human form. No
wonder the *manufacturers* like to draft, occasionally,
from the *rural districts*.

In examining the Manchester list of prices for
mule-spinning, I find the same premium held out to
the manufacturers, as at Bolton and elsewhere, to
enlarge their wheels, and do with fewer hands; and
this will account for the many cotton spinners I have
met with out of employment. In 1836, there were upwards of 2000 cotton spinners in full work, in Manchester; in 1841, there were only 600 employed.
Knowing this, I was not surprised to see scores
walking about the streets with nothing to do; others
employed in going errands, waiting upon the market-
people, selling pins and needles, ballads, tapes and
laces, oranges, gingerbread, &c. &c.; while those
who are in work, are killing themselves by over-exertion.

I would fain hope, that Dr. KAY, from whose work
I have had occasion so often to quote, is a cordial
friend of the "Ten-Hours' Bill." Attached as he
is to the cause of National Education, and knowing
the factory system, as he evidently does, to be reducing the operatives to the lowest state of degradation—bringing them down to the condition of the mere
animal—I must assume, unless I hear to the contrary, that he is among your Lordship's most zealous
supporters. One extract more, and I have done with
this gentleman.

"The dull routine of a ceaseless drudgery, in which
the same mechanical process is incessantly repeated,
resembles the torment of Sisyphus—the toil, like the
rock, recoils perpetually on the wearied operative.
The mind gathers neither stores nor strength from
the constant extension and retraction of the same
muscles. The intellect slumbers in supine inertness;
but the grosser parts of our nature attain a rank development. To condemn man to such severity of
toil, is, in some measure, to cultivate in him the
habits of an animal. He becomes reckless; he dis-
regards the distinguishing appetites and habits of his
species; he neglects the comforts and delicacies of
life; he lives in squalid wretchedness, on meagre
food, and expends his superfluous gains in debauchery."

I was told it was becoming common for the masters to keep an extra spinner or two, in order that
the regular hands might have a day's rest occasionally. Some will not allow their spinners to work the

double-deckers more than five days in a week, well knowing what the consequence will be; but even this extra day's rest will not repair their wasted powers, nor will it guard them from that premature old age, which is the inevitable portion of those who follow this work in the present day.

There seems to be a general wish on the part of the manufacturers to work long hours, increase the labour, and diminish the wages of the work-people. Several masters are now at variance with their spinners, in consequence of this grasping disposition. The spinners, are bowed down beneath a complication of evils, which must crush them in the end. The system of double-decking is carried on to a prodigious extent in one factory (Mr. KENNEDY's). They have actually coupled five pairs of spinning-mules together, and these are worked by *one man, instead of five as formerly ;* and thus one man is made to do the work of five, and throw four out of employment. These spinning-mules are what they call " 336's," or containing 336 spindles in each separate mule, or 672 in a pair; which, till lately, was thought as much as a man could manage : consequently, five times 672, or 3360, is the number of spindles in this *quintuple* decker.

The spinner who works these five pairs of wheels, is earning about 27s. per week, which is about as much as *each of the five men* could earn in 1829, on a single pair of 336 spindle-mules. The piecers are also fewer than before. There are other factories where they have the wheels coupled in a similar manner; but I have not heard of any, where so many spindles are superintended by one man.

There is also a great number of *self-acting mules,* or mules made to spin without a spinner, in use in Manchester. Some factories have self-actors only; in those establishments, of course, the spinners are not wanted, but are cast off, to increase the number already out of employment. The little scavengers who attend upon these self-actors, run imminent risk of their limbs and lives. Several terrible accidents have occurred with them.

I was glad to learn that one or two of the manufacturers of Manchester, had built schools on their premises for the education of young children; but these are exceptions. Generally speaking, they care nothing about the education of their workpeople; all they want is, a great quantity of work done for a little money. Education, or moral discipline, are only matters of merely secondary consideration, and very often of no consideration at all, with the manufacturers. There are several Sunday-schools in this town, some of them large ones; but anything that a child will learn there, will be, almost certainly, very soon counteracted in the factories, as at present conducted; I mean, where the parents do not take an active part in the education of their children. And it is a fact, that the parents themselves want teaching generally.

There are a great many cases of deformity and mutilation here, a few of which I shall forward on Monday.   I am, &c.

LETTER XV.

Manchester, October 18, 1841.

My Lord :

I now come to that part of my inquiries here, relating to the cripples. I have met with many ; but they are in Manchester, as I find them in most places, extremely shy. In passing along the street this morning, I overtook a young man with a wheelbarrow, in which were a few potatoes, a pair of scales, and some weights, and as he was very much crippled, I asked him if he had been in the factories. He said, yes ; so I inquired how he had become so decrepid. He said, if I would wait till he had served his customers with potatoes, he would tell me all about it. I did wait, and went home with him ; when he gave me his history, as follows :—

"WILLIAM FINDLOW, No. 67, Booth-street, Chorlton-upon-Medlock, near Manchester, went to work at eleven years of age, at the cotton factory belonging to SAMUEL and HENRY MARSDEN, as a creel-filler, at 3s. per week. He worked two years, and then had 4s. per week; worked three years longer, and then he had 5s. per week, and continued at these wages till he was done up, past work. He was ill six weeks, and at the age of eighteen was obliged to give up factory work entirely. He was perfectly straight when he went to the mill, and is now a miserable cripple, although in the prime of life. His masters, who are very wealthy, have made him no compensation in any way. His knees are both *turned in and*

wrap over each other.   He is a sad spectacle to look
upon; he only stands four feet ten inches high, although he spans five feet eight inches with his arms
extended.   He can read a little, but cannot write.
He depends upon his father, and what he can make
by selling little odd things to the neighbours, for a
living."

The second case is that of "RICHARD TAYLOR,
Stockton-street, Chorlton-upon-Medlock.   He went
to work at six years of age as a piecer; and had to
work from half-past five in the morning, with no time
allowed for breakfast, or for drinking in the afternoon,
and had only three-quarters of an hour for dinner.
He was quite straight when he went to the mill, and
is now a sad cripple.   The right knee is turned in,
and the left knee out.   He is now about thirty years
of age, and walks with a stick; he cannot walk without.   His brother EDMUND is a cripple also; but
not to the same extent."   These young men say, that
*their father was obliged to send them as piecers, or
he would have lost his work.*   It is worthy of remark,
that two other brothers, who have not been treated
in the same way, are fine young men; one of them
a *soldier.*

"BRIDGET LYONS, an interesting young Irish girl,
about nineteen years of age, went to work at the
Hanover Mill, in 1836, as a piecer.   She had worked
there about twenty weeks, when she met with an
accident in the following manner.   She was in the
act of picking up some waste cotton near an upright
shaft, which was not sufficiently guarded; the shaft

caught her clothes, and wound her round it, dashing her against the wall, and other obstructions. Being dreadfully crushed and bruised, she was taken to the Infirmary, where she remained thirty-eight weeks, and had *both of her legs amputated,* the *right leg above,* and the left *below the knee.* She recovered, and now walks with a pair of crutches, and one wooden leg. It is but justice to her masters to say, that they have behaved very kindly to her after the accident occurred. When she came out of the Infirmary, she had a small allowance monthly; besides which, they let her and her mother live in a cellar rent-free. After a short time, her allowance was sent weekly. They then bound her an apprentice to a dressmaker, which cost them 5*l.* 5*s.* She was bound for eighteen months, which will expire in May, 1842. When I saw her, her weekly allowance was 4*s.* She began her factory life in 1833 or 1834. Her wages, at the time of the accident, were 6*s.* 2*d.* per week. She can read a little; but not write." Without wishing to throw any blame, or find fault with her masters (who, as we have seen, have behaved very handsomely), I would ask the question, What compensation ought this girl to have, and where ought that compensation to come from? This is a question of the utmost importance to factory cripples generally; nor is it unimportant to the rate-payers, who frequently have them to maintain.

The following case I had from an eye-witness:—

"MARY JONES, being the mother of several children, worked as a winder at Mr. HOPE's mill,

Hulme, near Manchester; she worked near an upright shaft, the *coupling boxes* of which were considerably above the floor, and the *key* that fastened them together *projected about two or three inches.* These coupling boxes are for the purpose of coupling the shaft, nearly similar to the manner in which the several lengths of a fishing-rod are put together, only not so neatly. In passing the shaft one night, a few weeks ago, the *key* (which of course revolved with the shaft) caught her clothes, and dragged her round for several minutes, as no one could find the engineer to stop the engine. The shaft was but a short distance from the wall, and her head and legs were dashed against the wall every time the shaft went round. The wall was so covered with blood and hair, that it had to be immediately white-washed. *She was taken away a lifeless corpse.* The shaft had formerly been protected by some machinery, but which had been removed. Such employers have much to answer for.

In looking over the Reports of the Manchester Royal Infirmary for 1839 and 1840, I find that there were entered on the books in 1839, 3496 cases of accident; 2760 of which were *out-patients,* and 736 *in-patients.* Of the out-patient accidents, 490, we are told, were caused by machinery; of the 736 *in-patients,* we are left in the dark as to the cause; but supposing an equal proportion of them— *i.e.* 131—to be mill-accidents, this would make a total of 621; and, in addition to several other operations, there were, in 1838 and 1839, 35 legs and arms amputated, from accidents, and some of those we may reasonably suppose to be factory cases; besides which, many who are caught by mill-work have their limbs torn clean out of the sockets, and thus escape amputation.

Again, in 1840, there were 3749 cases of accident, of which 3018 are entered as those of out-patients, and 731 as those of in-patients. Of the 3018 cases of out-patients, 590, we are told, were occasioned by machinery, and if we take 142 as a fair proportion of the in-patients, we have a total of 732 cases of accidents by machinery; and, besides a great many other operations, there were 21 amputations of arms, hands, legs, and feet, some of which we may reasonably suppose were caused by machinery.

Your Lordship will please to bear in mind, that this account does not include the number of those who have been killed outright by machinery, neither does it include accidents taken to other Institutions; and I cannot help fearing, that of these 7245 cases of accidents in two years, a far greater proportion arises out of mills and factories than is discoverable by the books of the Infirmary. All I hear and see confirms me in this suspicion.

Your Lordship has most probably heard of the melancholy accident which happened in a machine-makers' shop, on the 13th inst., from the explosion of a steam-boiler, by which eight lives have been lost, and many others are in a dangerous state. I was not far from the place when it happened, and I visited it: it is little better than a heap of ruins.

One end of the shop is blown quite out, and the boiler is lying at a short distance in the canal. Many proofs are here to be seen, of the amazing power of steam: a large tool-chest, belonging to one of the men, has been thrown across the canal, a distance of about fifteen or twenty yards; an iron pipe, about four inches diameter, has been driven nine inches into a brick wall, nearly twenty yards from the shop. The tall chimney is standing, but in a dangerous position: there are several dwelling-houses near, which, I think, are in danger of being crushed, if it should fall.

It is melancholy to think of the many lives and limbs which are lost in this town in a year. I am told (but could not get in to see) that the Work-house is like an hospital, and contains many cripples from the factories. Something better than this ought to be provided for these poor creatures.

Yesterday, being Sunday, I visited the houses of several spinners, a little before church-time in the forenoon. Most of these operatives were in bed, or had only just got up. When I went home to dinner, the young woman, of whom I wrote in a former letter, had only just risen from her bed; such is the effect of the labour they have to endure. With re-spect to religious matters, there appears, on the part of these over-worked people, an apathy amounting almost to carelessness; and I am sorry to add, that infidelity, in many cases, has taken deep root. And unless something is done to counteract these per-nicious principles,—ruinous alike to individuals and to states,—I am afraid your Lordship's good intentions to improve their condition will accomplish little. The domestic tie seems to be broken; they live together as so many isolated beings, each having a separate interest. The rites and ceremonies of the Church (particularly that of marriage) seem to be disregarded; and very many of them study only how they shall best gratify their animal appetites and passions.

I intend to leave this place to-morrow for Wigan, and will write again in a day or two from thence.

I am, &c.

"Yes, this reproach is added; (infamous
In realms which own a Christian monarch's sway!)
Not suffering only is their portion, thus
Compelled to toil their youthful lives away:
Excessive labour works the soul's decay,
Quenches the intellectual light within,
Crushes with iron weight the mind's free play,
Steals from us leisure purer thoughts to win,
And leaves us sunk and lost in dull and native-sin."
A Voice from the Factories, p. 18.

LETTER XVI.

Wigan, October 21, 1841.

MY LORD:

Since I reached this town, I have been pursuing my usual inquiries as to the state of trade, the condition of the inhabitants, &c. The first answers to my queries furnished me with so melancholy a view of things, that I at once set them down for exaggerated

statements, and determined to examine for myself.
Accordingly, I hired an intelligent man, a cotton
yarn-dresser out of employment, as a guide, to pilot
me through the town; and I confess that, so far from
the statement I had heard exceeding, it fell far short
of the truth. I do not remember, in the whole
course of my existence, ever to have seen so much
misery and wretchedness, in such a small compass
before.

I travelled with my guide through one street after
another, till he was fairly sick of his undertaking,
and refused to accompany me further. On the following day I set out alone, as I found that I had
nothing to fear from the half-famished inhabitants:
in this manner I traversed fifteen or sixteen streets
and lanes, in that part of the town where the lower
orders generally reside. These streets were unsew-
ered, unpaved; every few yards a pool of stagnant
water, and heaps of accumulated filth of every description. The windows of the houses were more or
less broken, and pasted over with brown paper, or
stuffed with rags, affording a certain proof of poverty
within. In some streets, every fourth or fifth house
was empty, and boarded up; in the other houses
were living two, three, and in some four families,
crowded together. The lower parts, or cellars of the
houses, were occupied as weaving shops for hand-
loom weavers. The floors of these cellars were several feet below the surface of the street, *the walls
being damp half-way up*. The smell pervading these
streets and houses was most noxious and sickening.

I entered several houses, which were miserably furnished, and agreed with the general aspect of the exterior. The first I entered was occupied by a collier, and his family, consisting of a wife, and six children; the furniture of this house, that is, bed, bedding, chairs, tables, kitchen-utensils, &c., if put up to the hammer, might probably have realised 10s. A few days previously to my visit, the father and the eldest son, who worked in the coal-pits, and were the support of the family, had both been seriously burned by an explosion of gas, or as they call it, "firedamp" in the pit, and were both disabled. The father expected soon to be able to resume his work, but the son was so dreadfully burned on the face, head, and arms, that it was thought at one time he would lose his sight; however, when I called, he had hopes that would not be the case; but it was thought he would not be able to work for three months. I called on another family, similarly situated in every respect, except that the father only was burned by the firedamp, and that they had seven children, being one more than the other. I had an invitation given me to go down the pit, and examine the place where the explosion occurred; but, thinking this would be incurring unnecessary danger, I declined.

I then went to another house, in which I found a young woman of the name of ELIZABETH ASHCROFT, about twenty-four years of age, who had lost her right leg, a little below the knee, in WILLIAM WOOD's factory. She was a drawing-frame tenter, at 7s. per week. She had worked between five and six years, and had received no allowance from her master. Her father, a hand-loom weaver, who could now earn about 5*s*. or 6*s*. per week, formerly earned 20*s*. to 25*s*. per week, in the same business; they have children, and are very poor.

In another house I found a young woman about sixteen years of age, lying on a mattress in a corner of the room. She had met with an accident in the factories, a few days before, but, being afraid of offending her masters, she declined giving me their names, or her own. However, she told me that her right arm had got into the machinery, and the flesh was scraped off, leaving the bones and sinews bare, from a little below her elbow to her fingers. Her masters were not expected to do anything for her, as it is not their general custom, I was told. Beside her, on the same mattress (which was all they had for eight persons to lay on) and covered with an old cloak, lay a dying infant (on my second visit, this infant was dead). The father, a hand-loom weaver, stated, with melancholy aspect, that he could only earn 6*s*. per week when he had work; that the family depended for support on the united earnings of himself and the daughter who had got lamed; that they were almost starved, and that he did not know what was to become of them. He looked the picture of misery: his long beard (which was about three weeks' growth) and haggard looks, gave him a ghastly appearance. I would not have given 5*s*. for all the furniture in the place. I visited some other families, mostly agreeing with those above described, excepting the accidents;

and after three hours spent in this manner, I was compelled, by a sickening sensation, to leave the place.

There is a great number of factory cripples by accident, and long hours of labour, in Wigan ; my guide had run over the names of thirty or forty in a short time. A few cases I shall lay before your Lordship : those having friends in the mills were not willing to let me have their cases, as it might give offence, if it came to the ears of the manufacturers.

"MARY BROWN, a young woman about twenty-three years of age, was attending a throstle-frame in Messrs. JOHNSON and AINSWORTH's cotton factory, in November, 1839, and was cleaning the machine while it was going (as she was not allowed to stop it for that purpose), about four o'clock in the afternoon. She was so unfortunate as to get her left arm in among the wheels, just above the wrist, by which both bones in the fore-arm were broken, the flesh dreadfully crushed and lacerated, and the hand almost severed. By great care and skill of the surgeon she recovered, without amputation. Her hand is *stiff and contracted*, the *wrist immoveable*. She gets a scanty living by selling cakes, &c. Her masters, who are wealthy, have done very little for her."

"WILLIAM SAYER lost his right arm, a few inches below the shoulder, in the scutcher in Messrs. ACTON and ROBY's mill. The firm is rich, but I cannot learn that they have done anything for him. He is about twenty-four years of age, and stands six feet high. His sight is very much impaired ; he is endeavouring to pick up a living by attending on the market-people."

"EDWARD LEATHERLAND, a young man about nineteen years of age, lost his right arm in the scutcher in WILLIAM WOOD's factory. He has received nothing from his masters, and is endeavouring to gain a living by gathering manure in the streets. He lives with his parents, who are very poor."

"HENRY ROBINSON lost his right arm in the scutcher in Messrs. ECKERSLEY and SON's factory. He now goes with a boat on the canal: his masters have done a little for him."

"WILLIAM THOMPSON lost an arm in the scutcher at Messrs. ACTON and ROBY's factory. Goes with a horse and cart subscribed for him by masters and work-people."

"ANN SIDDLE lost her right arm in Messrs. RYLAND and SON's factory. She is now about twenty-two years of age, and, having been educated at the expense of the firm, is now acting as schoolmistress, in a school built on the premises for the education of the factory children."

The above five cases of accidents occurred nearly in a similar manner; they have all lost an arm; *all the right arm;* and all, I believe, a few inches from the shoulder; but, with the exception of ANN SIDDLE, none have been made comfortable.

"ESTHER TOPPING lost her left hand in WILLIAM WOOD's factory. She has not been in any way provided for, is not able to get a living, and is now assisting her mother who is very poor." These cases of accidents will show your Lordship the necessity of the machinery being well boxed-off, which, generally speaking, is not the case.

Throstle spinning, I find, is very much blamed in this neighbourhood, for making in-knee'd cripples; but people very seldom set the saddle on the right horse in this matter. I have seen very bad cases of in-knee'd cripples in silk mills (power-loom weavers, and others), who never worked at a throstle in their lives. The fact is, the great evil to be blamed is the long hours of labour, and standing chiefly in one position; and I am persuaded that, if they had no work to do at all, but were compelled to stand in the position they do, from morning to night, as at present, still there would be a great number of cripples made.

As I was standing at my window, which commands a full view of the principal street, about eight o'clock this morning, I was surprised to see about forty or fifty elderly men and women, and almost double that number of children, going down the street with the breakfasts of their sons and daughters, or brothers and sisters, who were working in the factories. Some of these people had three, four, or five, tin cans, and a little basket; and, although it was a cold wet morning, and snow lying upon the ground, many of those children had neither stockings nor shoes to their feet, nor covering of any kind for their head. In about half-an-hour I saw them returning, in a very drabbled condition. This is one of the drawbacks from the earnings of the factory people. Stimulants I find are much resorted to by the operatives here.

On looking into the origin of the manufacturing firms in this town, I find that the masters have, almost to a man, begun with nothing, and risen by little and little, till many of them have got to be very wealthy. One man, Mr. WILLIAM WOOD, died in the early part of this year, worth, as stated in the newspapers of the day, 300,000*l*., nearly all of which had been acquired by the factory system.

As men of figures they are often almost without a parallel; they can tell to a nicety how much money will be gained by reducing their hands 6*d*. per head throughout the factory, or to what the fraction of a farthing per pound or per yard, upon the goods produced, will amount. To their ability in calculating these minute details, may be attributed much of their success as accumulators of wealth.

There are a great many women working in the factories here; I saw many in an advanced state of pregnancy. Their average wages are about 6*s*. to 6*s*. 6*d*. per week for full time. They are mostly working short time at present. The men have very low wages here; the fines are frequent and heavy, amounting, in many cases, to several shillings per week, and yet the masters here very generally profess to be religious men.

In this, as in other manufacturing towns, I was surprised to find so very few book-shops, or other places indicating intellectual pursuits in the inhabitants, and seeing in my room a copy of " Pigot's

Pocket Atlas," I amused myself with making the following calculation. I took from this work an account of the population of six towns in Lancashire, and six towns in Dorsetshire; the one a manufacturing, the other an agricultural county, viz.: Ashton-under-Lyne, Blackburn, Bury, Bolton, Rochdale, and Wigan, the population of which, in 1831, was 183,288, and Poole, Sherborne, Bridport, Dorchester, Shaftesbury, and Weymouth, with a population of 28,535.

In the six towns in Lancashire, I found 142 academies, twenty-nine booksellers, and fifty-seven pawnbrokers.

In the six towns of Dorsetshire, fifty academies, twenty booksellers, and four pawnbrokers; or

	In Lancashire.		In Dorsetshire.
1 Academy for every	1293	persons	570
1 Bookseller —	6320	—	1420
1 Pawnbroker —	3215	—	7134

Thus affording a striking proof of the difference in the pursuits of the inhabitants of those towns.

While I was in Wigan, I entered a public-house, and, in conversation with the landlord, was told that the manufacturing labourers were very fond of, and very clever at, card-playing; and, as a proof of what he said, he showed me *four packs of cards*, all of which were nearly black from use; and he assured me that he had frequently all the four packs in full play, among his customers, at one time. He told me, also, that it would be no difficult matter to select

twelve, or almost any number of men, out of the factories in this town, willing to play at cards with an
equal number of men from any other trade in Great
Britain, and he had no fear as to the result.   But,
to a question I asked, if he would undertake to prove
that a small majority of those men could read and
write their own names?   He shook his head and answered " No !"

I intend to leave this place for Leigh to-morrow.

I am, &c.

L E T T E R   XVII.

Leigh, October 22, 1841.

My Lord :

I arrived in Leigh (a small manufacturing town
near Bedford, in Lancashire) yesterday.   In this
town there are a few silk and cotton mills, the former chiefly running short time at present.   The chief
cotton factory is that of Messrs. Jones, Brothers,
and Co.   All the people with whom I have conversed, speak highly of these gentlemen.   It appears
they are not men who have risen from a low beginning, but have brought 20,000*l.* or 30,000*l.* into the
trade, and evidently study the comfort and happiness
of their work-people. I have not heard of any manufacturers who are more respected by the working classes.
In the spring of this year, a boy of the name of
Joseph Smith, working in their factory, got his
hand into the scutcher, which was obliged to be amputated, and, to the credit of the firm be it said, he

has been properly taken care of ; his wages have been and are still paid, the same as if he had been at work, although he can now do little or nothing for them.

Working under the same firm, I found a young man, about twenty years of age, who had come with his parents, in 1836, from Suffolk, to Turton, near Bolton, where his father, himself, and others of the family, had been engaged by Messrs. HENRY and EDMUND ASHWORTH for three years. At the expiration of this term, they left Messrs. ASHWORTH, and went to work for their present masters. This young man, whose name I know, but do not feel at liberty to publish, was perfectly straight when he left Suffolk, and is now obliged, in the short space of five years, *to walk in* IRONS, and cannot walk without them. These irons are strapped round the waist, and come down to the ankles, with joints opposite the knees. The strain upon these irons is so great that, though well made, they have given way several times. His legs are very much deformed, and resemble those of R—— H——, of Bradford, before described. He does not complain of bad treatment from his former masters; but lays the blame to the long hours of labour, and his constantly standing. He walked without irons till he was obliged to be carried home from his work. His present masters are very kind to him; they have humanely given him a job, where he can sit to his work, and pay him 8*s*. per week ; and he may, probably, in a few years, get raised to 10*s*. per week. His two sisters, who were also quite straight, are nearly as bad as he is.

It is very clear, my Lord, that this family have reason bitterly to regret having ever come into the manufacturing districts.

The external appearance of this mill, and the cottages near, is very much superior to what we find in large manufacturing towns ; and from what I saw and heard, I should say the interior bears a corresponding character. Messrs. JONES, BROTHERS, and Co., I was told, prefer employing the poor families who belong to the parish ; and consequently there is not that shifting and changing from place to place, to which the manufacturing labourers generally are too much accustomed.

I am, &c.

LETTER XVIII.

'Bury, October 28, 1841.

MY LORD :

I arrived here yesterday, and immediately waited upon Mr. FLETCHER, an eminent surgeon of long experience, who received me kindly, and after some general conversation, introduced me to a working man, who had spent the most part of his life in connection with the factories. From these, and some other persons, I gathered an account of the condition of the factory labourers in this town. From what I have heard, it is something better than what I have ordinarily met with, in the course of my journey. There are a few manufacturers here, who seem to feel the responsibility of their situation. One, in particular, of the name of OPENSHAW, I am told, is doing much good among his work-people; he has a good school on the premises for the education of the children. There are two new churches here, built within a short time (one of them not quite finished); and I understand some of the manufacturers have been large subscribers towards their erection.

One of the mill-owners of Bury, Mr. WILLIAM RATHBONE GREG, published a pamphlet in 1831, descriptive of the condition of the factory people in the neighbourhood, from which I will make a few extracts, in order to show your Lordship that the manufacturers are themselves aware of the evils which the system has been creating.

In my travels through this part of the country, immense numbers of houses on the hill-sides were pointed out to me, as having formerly been occupied by the small domestic manufacturers. As the trade of those industrious families became monopolized by the mill-owners, they were obliged to quit their places of residence (in which some of them had been born), and repair to the towns, to get work in the factories. These houses, which formerly contained so many happy families, where the father could superintend his own children, some carding, some spinning, weaving, or knitting,—all busily employed at labour which would not ruin their health or strength, cripple their body, or demoralize their mind; these buildings, which, but a few years ago, were the scenes of so many happy hours for hundreds of contented

families, are now roofless, doorless, and sinking fast
into decay. And the land adjoining, for miles around,
which was formerly cultivated by these industrious
people, is now of comparatively little value, and in
many places lying waste. Mr. WILLIAM RATH-
BONE GREG, the mill-master above alluded to (he
being a partner in the largest cotton-spinning firm
in the kingdom), says, " Domestic manufacturers are
almost extinct; the population, which was formerly
scattered throughout the country, is now congregated
in large towns, and is impressed with a distinct character." What that character is, Mr. GREG will
best inform your Lordship. He continues thus : —

" From the long hours of labour, and the warm
and often close atmosphere in which they are confined, a very large proportion of our manufacturing labourers feel the necessity of some artificial stimulus;
and, we regret to say, that many of them, especially
those who receive the highest wages, are in the
habit of spending a portion of their leisure, after
working hours, more particularly on a Saturday evening, and during the Sunday, in besotting themselves
with ale and beer; and, still oftener, with the more
efficient stimulus of gin. It is customary for them,
in many of the towns, to stop at the gin-shops, and
take a dram as they go to their work in the morning,
and another as they return at night; and where, as
is frequently the case, the houses of the work-people
lie in a cluster round the factory, it is not uncommon for a wholesale vendor of spirits to leave two
gallons (the smallest quantity which can be sold with-

out a license) at one of the houses, which is distributed in small quantities to the others ; and payment
is made to the merchant through the original re-
ceiver. The quantity of gin drunk in this way is
enormous ; and it is painful to know, that children,
and even girls, are initiated into this fatal practice at
a very tender age. This is a picture which it is impossible to contemplate without sentiments of sorrow
and regret, that such a state of things should exist
within reach of a remedy, and yet that remedy not
be applied ; for, as we shall endeavour to show in the
subsequent pages, all these evils may be greatly miti-
gated, if not altogether removed. But this is not all.
Ardent spirits are not the only stimulus which this
class of people indulge in. Many of them take large
quantities of opium, in one form or another ; sometimes in pills, sometimes as laudanum, sometimes in
what they call an *anodyne* draught, which is a narcotic
of the same kind. They find this a cheaper stimulus
than gin, and many of them prefer it. It has been
in vogue among them for many years, and the use of
it is still continued."

Speaking of the labour in factories, Mr. GREG
says :

" As a second cause of the unhealthiness of manufacturing towns, we place the *severe and unremitting
labour*. The operatives in cotton factories begin to
work at half-past five, or six, in the morning, and
cease at half-past seven, or eight, at night. The
work of *spinners* and *stretchers* is among the most
laborious that exist, and is exceeded, perhaps, by that

of mowing alone; and few mowers, we believe, think
of continuing their labour for twelve hours without
intermission. Add to this, that these men never rest
for an instant, during the hours of working, except
while their mules are doffing, in which process they
also assist; and it must be obvious to every one, that
it is next to impossible for any human being, however hardy or robust, to sustain this exertion for any
length of time, without permanently injuring his
constitution.

" The labour of the other classes of hands employed in factories, as *carders, rovers, piecers,* and
weavers, consists not so much in their actual manual
exertion, which is very moderate, as in the constant
attention which they are required to keep up, and the
intolerable fatigue of standing for so great a length
of time. We know, that incessant walking for twenty-
four hours was considered one of the most intolerable
tortures to which witches, in former times, were subjected, for the purpose of compelling them to own
their guilt; and that few of them could hold out for
twelve; and the fatigue of standing for twelve hours,
without being permitted to lean or sit down, must be
scarcely less extreme. Accordingly, some sink under
it, and many more have their constitutions permanently weakened and undermined."

With respect to the evils arising from the unwholesomeness, and impurities of the atmosphere in factories, Mr. GREG says :

" The third cause we shall assign is, perhaps, even
more efficient than the last. The air in almost all

factories is more or less unwholesome. This, of itself, is sufficient to enervate and destroy all energy of
frame ; but, in addition to mere heat, the rooms are
often ill-ventilated, the air is filled with the effluvia
of oil, and with emanations from the uncleanly persons of a large number of individuals; and from the
want of free ventilation, the air is very imperfect-
ly oxygenated, and has occasionally a most overpowering smell. In a word, the hands employed in
these large manufactories, breathe foul air for twelve
hours out of the twenty-four; and we know that
few things have so specific and injurious an action on
the digestive organs, as the inhalation of impure air.

" The small particles of cotton and dust with
which the air in most rooms of factories is impreg-
nated, not unfrequently lay the foundation of distressing and fatal diseases. When inhaled, they are a
source of great pulmonary irritation ; which, if it continues long, induces a species of chronic bronchitis,
which not rarely degenerates into tubercular consumption."

Of the evil tendency of factory life on women and
children, Mr. GREG speaks thus :

" The fourth cause of ill-health, which prevails
among the manufacturing population, may be traced
to the injurious influence which the weakened and
vitiated constitution of women has upon their children.

" They are often employed in factories some years
after their marriage, and during their pregnancy, and
up to the very period of their confinement,—which,

all who have attended to the physiology of this subject know, must send their offspring into the world
with a debilitated and unhealthy frame, which the
circumstances of their infancy are ill-calculated to
renovate ; and hence, when these children begin to
work themselves, they are prepared at once to suc-
cumb to the evil influences by which they are surrounded.

" We will boldly appeal for the confirmation of
our views on the *present* unwholesomeness of large
manufactories, to any one who has been long and intimately acquainted with the interior of these establishments ; who has seen children enter them at ten
or twelve years of age, with the beaming eye, and the
rosy cheek, and the elastic step of youth ; and who
has seen them gradually lose the gaiety and light-
heartedness of early existence, and the colour and
complexion of health, and the vivacity of intellect,
and the insensibility to care, which are the natural
characteristics of that tender age, under the withering influence of laborious confinement, ill-oxygenated
air, and a meagre and unwholesome diet. We have
witnessed all this repeatedly, and we have found it
impossible to resist the obvious conclusion—a conclusion which, we think, cannot be gainsaid by any
man of experience and observation."

Speaking of the immorality of the factories, Mr.
GREG says :

" On the subject of the general licentiousness and
illicit intercourse between the sexes, which prevails in
manufacturing districts, we cannot, for obvious rea-

sons, dwell as long, nor as minutely, as the extreme
importance of the subject would justify. In the few
words we shall devote to this branch of our investigation, we shall be careful to keep within the limits of
the most scrupulous accuracy, and to affirm nothing
which we do not possess the materials of proving.

" The fact, then, undoubtedly is, that the licentiousness which prevails among the dense population
of manufacturing towns is carried to a degree which
it is appalling to contemplate, which baffles all statis-
tical inquiries, and which can be learned only from
the testimony of personal observers. And, in addition to overt acts of vice, there is a coarseness and
grossness of feeling, and an habitual indecency of
conversation, which we would fain hope and believe
are not the prevailing characteristics of our country.
The effect of this upon the minds of the young will
readily be conceived; and is it likely that any instruction, or education, or Sunday-schools, or ser-
mons, can counteract the baneful influence, the in-
sinuating *virus*, the putrefaction, the contagion of
this moral depravity which reigns around them.
After all, what motive has either sex, in the class
and situation to which we allude, for being virtuous
and chaste? Where they are unshackled by religious
principle, as is too generally the case, they have no
delicate sentiments of morality and taste to restrain
them from gratifying every passion; they have few
or no pleasures beyond those which arise from sensual indulgence; it involves no loss of character, for
their companions are as reckless as themselves; it

brings no risk of losing their employment, for their
employers know, that it would be unsafe to inquire
into these matters ; it is often a cause of no pecuniary
loss, for in many cases the Poor-laws provide against
this; and, all these circumstances considered, the
licentiousness of the manufacturing population is a
source of bitter lamentation to us, but of no astonishment whatever."

This, my Lord, is a picture of factory life, by one
who has had many opportunities of studying it; and
with what he states, I, who have been brought up
from infancy in the factories, perfectly agree, and
believe it to be applicable to the present day.

An accident of a serious nature happened this
morning, to a boy, who was brought to the surgery
of Mr. FLETCHER, with whom I dined. The boy
had had his head dreadfully cut between the carriage
of a self-acting spinning-mule and a gas-pipe, and if
the latter had not given way, the boy's head would
have been smashed to atoms. When I left, it was
not expected the boy would retain his reasoning
powers, if he recovered at all. I have not heard
since, how he has got on.

The wages at Bury are low, but distress does not
seem to prevail to the same extent as in some of our
large towns. In my journey from Bury to Heywood,
I met a cotton-spinner on the road, from whom I
learned that he had been thrown out of employment, in consequence of his master having made his
wheels into *self-actors.* He had had three children
by his wife, who was again pregnant: his master

had offered to give him 8*s.* per week as a piecer, but he had not decided whether he should take it, or at once go into the workhouse. He did not see how he could support himself, his three children, and his wife, especially in the way in which she was, on such slender means.

There is a large establishment in this town for making machinery, under the firm of Messrs. WALK-ER and Co. : I am told, that the only orders they have at present, are for *self-acting spinning mules*, of which they had a great number to make. I was also informed, that they had been making some power-looms, to go into Italy along with some Italian gentlemen, who had been learning to weave here, and manage machinery of this description. Many machine-makers are leaving this part of the country for the Continent.

I remain, &c.

" Mark the result. Unnaturally debarred
  All nature's fresh and innocent delights,
  While yet each germing energy strives hard,
  And pristine good with pristine evil fights ;
  When every passing dream the heart excites,
  And makes even guarded virtue insecure ;
  Untaught, unchecked, they yield as vice invites :
  With all around them cramped, confined, impure,
Fast spreads the moral plague, which nothing new shall cure."
               A Voice from the Factories, p. 18.

LETTER XIX.

Todmorden, November 1, 1841.

My Lord :

On my arrival here, I waited upon the Messrs.
FIELDEN, BROTHERS, and Company, from whom I
experienced every kindness, being permitted by them
to go over the whole of their extensive works, and
make any observations and inquiries I thought proper.
I spent a short time on Saturday in this way, and
renewed my inquiries again on Monday.   On the
latter occasion I devoted several hours to viewing the
different parts of their factories, and conversing with
various overlookers and workmen.   I have also conversed with many workmen in the town and neighbourhood, by whom I have been informed that the
condition of the people in the cotton mills here is
very little better than in large towns.   This is not
much to be wondered at, as the population is large,
and exposed to the same evils and temptations as at
most other places.   Many of the single women have
had illegitimate children ; some of them very early in
life.   I was told that one young woman had been

brought to bed, a short time before I arrived; the
united ages of herself, and the young man the father
of the child, being just thirty years. These young
women are permitted to resume their work as soon as
they are able.

It is very difficult for the manufacturer, who wishes
well to his work-people, to judge how to act for the
best in such cases. He very well knows, if he is a
thinking man, that young women who have been
brought up in the factories, very rarely get employed as domestic servants, or in any other capacity
than as factory labourers. He also is well aware,
that if he turns them out of employment, the result
will be, in nine cases out of ten, that the unhappy
girls will be driven for shelter to a workhouse; or,
what is more probable (as Union-workhouses are now
conducted) to a worse fate; that of prostitution, in
order to obtain a living. I have noticed that, generally speaking, where the manufacturers are inclined
to look over this fault (as in the case before us), and
permit the girls to return to their work, the streets
are kept comparatively free from prostitutes.

In Messrs. FIELDEN's mills I had an opportunity
of seeing several self-acting mules (for spinning yarn)
in full operation, and had some conversation with
the overlooker on the subject of spinning, generally;
by which I learned that a great reduction in wages
had taken place since he knew the business;* and

* The Messrs. FIELDEN have always shown a reluctance to
reduce wages, at the same time that they have been distinguished by a strong desire to shorten the hours of labour.

that in 1810, it was considered a good week's work if a person could spin $2\frac{1}{2}$ cwt. of a certain description of yarn, on a pair of mules of 228 spindles each. At the present day, a person *must* turn off 15 cwt. per week of the same description of yarn (which is just *six times as much*), from a pair of wheels containing about three times the number of spindles.

By conversing with the manager of this room, I attracted the attention of the work-people ; one young woman, turning half round for the purpose of looking at me, gave a motion to the lower portion of her dress, which was instantly caught by the machinery. However, as it was not a very dangerous part, and the manager was close at hand, the machine (a self-actor) was stopped, her clothes disentangled, and in about seven minutes all was right again.

I was very much surprised with the great room here for power-loom weaving, which is, perhaps, the largest in Lancashire ; containing 1058 power-looms all busily at work, excepting a few which were undergoing repairs. These looms give employment to 521 weavers, chiefly young men and women ; 22 overlookers, 18 twisters, 6 winders, 2 drawers, and 2 heald-pickers ; in all 571 persons. They are now working only 8 hours per day. These 1058 power-looms are capable of weaving, when working full time, 3900 cuts per week, each averaging 46 yards long, 36 inches wide, and 52 picks of weft to the inch. They are weaving, generally, strong cotton shirtings, sheetings, &c. I was taken through a store-room nearly filled with these goods, standing pile upon

pile, over a great extent of ground; and to a question
I asked, as to the number, I was told there were
nearly 300,000 pieces, all ready for the market.

In the dressing-room, I was astonished to see the
great quantity of flour in use. In one room there
were about 30 large tubs, about the size of half a
wine-pipe, filled with flour and water, undergoing a
sort of fermentation or preparation, previously to being
used by the dressers, the oldest being taken the first.
In another room I saw a great number of *packs of
flour*, and I asked the person whose duty it was to
attend to this department, how much flour they consumed in dressing yarn; and was told that, when
they were working full time, they used 36 packs per
week, or 1872 packs per annum; which, at 2*l.* per
pack, would cost 3744*l.* per annum, in one establishment only; which, I am persuaded, is as much, or
more, than is consumed *for food* by all the work-
people under the firm. I was also told, that in some
establishments in Manchester, the consumption of
flour is considerably greater, amounting in some cases
to 6000*l.* per annum. Can anybody wonder at the
manufacturers wanting cheap corn?

The wages paid to the work-people in this neighbourhood are better than in many places; many of
them are receiving nearly as much for eight hours
work per day, as those in the same branch at some
other places are, for twelve hours. Of this I was assured by the work-people themselves, and by comparing their statements with those of other opera-

tives at Matlock Baths, and elsewhere. This fact is worthy of particular notice.

There is a good school in Todmorden, supported by the Messrs. FIELDEN, for the education of the children of the poor, many of whom work in the factory.

The distress, which at present is felt more or less throughout the manufacturing districts, does not prevail here to the same extent as in large towns; but it is quite sufficient to make the population feel the necessity of a change.

I leave here to-morrow for Halifax, from whence your Lordship may expect a letter in a day or two.

I am, &c.

LETTER XX.

Halifax, November 4, 1841.

My LORD:

I beg to lay before your Lordship an account of my sojourn in Halifax and its neighbourhood. Soon after my arrival I waited upon Mr. HOLROYD, surgeon, who received me very kindly, and offered to assist me in any way I might point out; and, being informed of the nature of my errand, he mentioned several individuals whom he thought I had better see, particularly Mr. AMBLER, who has interested himself very much on behalf of the factory people. I am sorry to say he was ill in bed, and scarcely able to speak to me. I then tried to get into the mills, but without success; after which I mixed with the working people, and from some sensible men I collected the following particulars. The children seem to be pretty well attended to in the schooling department. I had an opportunity of hearing some read. Mr. HOLROYD, who is a certificating surgeon (being appointed to that duty by Mr. SAUNDERS, the factory inspector), keeps a sharp look-out after their *health* and *age*. He has a very good plan of passing them from mill to mill, by means of certificates, a specimen of which I enclose. This prevents that deception practised in most towns by all parties interested in working children a greater length of time than is allowed by law. The manufacturers have, on several occasions, manifested a disposition to break the law, and it requires all the watchfulness and care of Mr. HOLROYD, and others, to keep them in order.

The married and single females are much the same here as at most other places; generally working till the last day in a state of pregnancy, and going to the mills again, in three or four weeks after the birth of the child. They have a plan here of giving the infant a rag to suck, in which is tied a piece of bread soaked in milk and water. The children get so habituated to this, that it is found very difficult to break them of it afterwards. It is no uncommon sight, I am told, to see children from two to three years of age running about with these rags in their mouth, in the neighbourhood of factories.

The condition of the men is very bad: they are generally working for very low wages.   One man told me, with tears in his eyes, that he had been *four weeks* (six days in a week, and twelve hours a-day) in earning 19*s.* 6*d.*, at weaving with the power-loom. Formerly he could earn upwards of 20*s.* a-week, by hand.   He has a wife and three children; the two eldest go to the factories, and earn between them 6*s.* 6*d.* ; and this, with his earnings, is all the family has to subsist upon.   He said, he was quite aware it was wrong to send his children to the factories ; but he could not keep them at home with his present income.   He attributes all his sufferings to machinery. Some of the factory people are very low in circumstances.

My Lord, I have received a letter in which I am informed of a *fatal* accident which took place in October last, to a boy of the name of ROBINSON, in a mill belonging to Messrs. BRAITHWAITE, situate at Meal Bank, near Kendal, in Westmoreland.   The writer of the letter which alludes to this accident, is evidently afraid to speak out ; but he says sufficient to inform me, that the boy, by some means, got taken in by the teasor (or devil, as it is commonly called), and was killed ; also that, about twelve months before, the boy's father-in-law, an old friend of mine, was killed by a similar machine.   What must have been the feelings of the poor widow, at seeing first her husband brought home, and in a few months after her son, a fine lad of fifteen years of age, both killed by machinery; it is much easier to imagine than describe. The facts, my Lord, have been confirmed by other parties; and, I believe, are correctly stated.

I have not seen many cripples in Halifax, but I have been told that this town has its share. At Keighley, a place about twelve miles from here, there is a great number of bad cases, two of which I have got the history of. I have not time to go over and see them myself; but the respectability of the party from whom I have the information, leaves no doubt of its being correct. It is as follows :—

" JOSEPH DRIVER, Lowbridge, Keighley, went to work in a factory when between five and six years old; he has worked in factories ever since. He was a fine strong boy, and quite straight on entering the mill; but long hours have made him a shocking figure. He stands four feet six-and-a-half inches, and spans five feet five-and-a-half inches. He has a wife and two children."

The other case is as follows :—

" SAMUEL RHODES, of Keighley, began to work at Mr. MITCHELL's worsted mill, when he was six-and-a-half years old: this was in 1819. He was then perfectly straight, strong, and active. He had 1s. 6d. per week, as a piecer, and worked from six to seven, with an hour off for dinner; no time for breakfast and drinking. Sometimes he had to go entirely without breakfast ; sometimes he got a part and took the rest home. He was treated very badly by the overlooker at MITCHELL's mill. Sometimes he was beaten with a strap *with nails in it*. ' I don't believe,' says he, Mr. MITCHELL knew any thing about that.' " He also says, " I remained with Mr. MITCHELL one year. I then went to Mr. WILKINSON's, where I had 2*s.* 6*d.* per week. I stayed with him nearly a year. I afterwards went to BURY SMITH's mill, when I was between eight and nine years old. We generally began at six, and wrought till eight at night. There was nothing allowed for breakfast, three-quarters of an hour for dinner, and nothing for drinking. I felt that length of labour fatigue me excessively. I got stiff in my limbs. I had much pain, and began growing deformed in my knees. *There were seven or eight boys beside myself in that mill, who were deformed, from the long hours of labour;* some more and some less deformed than myself. There were about thirty boys in the mill altogether. I was perfectly straight when I was between eight and nine years old, and quite active and strong. *In Keighley, you may find waggon-loads of children deformed from working in mills.* Deformity is exceedingly common in the town of Keighley. There are a great many cripples with whom I am acquainted; *I know, of my own knowledge, a great many cases of children being crooked who were perfectly straight before they went to the mill.* I was forced to go to a Sunday-school; our parents made us go, or else we should not have gone. Very few factory children can read or write. Their conduct and language is unruly and immodest. I believe they would be better, if they were not so long in the mills, and had time to employ themselves in reading and other proper engagements. I remained with BURY SMITH five years ; and then learned to comb wool." SAMUEL RHODES stands four feet eleven inches high : his father stood six feet.

The above two cases are a fair sample, I am informed, of factory cripples at Keighley, which town, I fear, I shall not be able to visit ; a circumstance which I greatly regret, as I am assured that there is in that town an awful number of cripples, " cartloads of them," was the expression made use of by my informant, a female factory worker, who could not speak of them without emotion. Nothing on earth can compensate these poor creatures for the injuries they have sustained.

I am, &c.

LETTER XXI.

Huddersfield, Nov. 16, 1841.

MY LORD :

On my way here, I stopped at Dewsbury a day or two, but in consequence of the unfavourable state of the weather, I could not visit the factories in that neighbourhood. On inquiring, however, of parties on whom I could rely, I was told that the manufacturers of Dewsbury have not much inducement at present to work contrary to law ; but if good orders should pour in, many of them would soon set the law at defiance. The country mills, especially, require good looking after.

On my arrival in Dewsbury, I was informed that a young man, about eighteen years of age, of the name

of WILLIAM WALKER, had met with an accident in
the machinery of Messrs. BREARLEY, HALL, and
Co., of Batley, about a mile from Dewsbury, on the
preceding day, by which he lost his life. I was
shown the mill in which this accident occurred; and
the account I received from a person living near,
and which was afterwards corroborated by the newspapers, is as follows : " He had been cleaning the
machinery, I believe a carding-engine; and to do this
properly, it is necessary to take the rollers off the
cylinders, or, in other words, to take the machine
in pieces; the same as a clock when it wants dressing. When a carding-engine is put together, after
cleaning, and again set in motion, it is requisite that
the person in attendance should ascertain if all the
rollers are working right. This can only be done
by *listening,* to hear if the cards graze equally and
rightly upon each other. The young man above-
mentioned was attending to this duty, and while in
the act of *listening,* his neckcloth (the ends of which
were hanging down) was caught by one of the rollers,
and wound round it, and drawn tight, so as to produce strangulation. He died in less than an hour.
An inquest was held on the following day, before
THOMAS LEE, Esq., when a verdict of ' Accidental
Death,' was returned."

On the 11th, I proceeded on my way to this place,
and have waited on many clergymen, gentlemen,
work-people, &c. ; particularly on the Rev. J. OLD-
HAM, the Rev. WYNDHAM MADDENS, Mr. WHITE-
ACRE a retired manufacturer, Mr. STOCKS, and Mr.

LEACH ; all of whom received me very kindly, and
entered freely into conversation on the subject of my
inquiries.   I have drawn the attention of the clergymen to several cases of cripples which I met with in
this town, and have reason to hope that they will all
assist us.   Mr. WHITEACRE, and two other gentlemen, kindly conversed with me on the factory system,
for about half an hour ; they then were pleased to
say, that I had told them many things connected
with the working of the system which they had
not known before ; and, wishing me every success,
one of them presented me with half a sovereign,
to assist in defraying my expenses.   I think we have
not much to fear from the manufacturers of Huddersfield.   One of them, I hear, is going to com-
mence, to-morrow, working ten hours and a half per
day ; another is gradually withdrawing the *married*
females from his mills, and nearly all seem favourable
to a factory *reform*.

   It struck me very forcibly, since I came here, that
if we get an increase of leisure-time for the factory
labourers, inducements must be held out to them to
employ it in a way which may be beneficial to themselves, and their employers.   My opinion is, that it
would be a great point gained, if small societies were
established, for instruction in reading, writing, arithmetic, and singing, so that utility, and cheerful and
innocent recreation, might be combined.   There should
also be a library of religious and other books, and no
work should be admitted but what would bear the
strictest scrutiny.   These societies should be under

the superintendence of the resident clergyman in each
town or village. I have no doubt that this plan
would meet with encouragement from some of the
most influential manufacturers. The people would
thus be brought to read publications which would do
them good, instead of the infidel productions of
PAINE, VOLNEY, &c., which are now very often
thrown in their way; and also to sing something
that would be worth hearing, instead of those filthy
and obscene songs, so much in use in our factories at
present.

I have met with a variety of original documents
relating to the migrant families, who were induced to
leave their homes, in Suffolk and elsewhere, in 1835-6,
and come to work in the factories. One class of
these documents is in the form of *plans* of distressed
families, made out by the guardians of the poor in
different parishes, which plans were forwarded to
Mr. MUGGERIDGE, the migration agent at Manchester, for the purpose of getting masters for the said
families. The other class of documents consists of
agreements entered into between the manufacturers
and the agent, and are a species of invoices of the
families, as sent by the parishes to the manufacturers.
These two kinds of documents are of importance, and
I think are likely to interest your Lordship. I shall
therefore inclose in this letter correct copies of two
plans of families, which original plans are in the
handwriting of the guardians, by whom they were
transmitted to Manchester. By these copies your
Lordship will perceive that six families, and three

orphans, in all forty-eight persons, were entered upon a list, with their names, ages, characters, &c., which list was sent to the *labour-market* (I had very nearly written *slave-market*) at Manchester; and there offered to the highest bidder.*

Your Lordship will also perceive, that three of those six families were selected, and engaged; the one with the *orphan children* attached to it, by ROBERT MANN and Co., of Manchester, another by Mr. J. J. CLEGG, of Heywood, and the third by Mr. HAYNES, of Congleton. The said families were then sent by the parishes to their several destinations, without daring to say a word, or in any way refuse. Your Lordship will please to observe the remarks made by the guardian, in the right-hand column of the plan No. 1, which show him to be a man of business, and that he understood the nature of the work he was upon.

This will give your Lordship a clear view of the manner in which vast numbers of families were brought from the agricultural counties into the manufacturing districts during the above years.

I have endeavoured to find some of these agricultural families, and, to my surprise, have been told that they have all left the neighbourhood; some have gone back to their old places of residence, many are dead, and others have turned to different sorts of labour, more congenial to their former habits. It would seem that they have suffered great hardships

* *See* APPENDIX (B).

from sickness, lameness, accidents, and privation; but, as it may be desirable to give the recital of their sufferings in their own words, I will content myself with transcribing for your Lordship's perusal, the history of a few families, as related by themselves to several gentlemen in this neighbourhood. These histories were taken soon after these poor people came into this district, by gentlemen who had no wish to exaggerate any statement made to them, and who were actuated solely by a philanthropic feeling, in their visits. The statements I will furnish as a separate document.*

These cases, my Lord, will furnish a tolerable picture of the sufferings and misery of these wretched beings, who, in many instances, I might say, were decoyed and kidnapped from their homes. And if we bear in mind that 10,000 persons were brought from the agricultural counties in a few short months, through the arrangements of the Poor-law Commissioners, independently of the tens of thousands who were induced to migrate by other means, we may form some idea of the misery occasioned.

Nearly all these migrants are now dead, or dispersed. There is occasionally a family of them to be met with; but very rarely, and they are generally in a sad plight.

I am, &c.

---

* *See* APPENDIX (C).

LETTER XXII.

Ashton-under-Lyne, November 20, 1841.

My Lord:

I have now to lay before your Lordship the result of my observations in Ashton-under-Lyne, Staley Bridge, Duckingfield, &c.; previously to which, however, I beg to mention that I have heard of a serious accident which happened the early part of this week. On Monday morning, a young man of the name of WILLIAM FIRTH, in the employment of Messrs. ROBERTS and LUPTON, of Junction Mill, Laister Dyke, near Bradford, whilst in the act of greasing a part of the machinery in an upper room, had his foot caught between two revolving shafts running near the floor. Before assistance could be rendered, the shafts made several revolutions, wrapping the leg round, and *crushing bone and muscle into one indiscriminate mass.* In the course of the forenoon the leg was amputated by Messrs. ILLINGWORTH and MUIR, surgeons, Bradford. Poor man! what earthly possessions can repair or compensate his loss?

It appears there are a great number of accidents in *this* neighbourhood, some very serious ones; the *eyes* seem to be in great danger from the shuttle flying out, in the act of weaving in power-looms.

In order to make this matter clear, your Lordship will please to observe, that the longitudinal threads (or what is termed the warp) of a piece of plain shirting, are divided into two equal numbers; or, in

other words, that all the odd threads, counting from
the side of the warp, viz., the first, third, fifth, &c.,
move *up* and *down* together. So, likewise, all the even
threads, viz., the second, fourth, sixth, &c. Now, if
we suppose that by a movement of the loom the
odd threads are made to *ascend*, and the *even* threads
to *descend*, they will form a sufficient space between
the rows of threads for the shuttle to pass through,
and leave behind it a thread of weft. The next movement of the loom will be to knock close up the weft
left by the shuttle, and reverse the order of the threads
of the warp, or cause the *odd* threads to *descend*, and
the *even* ones to *ascend*. This movement is repeated
in a power-loom from 100 to 130 times per minute;
being as quick as the eye can follow the shuttle.
Now, should one of the threads of the warp break
(as is frequently the case) while the loom is in full
operation, the shuttle will most probably trail the
broken thread across the warp, which will thus prevent the threads of the warp passing each other
freely. The shuttle is thus checked on its journey,
and as it is going at a railway pace, it flies out, and
strikes any object that may be in its way, with a force
which I am not able to calculate.

However, some idea may be formed of its momentum by taking into account the picks which it
makes per minute, which, I before observed, are
from 100 to 130; thus travelling at the rate of
9 miles per hour, and making between 7000 and
8000 turnings on the road, from side to side. In addition to the force with which it travels, the ends of

the shuttle are tipped with *steel*, and ground to a point, so sharp as to prick the finger when pressed against it. This instrument, when thrown out as above described, will not unfrequently turn the eye *quite out on the cheek*. But the most remarkable thing is, that the shuttle very seldom strikes its own workman, but generally those attending the adjoining looms, either right or left of the one in which it works. It is frequently thrown to a great distance; sometimes through the window into the street, and may, perchance, hit a passer-by, before he is aware of danger.

Several persons whom I have met with, have lost *one eye* from this cause. One young woman deplored her loss very much; she was on the point of marriage when the accident took place, and, as is sometimes the case with factory girls, on such occasions, she was in the family-way. The loss of her eye disfigured her countenance so much, that her intended husband altered his mind. Thus was this poor girl deprived of her *eye*, her *husband*, and a *father for her child*, all by the *breaking of a thread of cotton yarn*.

I have also met with a young man who is *totally blind*, from the same cause. He lost one eye by the shuttle, which so affected the other, as to deprive him of the sight of that also. Shortly after this, his sister (also a weaver) had a similar accident ; but the shuttle in this case only cut the corner of her eye, and did not injure her sight.

These people have all declined to give me their names, in consequence of having relations working in

the factories, who would inevitably lose their employment, if it were known to the manufacturers that
they had given any information about it.   Besides the
eyes, the cheeks and forehead come in for a considerable share of wounds and bruises.

I have seen and conversed with two young women,
who have each lost an arm by one and the same
machine.   The first I called upon was SARAH ANN
GODDARD, of Hurst Brook, in the parish of Ashton-
under-Lyne.   She lost her arm on the 9th of December, 1833, by the blower, at Mr. GARSIDE's mill,
situate in Charlestown in this parish.   She was
fourteen years of age at the time the accident happened ; she was off work about twelve months,
during which time she had very little assistance
from her master.   She then applied for work, and
was set to a job, for which she received 3s. per week,
while the manufacturer was paying 8s. to other
people for the same work.   Shortly after, she got
4s. 6d.   Her master then became a bankrupt, and
she was thrown out of employment, and has not
been able to obtain any work in factories since.

The other case is HANNAH WALKER's, of the
same place, who lost her arm at the same mill,
and by the same machine, in the year 1836 :
she was nineteen years of age at the time, and
she only received 5s. from her master ; she applied
for work on several occasions, but without success ;
she has not had any since.   Both these young women
are in a wretched condition as regards worldly comforts, and are wholly dependent upon their friends.

But, besides the accidents which it occasions, I find that power-loom weaving makes cripples by long hours, as well as other branches of the system. As I was going along the street yesterday, I overtook a poor cripple walking with crutches, and asked him to go with me to take a little refreshment, when he gave me his history as follows :

" WILLIAM GREGSON went to work in the power-loom factory of Mr. THOMAS ASHTON, in Hyde, as a weaver, at the age of twelve years. He was then a stout, strong, hardy lad. He worked generally fifteen hours per day, attending to a pair of looms, always standing from morning till night. His average wages, when he got to know his business, were about 12s. or 13s. a-week. He continued to work in this manner for about seven years, when he became a complete cripple. A short time after, he was so overcome with the long hours of labour, as to be obliged to be carried home from his work ; and has not since been able to resume it. He never worked for any other master than Mr. ASHTON, of Hyde. He has had no allowance or compensation from his master. He is now, although a stout-made man, and in the prime of life, obliged to walk with crutches. His legs are dreadfully deformed ; both knees are *in*, and wrap one over the other. When sitting in an ordinary-sized chair, he appears to be a well-proportioned man, and in this position he is full two inches *higher* than when standing, or rather leaning upon his crutches. He gets a living by selling toys, and hardware, in the market of Ashton-under-Lyne."

The effects of factory labour on females are in part illustrated by the following anecdote, related to me by a respectable linen and woollen draper of this town, with whom I had the pleasure of dining.

"A poor woman came into my shop," said he, " one Saturday night in September last, for the purpose of purchasing some small article. She had a child about twelve months old in her arms, which she set upon the counter, with its back against a pile of goods, in order that she might have her hands at liberty to examine the article she wanted. The child was not noticed by the shopmen till it became troublesome ; and being Saturday night, and a great many women in the shop, I asked whose child it was, but none of the women present would take to it. A thought instantly struck me, that some one had been playing the trick of child-dropping with me ; however, as we were busy, I ordered the child to be brought into my parlour, and laid upon the sofa, upon which you are now sitting, where it soon fell fast asleep. About an hour afterwards, a woman came into the shop in great haste, and inquired if she had left a child there? She was brought into the parlour to see if the one lying asleep on the sofa was hers. As soon as she saw it, she cried out, ' Yes; bless thee, it is thee!' She was then asked, how she came to leave it, and by what means she had discovered her loss? To which she answered, ' That while attending to the purchase she had been making, she had quite forgotten her child. That she had been through the Market, and in

many other shops, and had bought all the things she
wanted, but never once found out her loss till she
got home, and was asked by her husband where she
had left the child? To which she said, ' Why, the
child is up-stairs asleep in bed, to be sure.' But,
being convinced to the contrary, and that she had
taken it out with her, she began to think where she
had left it. There was then no alternative but going
round to every shop at which she had called; and,
at last, she came to the right one. She had left the
child in the same manner as people sometimes forget
their umbrellas, or a paper parcel. So you may
judge," said the draper to me, "what is the effect
of the system of factory labour upon these poor
people and their offspring!"

I was not surprised to hear this account, well
knowing, as I did, that the mothers only see their
infants at morning, noon, and night, except they are
brought to the factory to be suckled in some other
part of the day; and that, for the most part, the
children are in the care of strangers.

Another circumstance to which this gentleman
drew my attention, was the fact of his having ten or
twelve men and women, all power-loom weavers,
calling at his shop every week with damaged pieces
(chiefly cotton goods) to sell, which the manufacturers, for the most trifling fault, had thrown upon
their hands; and, to make the matter worse, he invariably found, on inquiry, that the work-people had
been charged 1s. or 1s. 6d. more than the market
price.

The work-people generally dispose of these pieces at considerable loss, in the way of barter ; shops being open in many places for the purpose of receiving such goods in exchange for others, of which they may stand in need. The work-people have no remedy for this, but leaving their places.

It appears that the manufacturers of this town have agreed with the sexton of the parish, to ring the church-bell every morning (except on Sundays), at five o'clock, for the purpose of waking the factory people. Immediately after the tolling of this bell, a curious scene takes place in the streets, something similar to what we are informed took place in the streets of Brussels, on the memorable 16th of June, 1815, when the drum beat to arms at the dead of night. The chief points of difference being, that instead of soldiers running to and fro to their several regiments, we have men, women, and swarms of children, running to their several mills (the mothers first hurrying with their suckling babes to some hireling nurse) ; and also that while, in the former case, thousands went forth to a speedy and honourable death in the service of their common country ; in the latter case they go to a lingering death—a death by inches—for the pleasure of capitalists, who, for the most part, have not a single thought beyond the sordid accumulation of wealth.

There is also a wide difference in the event of meeting with wounds, which may not produce death, or in the case of either party losing limbs ; the soldier being quartered on the country with a comfortable allowance, and the factory slave upon the rate-payers, and kept down, too often, to the starvation point.

There is still a part of the truck system carried on in this neighbourhood. I have conversed with spinners who have been *obliged* to take a great part of their earnings in beef; they mostly have the key of a house forced upon them also, even if they are single men, and do not want one. Many young men have kept houses empty for a long time, paying 2s. 6d. a-week rent, rather than lose their work.

The system here is much the same as at Manchester and Bolton, in all its prominent features. On Monday I intend to proceed to Stockport, and will write again in a few days. In the meantime,

I am, &c.

See, left but life enough and breathing-room
The hunger and the hope of life to feel,
Yon pale mechanic bending o'er his loom,
And childhood's self as at Ixion's wheel,
From morn till midnight tasked to earn its little meal.
Is this improvement?—where the human breed
Degenerates as they swarm and overflow,
Till toil grows cheaper than the trodden weed,
And man competes with man, like foe with foe ;
Till death, that thins them, scarce seems public woe ?
Improvement!—smiles it in the poor man's eyes,
Or blooms it on the cheek of labour ?—No—
To gorge a few with trade's precarious prize,
We banish rural life, and breathe unwholesome skies.—*Campbell.*

LETTER XXIII.

Stockport, November 23, 1841.

My Lord:

When I began my tour, I imposed upon myself
the task of visiting the sick, maimed, and distressed
part of my fellow work-people, in their dwellings ;
and it was a source of pleasure to me to go among
them, to inquire into their wants, and listen to their
opinions of the cause of the evils under which they
labour ; but, latterly, this duty has been rather more
painful than otherwise. Distressing cases have crowded upon me very thickly indeed, of late ; and not having the power to relieve them as I could wish, it has
made me feel almost a desire to quit a district in
which misery is so prominent a feature.

The cases of accident in Stockport are numerous,
and often serious. This very afternoon, as I was
walking along the streets in company with a spinner

out of employment, we saw a crowd of people at a little distance, and, on inquiring the cause, I found they had collected to see a poor woman, who had met with an accident in Messrs. M——'s cotton factory, in H —— L—. *One man was carrying her left arm in a cloth,* while four others were bearing her along on a litter, a little behind. She presented a sad spectacle : her head, face, and neck, were dreadfully cut and bruised, and blood was trickling out of her boots, and leaving a track behind, as they took her to the Infirmary. I have made inquiry into the cause of the accident, but the accounts I hear are so various, that I intend to wait till I can get a correct statement of the particulars.

I have heard of several serious accidents from power-loom weaving. One young man, of the name of WILLIAM JONES, a weaver, had the misfortune to lose his right eye, a short time ago, in consequence of the shuttle flying out of its place. *The eye was knocked completely out of the socket.* He went to the Eye Institution at Manchester, and got well ; but, of course, with the loss of his eye. He then applied for work again, but was told they could not employ him, unless he would take *four shillings per week;* his former earnings were about *twelve shillings.* He has not received a penny in the form of compensation for his loss. He is about nineteen years of age.

I have been informed of a similar case, which happened last week to a young woman working in the weaving department of Mr. ORRELL's factory. She was struck by the shuttle, and *her eye was turned out on her cheek*.   This is a very common occurrence among the weavers : they ought to be in some way protected from the danger.   If the shuttles broke some part of the machinery every time they were thrown out, we should soon hear of patents being taken out to prevent the evil ; and surely, where it is *an eye of the weaver*, although a substitute for him can easily be found, and it does not affect the pockets of the manufacturer, it should not be allowed to go on without remedy.   The power-looms are placed so close to one another, that without further precaution, which, be it observed, can originate with the masters only, the poor weavers are constantly exposed to danger from the shuttles.

Many accidents occur from the self-acting spinning-mules.   The following is one of several cases which have come to my knowledge: "A boy of the name of JOHN EDERSON, about fourteen years of age, working in the cotton factory of Mr. JESSE HOWARD, New-bridge-lane, came by his death in the following man-ner.   He was learning to attend a self-acting spin-ning-mule, in the early part of this month, and being in the act of preparing a broken thread for piecing, the carriage of the machine caught him in going back, and crushed him so dreadfully against an iron pillar which served as a prop to support the ceiling, that he died in consequence, in about six days.   The verdict of the jury was 'Accidental Death,' without any deo-dand whatever on the machinery."   The mother of this boy states that *his shopmates* subscribed 7s. 2d.

towards defraying the expenses of his funeral, and
his *master nothing;* not a single penny!

I have also heard, my Lord, of a fatal accident
which took place in Mr. BOLD's factory, at Craw-
shaw-brook, near Halifax. It appears that a boy received a severe injury from some part of the machinery, about the 16th instant, and lingered on, in
great agony, till Saturday last (three days ago), when
death put a period to his sufferings. I have not
heard whether a coroner's inquest has sat upon the case.

Mr. CHARLES TRIMMER, assistant-inspector of
factories, speaking of accidents, says, " I have taken
some pains in collecting, for the last three years, from
the books of the Stockport Infirmary, the number of
factory accidents. The number of accidents from
March 1837, to March 1838, in Stockport, was 120;
from 1838 to 1839, 134; from March 1839 to 1840,
86; out of which 36 *were owing to their being caught
whilst cleaning the machinery, the machinery being in
motion at the time.*"

"In the Report of the Stockport Infirmary for 1839
[says Mr. TRIMMER], there is the following passage:
' The Committee cannot conclude their Report without stating a fact which was painfully impressed
on their minds during the last year. They refer to
the manner in which accidents generally occur in our
cotton mills. *Almost all the accidents that have
come under the notice of the Committee, have happened in consequence of the cleaning of the machinery
while it is in motion.*' It is earnestly hoped that
the owners and managers of our manufactories will

adopt effectual means for the discontinuance of so dangerous a practice." "The practice (adds Mr. TRIMMER) *has not been discontinued;* because, in the following year, when the cotton trade was very bad, there were 36 accidents in Stockport, owing to clean-ing machinery while it was in motion."

He adds, "that of 340 cases, he only knows of TWO in which the manufacturers have made any re-paration or compensation to the injured party!"

It is peculiarly painful to contemplate the condi-tion of the factory people in this town. As far as I have had an opportunity of judging, Stockport and Wigan, and, perhaps I might add Holbeck, a town-ship forming part of the suburbs of Leeds, are the worst neighbourhoods which it has ever been my lot to visit, and the factory population of those districts are in the most awful state of degradation.

I have been sometimes asked, in the course of my travels, what good we have gained by legislative in-terference in the regulation of factories? And al-though I must acknowledge that we have not ob-tained all that is desirable in the forty years during which this question has been agitated, in and out of Parliament; yet, viewing the condition of the factory labourers even in this very town of Stockport, as re-ported to the House of Lords in 1819, I find that, bad as things still are here, some good has result-ed from legislative interference. I have carefully condensed a part of the evidence, on oath, given three-and-twenty years ago by two medical men of eminence in this town, and I beg to draw your Lordship's attention to it, as showing what an unbridled factory system would soon again become.*

It has long been my opinion, my Lord, that every working man ought to have it in his power, by means of rightly-constituted Benefit Societies, to make himself independent, during sickness and old age, and insure something for his wife and children to look to, in the event of his death. But, how is this to be done by people working in the factories? No scale of rates ever yet calculated would ensure the above benefits to them; and the rates which would be sufficient, it is entirely out of their power to pay. Some of the very best-regulated societies have found that, between twenty and thirty years of age, a man in other occupations has a chance of being but little more than half a week per annum indisposed. Between thirty and forty, the annual duration of sickness is found to be about two-thirds of a week each. But, on referring to the Stockport tables, we find, that in the case of the 823 persons therein-mentioned, although 790 were under twenty years of age, the sickness was very nearly two weeks each. Again, the ordinary Benefit Societies calculate upon their members becoming superannuated at about sixty years of age; whereas the factory people, speaking generally, are superannuated before they are forty, and immense numbers never reach twenty. I am confident, that no system of insurance ever yet devised would, while the present long hours of labour are exacted,

* *See* APPENDIX (D).

secure the people working in factories from becoming, at some part of their lives, troublesome to their friends or the public.

Although, judging from these tables, it is clear that some benefit has been gained by the interference of·the Legislature, in so far, at least, as it has prevented children from working in factories (always excepting the silk and lace factories) before the age of nine years; yet the system of increasing the speed, enlarging the wheels, and compelling the hands to turn off a far greater quantity of work in a given time, leaves but little hope of finding the condition of the workpeople much improved. However, I shall visit this place again in a short time, and will then study their character and habits more closely.   I remain, &c.

L E T T E R   XXIV.

Stockport, December 13,* 1841.

My Lord :

Your Lordship may, perhaps, remember the case of accident which took place on the 23rd of November last, in Messrs. M——'s cotton factory, H—— L——, as mentioned in my letter of that date.   I have to inform your Lordship that I have since had some conversation with an eye-witness of the accident, and have learned the following particulars, which may be relied on as facts.   The husband of

---

* For the sake of bringing the information respecting Stockport into one place, the above letter is inserted here; although written on the occasion of a *second* visit to this town, the reason of which it is needless to enter upon.

this poor woman is a cotton yarn-dresser, of the name of JAMES LEES, living in Walker-street, Dawbank, about three-quarters of a mile from his work. On the day above-mentioned he felt exhausted, and did not go home, thinking to have a rest; and relying upon his wife bringing his dinner to the mill, as she had been accustomed to do before, when he had not gone home till half the hour had expired; this being understood between them. The wife brought the dinner, according to expectation, and while he was getting it the engine started, and he had to attend to his work, eating a bit occasionally, as he could find time. When he had finished his dinner, the wife had to return past the machinery, which was then in motion. About a yard distant from the machine which her husband was attending, there was an upright shaft, revolving at the rate of 140 times per minute. This shaft was four inches in diameter, and unpolished; situate five inches from the wall, and unboxed-off or guarded in any way whatever.

There was also a large wheel on the top of the shaft, about six feet from the floor. The indentation made in the wall for the wheel was about eight inches. The shaft and wheel being quite unguarded, the rotatory motion caused a strong current of air, which drew her shawl round the shaft; she shouted out, and when assistance was at last obtained, she was jammed fast between the shaft and the wall. All her clothes were torn off below her stays, *and her left arm was wrenched off a little below the elbow.* The engine was stopped, and on taking her clothes off the

shaft, her arm was found cased in the sleeve of her
gown. A surgeon was then sent for, who said the
stump would have to be amputated, about four inches
from her shoulder. She was then conveyed to the
Infirmary, where, on further examination, it was discovered that her right hand was broken in three
places; her left thigh was also severely burned by
the friction of the shaft; her neck and several other
parts of her person were also much burnt. She
is pregnant, and after the stump had been amputated, she was thrown in labour by the fright; but
the symptoms were repressed by opiates. JAMES
LEES has a family of two children. *The shaft was
immediately taken down after this accident happened.* The Messrs. M—— have not yet made any
compensation. The shaft which caused this accident was not only left *unguarded*, but was *useless;
it performed* 140 *revolutions per minute, close by
a thoroughfare* in the mill, and consequently was in
a dangerous position. If these gentlemen had used
that care which is requisite in such places, they
would have removed this useless shaft, before it had
done the mischief; and I hope I may be allowed to
add, that if they had been influenced by the dictates
of justice and humanity, as they ought to have been,
they would have soothed and alleviated the affliction
they had caused this poor family, by every act of
kindness in their power. But they have not only
not done this, but, if I have been correctly informed,
they have actually *stopped the husband's wages for
the time lost in waiting upon his wife.* Can this be

right ? [Since my return to London, I have heard
that JAMES LEES has got his wife home, but that
she is in a very weak state, and that his masters
have given him the sum of *ten shillings.*]

JAMES LEES is a well-informed steady man, and
appears to be a very affectionate husband.   When I
called, last night, to see him, he had been at the Infirmary with his wife most part of the day, and had
to go to sit up with her all night ; and had to work
to-day in an atmosphere from 90 to 100 degrees.
His work is ruining his constitution, and he does
not expect to be able to follow it after forty years of
age ; and what to do for a living after that, he could
not tell.   The poor man was almost melancholy at
the reflections on the past, and the gloomy anticipations of the future.

I called at the Infirmary to see his wife, and found
her in a very low state, but much better in spirits
than I expected.   Great credit is due to the surgeons
of this institution, for the care and attention shown
to this poor woman.   Another thing which, I think,
is favourable to her recovery, is the religious sentiments which she has evidently imbibed in early
youth, and the patience and cheerful resignation she
displays under her sufferings.   She described to me
some of the injuries she had sustained on different
parts of her person, and showed me her hand, arm,
neck, &c., which were nearly covered with plasters,
and were shockingly disfigured, being sadly cut, and
bruised ; her eyes, which are blue, have a remarkable
appearance, as that part which ought to be white, is

a bright scarlet. In short, my Lord, it is impossible to see this poor woman without feeling the most lively interest on her account, or the utmost abhorrence for a system, by which the lives and limbs of her Majesty's subjects are daily sacrificed, as if they were of no value.

I have heard, my Lord, of a fatal accident that took place, a few days ago, at a place called Glossop, twelve miles from this town. It appears that a young woman of the name of CATHERINE GUNNING, was working as a weaver in the factory of Mr. J—— W——, in a small room under the warehouse. She was combing her hair out, which was very long, and, combing it *upwards*, a shaft, which was not more than a foot above her head, caught her hair, and dragged her up, when she caught hold of the straps to save herself, which *broke both of her arms, took three fingers from the* RIGHT HAND, *and one finger and thumb from the* LEFT; *and the shaft took both hair and skin completely off her head, leaving the skull quite bare.*

This incident happened about mid-day; the girl was taken home, and a few days after she was conveyed to the Infirmary, where (I have since been informed) she died about a week after the accident occurred. My informant, who saw her carried home, says, " I assure you, I cannot describe my feelings at beholding the sight she presented, when she was carried from the mill." This, my Lord, is the *fifth death by machinery* that has taken place, to my knowledge, since I left home.

There appears to be a great deal of sickness among the female factory labourers in Stockport. In Mr. ORRELL's factory, I am told, there is a great number of young women absent from sickness; some have died. I have not been able to learn the immediate cause; but it is, no doubt, greatly owing to the long hours of factory labour, and breathing an atmosphere laden with impurities.

The men, also, suffer very much; for, in addition to the above evils, they have to contend with over-exertion, in consequence of increased speed, double-decking, &c. Some idea may be formed of this, by the following statement:

" By returns made to Parliament, dated 28th of March, 1836, and 20th of February, 1839, it appears, that in three counties only, viz., Lancashire, Cheshire, and the West Riding of Yorkshire, the steam and water power to turn machinery in factories, was increased, in three years, from 45,836 to 65,395 horse-power, or 42½ per cent. While the number of hands employed in those factories had only increased, in the same period, from 242,099 to 292,179: that is, only 20½ per cent."

This will be rendered still more clear by a quotation from the " Philosophy of Manufactures," by Dr. URE. He says at p. 23, " It is, in fact, the constant aim and tendency of every improvement in machinery, to supersede human labour altogether, or to diminish its cost, by substituting the industry of women and children for that of men; or that of ordinary labourers for trained artisans. In most of the water-twist, or throstle cotton-mills, the spinning is entirely managed by females of sixteen years and upwards. The effect of substituting the self-acting mule for the common mule, is to *discharge the greater part of the men spinners,* and to retain adolescents and children. The proprietor of a factory near Stockport states, in evidence to the Commissioners, that by such substitution he would *save* 50*l. a-week in wages,* in consequence of dispensing with nearly forty male spinners, at about 25*s.* of wages each.''

This, of itself, is sufficient, my Lord, to account for the distress which prevails in the factory districts. I am apprehensive, my Lord, that unless this tendency of things receives a timely and salutary check, it will lead to some terrible convulsion. Your Lordship, I trust, will excuse the liberty I take; from a poor factory cripple this warning may appear presumptuous, but I cannot conceal my fears.

Yesterday I visited the Stockport new Sunday-school, and was kindly shown over the large building by a gentleman, who, being informed that I was from London, took especial care to show me every thing about the place that could in any way interest me. This School is capable of holding 4000 scholars of both sexes. These children and young persons are divided into classes, according to the age, sex, and religious denomination to which they belong; each class occupying a separate apartment, of which there are a great number. The several classes are brought together at stated periods, in a very large

room, for the purpose of hearing lectures or ser-
mons from clergymen, and others, who may wish
to address them. On this occasion a gentleman
delivered a very impressive discourse, from the
words "What think ye of Christ." This discourse
formed a striking contrast to a discussion which took
place, about a fortnight before, in a town in this
neighbourhood in which I sojourned, on the words,
" What think ye of Christ, and *Robert Owen?*
Which of the two has done more good for mankind,
and which of the two characters is it more desirable
to *imitate?*" I did not hear this discussion myself,
but I had some conversation the following day with
one of the men who had taken a prominent part in
it, and who assured me (with evident marks of
pleasure) that the discussion had terminated in favour of *Robert Owen.*

In addition to this great School, there are several
Sunday-schools, belonging to the Church, the Wes-
leyan Methodists, and other bodies of Christians.
On the whole, Stockport seems well provided with
schools for the religious education of children on
the Sabbath-day. But, when we take into consideration that these children mostly have to work in the
cotton factories during the week, and are thus exposed, six days in the week, to debasing and de-
moralizing influences, we cannot be surprised at the
condition the young factory people of this town are
in. Under the existing factory system, Sunday-
schools cannot effect a thousandth part the good
which might, under more auspicious circumstances,

be expected from them.   The state of morals here is frightful, in spite of the corrective influence of Sunday-schools, churches, and meeting-houses.

In addition to the evils encountered with in the walls of the factories, the young people are exposed to much temptation in the low places of resort, the beer and public houses, with which Stockport abounds. On Saturday night I visited several of their favourite haunts, some of which were of the very lowest description.   It is usual for these places of rendezvous to be provided with a musician, whose business is to play upon the violin, piano-forte, or dulcimer.   In these houses dancing and singing are permitted to any one willing to exhibit.

There is another description of houses, in which professional performers are engaged to amuse the company.   I shall endeavour to describe one of each of these places, and thus enable your Lordship to judge of the arts made use of to amuse the overwrought population of Stockport, and extract a portion of their earnings.

The most respectable of these places is known by the sign of the "Jolly Hatters," and is in Hill-gate. The house appears to have good accommodation for all descriptions of customers.   There is a good parlour, tap-room, &c.; but the part of it to which I wish to draw your Lordship's particular attention, is the "Thespian Gallery, and Temple of the Muses." This is a long room, capable of holding from 400 to 500 persons, beautifully painted, and well furnished, at a cost to the publican (as I was informed) of 300*l.*

The walls are painted with historical subjects; the ceiling also is highly decorated. Near the entrance is painted the following inscription :—" This room is open on the evenings of *Sunday,* Monday, Tuesday, Friday, and Saturday." Your Lordship will please to bear in mind that it is closed on the Wednesday and Thursday evenings, the operatives having had their pockets thoroughly drained on the Tuesday night; and the only reason why it is re-opened on the evening of *Friday* is, because that is the market-day, and the publican looks for a different class of customers on that night. This "Thespian Gallery" is open at six o'clock in the evening, and closes at about twelve. Till very lately, the performances were carried on in the same manner on *Sundays* as on other evenings; but the magistrates at length interfering, the publican was glad to dispense with the singing &c. on those evenings, in order to save his license. There is still an exhibition of the Phantasmagoria on Sundays: it is of two kinds, one is called "The Temple," and the other "The Sun." The money paid for admittance to this gallery is 3*d.* each person; for this a ticket is given, which is convertible into liquor, &c. On Sundays this room is free; but, of course, it is expected that parties visiting it on that evening, will spend something. When I entered it on the Saturday evening, about seven o'clock, there was but little company; when I left, there might be from 200 to 250 present. People kept coming and going all the evening. Several men-waiters were constantly in attendance to take *orders.*

The company in this gallery have nothing to do
with the performances, and are there only as the
audience, and for the purpose of eating, drinking,
laughing, talking, and smoking; all which is going
on at one and the same time. The further end of
this gallery, which is opposite the entrance, is fitted
up as a theatre, with drop, and side-scenes, &c. &c.
Shortly after I entered the room, the curtain drew
up, and a young woman, in a *stylish undress*, came
forward, and sang "Meet me by the willow glen;"
after which she was rapturously applauded, and with-
drew. Presently a young man, dressed like a plough-
man, came forward, and sang the "Parson and the
pigs;" being a burlesque on the "cloth;" soon
after which I retired. With the exception of some
boys, about fifteen years of age, who seemed to take
a delight in puffing clouds of smoke towards the stage,
for the purpose of annoying the performers, as good
order as one could expect prevailed; but the room
would continue open at least three hours after I left.
In passing, I looked in last evening (Sunday), and
there was the exhibition going on of the "Sun,"
and the "Temple," which, I have no doubt, is produced by the moveable slides of a Phantasmagoria,
or Magic Lantern. The company present (about
fifty) appeared of a more sedate description than on
the previous night; there were not so many young
men and girls between fifteen to twenty years of age.
For persons of another grade, there is the tap-room,
which is also well fitted up, and *painted*.

Another description of amusement (if it is deserving of the name) is in taverns, where the customers themselves are the performers. I saw a specimen of this sort of "life in Stockport," at the "Highland Laddie," Hill-gate. I went into this beer-house, for such in modern phrase it is, on the Saturday evening, and had not been seated long, before I heard *music* in an upper room, and getting permission of the publican, I went up stairs. Although it was early in the evening, the room was nearly filled. There were seats all round for the audience, and a vacant space in the centre for any one who might choose to display his abilities. During my stay a dance took place, by two young women, and a young man. This dance consisted chiefly of an exhibition of disgusting attitudes and postures, the young man being the leader, and the women *copying or imitating his actions,* which were such as it would not be proper to mention. This mongrel kind of dance elicited bursts of laughter from the company, and when it was over the performers retired to their seats, covered with perspiration, and amid vociferous applause. I visited several places of this description, in most of which I observed a door leading to an inner room.

There is another class of beer-houses in Stockport, into which I did not venture, considering, from what I had heard of their profligate character, that I really should not be safe in them. These places have been described to me as being of so low a kind that, in many instances, the goods and chattels are worth but a few shillings, and consist of only two or three benches and a ricketty table. In these obscure haunts, youths between fifteen and twenty years of age, may be seen associating and revelling with poor abandoned girls, without the slightest check or restraint; and I am assured, by a very well-informed person, that many of these youths get so completely corrupted in these dens of iniquity, as in a very short space of time to be in the hands of the Police.

I have made several inquiries, but cannot learn that the factory people generally are in the habit of attending any place of worship on the Sabbath-day. Many allege as an excuse, their not having suitable clothes; others, their being exhausted by the labours of the week; others, again, candidly acknowledge that they have no inclination for such things. In a room in one factory, they told me that nine out of every ten frequent no place of worship.

The Sunday is spent by the majority of factory work-people, of mature age, in resting themselves; either by lying in bed, or collecting together in some one of their houses, to talk over grievances, and discuss the merits of a turn-out; or, if they have money to spend, by collecting in groups in beer and public houses; while others take a walk into the fields, or amuse themselves in any way that will serve to blunt or stifle their feelings of the injuries and wrongs under which they labour, and afford a temporary oblivion of the cares and troubles of their wretched life.

I passed several beer-shops on my way home, where I heard a great noise, as of people quarrelling; and, in one place, they were turning out to fight, mostly drunk, of course.

There are a great many pawnbrokers' shops in Stockport. I counted between twenty and thirty, many of them open till nearly twelve o'clock on Saturday night; and I noticed, in my walk round the town early this morning (Monday), that these shops were again open, and gas flaring up, as early as five and six o'clock. The gin-shops also were open for business, but I did not see many people frequenting them. I find, wherever I go, these two great temptations to evil infest the factory districts in a greater ratio than in other places.

As a matter of course, there are a great number of loose girls, and prostitutes here. I have been informed by a gentleman of great respectability, that *eight* out of *ten* of these poor girls have spent the early part of their lives in the factories. These girls are degraded to the lowest degree, and seem ready to catch at any thing which may offer the least chance of effacing their recollections of the past, or bettering their present condition.

The wages of the work-people here are very low. It would appear that this town has the unenviable reputation of always taking the lead in reducing wages. This practice has been pushed to such an extent, that some of the manufacturers of Stockport have lately received threatening letters; and from all I have learnt, there is ground for serious apprehension, if this state of depression and suffering should continue and increase.

This town, I need not remind your Lordship, is also notorious for unboxed machinery, and for the

dangerous practice of setting children to clean it while
it is at full speed.   But to this subject I have already
sufficiently adverted.   Stockport has long had a bad
pre-eminence in both these respects.

Great distress prevails among the calico-printers
of this town.   I have conversed with several very
intelligent block-printers, and they lay the blame of
their sufferings to the introduction of machinery;
and yet the goods printed by machinery are equally
high in price to the consumer, although much dete-
riorated in *value*, in consequence of the pernicious
quality of the colours and preparations used in ma-
chine-printing.   Thus, both the block-printers, and
the public have been losers.   Many of these men,
who were formerly able to maintain their families in
comfort, are now depending upon the assistance of
their wives and children.

I am, &c.

LETTER XXV.

Macclesfield, Nov. 27th, 1841.

MY LORD:

On my arrival here, I was recommended to call
upon Mr. THOMAS BRODERICK, a silk manufacturer.
He received me very kindly, accompanied me through
his mills, and explained anything which I did not
properly understand; allowing me at the same time
to ask any questions I liked of the work-people.
After he had shown me every thing worthy of notice
in his works, he accompanied me to a school in the

neighbourhood, where I was pleased to see that much care was taken to instruct the children in the various branches of education. Mr. BRODERICK repeated to me his opinion, as stated before the Select Committee of the House of Commons, that the children ought to be able to read and write before they are allowed to work in a factory at all. This, I am myself persuaded, would be a great benefit, not only as it would tend to counteract the general spread of ignorance; but, what is of much more importance, it would prepare them to meet, and more successfully grapple with, the evils by which they must, in the present state of things, be surrounded in the factories. I saw in this gentleman's mills a few children, who, I thought, would have been much better in the schools; one or two about eight years of age. I also met with some cases of deformity, which the parties themselves attributed to factory labour.

On the following day I called upon Messrs. BROCKLEHURST, who are very extensive silk manufacturers, having several mills in this neighbourhood, which furnish employment to between 4000 and 5000 hands. By the kindness of these gentlemen, I was allowed to inspect their works; one of them kindly accompanying me through the different rooms of the establishment. By this means I got a full insight into the various branches of the manufacture of silk. In this way I have made many observations bearing upon the condition and comfort of the workpeople; and, as far as I have hitherto seen, I am inclined to think that they are better off than are those who labour in cotton factories. But as it is impossible to form a correct opinion from hearing only one side of the question, I shall withhold the remarks I may have to make on some things, until I have seen and conversed with the work-people after mill-hours, and have heard their own statement of the working of the factory system here. I may, however, say, that in consequence of the material being much more valuable than cotton, flax, or wool, the discipline in some respects appears to be of a more rigorous nature. As the work-people have it in their power to do much harm to the valuable property intrusted to their care, they require to be more narrowly watched. In the silk mills, there are regulations respecting their dress, general conduct, and behaviour, which in flax, cotton, and woollen factories are not so rigidly enforced. The females, generally, seem to be clean, modest-looking young women. I have not observed the looseness of carriage among females here, which is so conspicuous in the factory girls of Manchester and Leeds. When I was in the mill of Mr. BRODERICK, and conversing with that gentleman upon the general licentiousness of factory people, he observed, that it was not so bad in silk mills as in other factories; and to convince me of the fact, he requested his manager to go through the rooms, and ascertain how many females had had illegitimate children; and, to my surprise, he made his report that there was not *one* unmarried female who had ever had a child.

The wages paid to the people in silk mills appear

to be generally about the same as in cotton factories, some branches being paid better, and others worse ; but I find this is a subject which requires a close investigation, before I give a decided opinion upon it, as there are regulations existing here between the masters and work-people which are quite new to me. There is much still to notice in this town. I will, therefore, take another opportunity of resuming the subject.

I am, &c.

LETTER XXVI.

Macclesfield, December 9th, 1841.*

My Lord :

Your Lordship will please to remember, that I addressed a letter to your Lordship on the 27th of November last, containing a few observations on the silk mills in this place : the present letter is a continuation of the subject. I regret exceedingly, however, that I cannot report so favourably as I was then disposed to do. The more I have mixed with parties connected with the silk mills, the greater I find the resemblance between them and the cotton factories ; so far at least as the work-people are concerned. Immediately after I had written the letter dated the 9th of November, it being Saturday evening, I took a

---

* In order to bring the information respecting Macclesfield together, into one part of the volume, the above letter is placed here, though written about a fortnight after the preceding one.

walk through the Market, and other places likely to afford me an opportunity of studying the habits and manners of the factory people of Macclesfield; I also visited a few of their places of rendezvous ; and from what I have observed, I have come to the painful conclusion that the females are equally degraded with those of Leeds, Manchester, and other places. In the beer and public houses, I saw a great number of young men and women, *some apparently not more than fifteen years of age,* drinking, singing, and smoking, and showing other indications of factory life. I was rather surprised at several well-dressed men mixing themselves with the factory girls, and treating them with French brandy and other spirits, till the poor girls lost all command of themselves, and left the place in a state bordering on intoxication. These scenes were, in every respect, similar to those I have witnessed in the cotton districts. I have, since then, had some conversation with a committee of working men, and have asked them, how they accounted for the fact of there being so many factory girls on the streets, endeavouring to get a livelihood by prostitution, while scarcely one immodest girl could be found in the mills. In answer to this I was told, that as soon as it is known that any of the single women in silk mills conduct themselves in an improper manner, they are immediately dismissed. This, they said, was the general practice ; and so rigidly is it observed in some mills, that were a girl pregnant, even by her own *master*, she must leave her work, just the same as if the intercourse had been with any of the men. In confirmation of this fact, one of them told me the following case : "M—— T——, a young woman in Sutton, Macclesfield, was in the family way in 1837-8, by her master, Mr. ——, of P —— G——. She continued to work until her mother was taken ill, on whom she had to attend for a short time, as she had occasionally done before ; but when the young woman went back to the mill, she was told that there was no more work for her there. She was brought to bed shortly after, and her master behaved pretty well to the child ; but as for the young woman, she might go beg, starve, or die in the street," continued my informant, "for anything her master cared." I looked upon this as a very serious charge against a manufacturer, and asked the man if he was sure that the information was correct ? "Yes," he replied, "I am certain it is correct, for *she is my own sister !*"

This piece of information, taken in connection with the evidence of THOMAS BRODRICK, Esq., silk manufacturer of Macclesfield, as given on the 8th of July, 1840, before the Select Committee on Mills and Factories, of which Committee your Lordship was chairman, will throw some light upon the unhappy condition of females here.*

---

* From the Evidence of THOMAS BRODRICK, Esq., silk manufacturer of Macclesfield, given July 8th, 1840.

9891.—"You have just been talking of the education which you say is necessary. Do you not think that in respect of the education of females, something more is required than a capacity to read and write ; is there no knowledge of domestic economy,

It will also account for the great number of factory
girls who nightly walk the streets of Macclesfield;
for it is very clear that, if they have not an opportunity of learning domestic duties and habits, in consequence of the long hours of labour in factories, and
if they are not allowed to remain in the mills, after
having made a false step, no alternative but the
workhouse remains; and few young people like to
bury themselves in such a place.

I find it very generally, I might almost say, universally the case, that where the mills and factories
are nearly free from mothers of illegitimate children,
there the streets are infested with prostitutes; and
on the contrary, where the girls are permitted to
return to their work, after giving birth to a child,
there the streets are kept comparatively clear of
those unhappy beings.

With respect to the cripples in Macclesfield, I have
been very much surprised at the great number of severe cases I have found. There are many to be seen
walking about the streets; but there is also a great

---

or the practice of domestic habits required?''—''I do not know
how they are to learn it, consistently with pursuing the manufactures. I agree with you, that it would be most essential, for the
further happiness of themselves, and those with whom they may
become connected, that they should be instructed in domestic
habits; but I know no means of making such a system of training consistent with getting their bread in a factory.''

9892.—'' You have given an opinion, that by long detention in
a mill, it is not possible to acquire that knowledge of domestic
economy, which would be useful to themselves, to make them
wives and *mothers?*''—'' No.''

number who cannot walk at all, and who are obliged to remain within doors. I have visited many of these poor creatures, and will lay the history of a few of them before your Lordship, in their own words.

" JOSEPH LOCKETT went to work, at seven years of age, at DAVID HIGGINBOTTOM's silk mill; he was hired for three years, to have 2s. per week the first year, 3s. the second year, and 4s. the third year. He continued to work in a silk mill until he was twenty years of age, when he was literally ' done up.' The highest rate of wages he ever obtained, was 5s. per week. For some time before he gave over, he was so lame as to be unable to go to his work, and they had him to carry both ways. He is now unable to walk across the floor; indeed, he cannot get out of his chair without assistance. He was off work thirty-six weeks, before he gave up entirely. For the last four years he has not been able to do anything whatever. He sits in an arm-chair, like an old man of ninety years of age, although he is but twenty-four; and he cannot get to bed without assistance. He can read a little, but not write. *His parents are both dead.* He has no friend, except an old woman, who has a little with him from the parish; but the ' workhouse test,' in all probability, will soon be applied to his case, and then he will have to pine away, or be incarcerated in some union workhouse, till death comes to release him. For thirteen years he worked in the silk mills, making with over-time about seven days per week. The sum total of his earnings during that period is about 170l.; for which he has been utterly ruined in

the prime of life.   His master has not done anything
for him."

A young woman, named ELIZABETH TOMKINSON,
tells her sad tale thus :—

"She went to work, at seven years of age, at Mr.
KNIGHT's silk mill, where she worked a fortnight
for nothing.   She then had 1s. 6d. per week, and
continued to work till she was fifteen years of age;
her wages being gradually raised, until she had
3s. 9d., the highest wages she ever had, and for
which she had to work sixty-nine hours a-week;
being a fraction more than five-eighths of a penny
per hour.   She was well formed, and quite straight
on entering the silk mill, and at fifteen was obliged
to give up work.   She is now about sixteen years old,
and cannot *walk without a stick*.   She is unable to do
anything for a living; has had no assistance or compensation from her master, and depends entirely
upon her friends."

Another cripple, of the name of JOHN COLLINS,
thus stated his case to me :

"I went to work at Mr. THOMAS JOHNSON's silk
mills, near Congleton, at seven years of age.   I had
2s. per week for about one year.   I then went to
work for Mr. SAMUEL CHEATHAM, where I had
2s. 6d. per week.   Afterwards I went to Messrs.
JOHN COOK and Co., the Depôt mills, Macclesfield;
where I stopped till they would not keep me any
longer.   I have been off work more than half my time.
I am now about eighteen years of age, and can earn
3s. per week, by winding quills for weavers."

JOHN COLLINS is obliged to walk with a stick, the right knee is in, and the left knee out. He stands only four feet one-and-a-half inch high, though, when sitting upon an ordinary-sized chair, he is four feet high. He spans between the tips of his fingers, when his arms are extended, five feet three inches. He has not received any compensation from any of his masters. This is a very pitiable case.

The next is that of WILLIAM KIRKHAM, whose account is as follows :—"I went to work at Mr. JACKSON's silk mills, at seven years of age, as a piecer at the engine. I had 1s. 1d. per week the first year, for nine hours per day; and 1s. 6d. the second year. I also worked for Mr. BARBER, and Mr. PEARSON. I worked in all about eight years. My highest wages were 4s. a-week, for twelve hours a-day. Several times I have been obliged to give up work. I am now learning the business of a tailor, and can earn about 1s. per day, when fully employed." WILLIAM KIRKHAM stands four feet six inches high.

Another case is that of JOHN GOODWIN; the following account I had from himself:

" I went to work in a silk mill at six years of age. I had 1s. 9d. per week at first. I have been working in silk mills ever since, for Mr. TAYLOR, Mr. AR-NOT, and Mr. WALKER. About the age of sixteen, I was bound an apprentice as a silk weaver for five years, allowing my masters half my earnings; I am now loose, and unable to earn as much as when I had to allow my masters half. I was quite well formed on entering the silk mills."

JOHN GOODWIN is now very much deformed, his
knees are both turned in.   He is about twenty-two
years of age.

My next visit, my Lord, was to a *whole family of
silk-mill cripples :* — " JOHN, GEORGE, MARY, and
THOMAS BOOTH, three brothers and one sister, of
the several ages of thirty, twenty-seven, twenty-six,
and twenty-five years ; were all well made, and quite
healthy and straight, when sent to work at Mr.
CHARLES KNIGHT's silk mill, where they all became
much deformed.   They were sent to work at the
several ages of ten, nine, eight, and seven.   They
had each 1*s*. 6*d*. per week at first, and got advanced
about 6*d*. a-year.   They had to work generally
thirteen hours a-day.   They never sat down, except
at meal-times.   They continued to work for Mr.
CHARLES KNIGHT about five years ; after that, they
went to work for Messrs. BAKER and PEARSON,
where they had about 5*s*. per week ; but, in a short
time, were all obliged to give up their work.   JOHN
was off work *twelve years,* during which time he
got about 1*s*. a-week for doing some trifling jobs.
GEORGE did not lose much time.   MARY was many
years off work ; she went on crutches six years, and
cannot entirely do without them now.   THOMAS, the
youngest, was off work four years.   JOHN and THO-
MAS walk with their *right knee in,* and *left knee out,*
very badly.   GEORGE and MARY have *both knees
in;* theirs are very bad cases.   They are all obliged
to walk with sticks or crutches, more or less.   JOHN
has bad eyes.   The brothers have each got some

work, where they can sit, generally at low wages; MARY has been instructed in making fancy trimmings."

It would almost melt a heart of stone, to hear the mother, a *poor widow*, bewail the unhappy fate of all her children; and to hear her describe the pleasing anticipations in which she had indulged in their infancy (when they lived in the country and kept a cow), of the pleasure she would enjoy when they all got up to maturity; " and, now," said she, " to see them all cripples, is the worst of miseries."

A person going through a silk mill, and viewing the operations of the various branches of the manufacture, would suppose that no human beings could be deformed and crippled by such light, clean, and beautiful work; consisting of little more than knotting threads of silk, clipping the edges of ribbon, and other things, which seem, to a casual observer, more suitable for a lady's parlour than a factory. But when we look more narrowly into the matter, we find causes for the awful effects of factory labour in silk mills. It may seem a very nice thing for a child or young person to be placed near a frame and have nothing to do but knot the threads of silk as they break; but, if we take into consideration that they are to remain close by that frame twelve hours per day, and never sit down, our astonishment at the great number of silk-mill cripples will vanish. Let us suppose, my Lord, that these young persons *had nothing to do whatever*, but were compelled to walk over a space of ground four yards long, and one yard

wide, for twelve hours per day, without having leave
to sit down, or rest themselves in any way, except
by leaning their knees against a rail which runs
along ; and this duty to be performed, day after day,
and year after year ; the consequences, I venture to
affirm, would be the same in both cases.

In order to make myself acquainted with the probable number of cripples in Macclesfield, I ventured
to suggest to my friends the propriety of having a
census taken, and I found several of the workmen had
formed short lists of cripples living in their immediate neighbourhood.   One had got sixty-three, in
about a tenth part of the town.   Acting upon this
suggestion, they are now taking an account, which
will, I have no doubt, be forwarded to your Lordship
when complete.   Since my return to London, I have
received a letter from a friend, of which the following is an extract :—" We have found more difficulty
in getting the cases of cripples, than I expected.   In
consequence of the great number, they are little noticed here, and people cannot tell much about them;
we have however taken 164 cases, and know of about
thirty more, besides others who are in the workhouse, and some who would not have their names
recorded.   The females, in particular, are very shy
in acknowledging their deformity ; but we are informed by dress-makers, stay-makers, &c., that many
of them are so deformed in person, as to require pad-
ding in different parts, in order to give them a tolerable shape."

I believe Macclesfield has as great a ratio of crip-

ples as any manufacturing town in Great Britain;
and I can see no reason why the silk mills should
be exempt from the same legislative interference as
the cotton, woollen, and flax mills. They may require greater protection from foreign competition,
but that does not justify the employers in ruining
the health and future prospects of their work-people.

Accidents in Macclesfield are but few, comparatively speaking. This may be accounted for by the
machinery being generally of a lighter description,
and the work-people not being required to clean it
while it is in motion, as in the cotton factories.
They do, however, sometimes meet with sad accidents, even in the silk mills.

The hours of labour are generally sixty-nine per
week; viz., twelve each day for five days, and nine
on the Saturday; besides which they make over-
time, generally a day in a week.

The wages for all branches of silk manufacture
appear rather lower than I expected to find them;
but this is a subject on which I cannot speak posi-
tively, as their exists a number of regulations between the masters and work-people, which few but
themselves know, and the masters seem to have a
desire to keep all knowledge on this head among
themselves. One of these regulations is explained
in the case of JOHN GOODWIN, the cripple just
mentioned, who says: " I was bound an apprentice
as a weaver for *five years*, allowing my master *one-
half of my earnings the whole of that time.*" This
plan of having apprentices, is very extensively prac-

tised, and is of much importance to the manufacturers ; for, as they are shareholders in the proceeds
of the labour of these young men, they give them
the *best work*.   JOHN GOODWIN further says (and
his story is confirmed by many), " that he could not
get so much money after he was loose, and when he
had all his earnings, as he had done when allowing
his masters one-half." I am also informed, that
some old weavers, seeing the effects of this system,
have actually placed themselves in a similar situation
with the apprentices, weaving the better description
of the work, and allowing the masters one-half their
earnings ; and find it advantageous to do so.   A
more oppressive system, it is difficult to conceive.

Many of the operations of the silk manufacture
are very tedious ; there are also exhalations from the
silk *in certain processes*, which, I am told, are pernicious to health.

In going through the silk mills, I was shown that
it was possible to leave the winding frames going,
without any one to attend them ; and that they
would continue running, till every thread of silk was
broken.   But the workmen said, there was not much,
if anything, gained by this practice; as, when a great
number of the threads were broken, in consequence of
the silk being very fine, it required several hours to
get all into working order again. This fact, my Lord,
furnishes the manufacturers with their chief argument for preventing any restrictive measures being
applied to the machinery.

I am, &c.

LETTER XXVII.

Belper, December 2, 1841.

My Lord:

Since my arrival here, the weather has been extremely unfavourable. I have, however, made a few trips to the large cotton factories of Messrs. Strutt, which present the most singular appearance of any establishment I have met with in the whole course of my travels. This is the principal, if not the only firm carrying on the cotton trade in this neighbourhood; besides their large factories in Belper, they have one at Milford, about a mile-and-a-half from the town. The factories here are surrounded by fortifications, and I have been told, that the other is guarded in a similar manner. The whole length of the works is about one hundred yards, and they extend along both sides of the road. Connecting the factories is a gallery across the road, about thirteen feet wide, supported by three arches. In this gallery are loop-holes for cannon, small arms, &c., which completely command all the approaches to the mills by the road. One part of their works is made bomb proof, with loop-holes similar to the above. The opposite building is nearly surrounded by water, over which a small bridge is thrown from the road, which, I was told, could be easily removed in case of danger. The river is made to cover two sides of the works; in addition to which there is a high wall nearly all round, with many hundred loop-holes, from which those within might fire upon any crowds assembled outside. There are also other means of protection, which are too numerous to mention in this letter.

I inquired the reason for all this formidable precaution, and was told by one party that Messrs. STRUTT, about twelve or thirteen years ago, had some misunderstanding with their work-people, concerning wages and other matters, and several threatening letters had been sent them; but, as they had not taken any notice of these letters, several large piles of cottons had been burned, and the whole premises placed in imminent danger. Another account is, that at the time above-mentioned, the Messrs. STRUTT were in the habit of slaughtering their own cattle, and compelling the work-people to buy of them, in preference to the town butchers, a covered cart being sent round each week to their dwellings, leaving a certain quantity at each. The butchers, conceiving this to be an unjust monopoly on the part of Messrs. STRUTT, entered (as is supposed) into a kind of league for their own protection, and some persons even go so far as to charge them as the incendiaries. Be this as it may, it had the desired effect, the slaughtering system having since been suspended, and this species of truck abolished.

The Messrs. STRUTT seem to have great influence over the town of Belper, which is nearly all their own, together with the land for some distance round. The eldest of the partners is popularly called the "God of Belper;" to him every one must yield, scarcely any thing of importance being done without his knowledge and approval. All parties seem to

consider that his smile can make, and his frown un-
make or ruin almost any tradesman, or workman
in the town.

The condition of the work-people is better than
one might expect under such a system. Their morals and general behaviour are of a higher order than
in some places. I passed several scores of them as
they were leaving for dinner, without hearing any
unbecoming language, and this is a rare thing among
factory workers. The Messrs. STRUTT's people have
constant work at low wages, and yet I am told the
wages here are better than at Matlock. I will inquire into this next week.

Being very peculiarly situated, and as is the case
with the work-people of the Messrs. ASHWORTH,
of Turton, mixing very little with any other factory population, a comparatively moral discipline is
here successfully maintained. Many of the hands,
no doubt, are well conducted, for no better reason
than that they dare not be otherwise : it is the
condition on which they remain in these establishments. This firm has the factory population entirely under its own management, and is fully
entitled to the credit of having, in many important
respects, exercised a salutary influence over it. But
were they not so peculiarly situated, I mean, as to
their respective localities, neither the Messrs. ASH-
WORTH, nor the Messrs. STRUTT, could have ac-
complished what they have. In the great establishment of Messrs. WOOD and WALKER, of Bradford,
we have a remarkable, but, I fear, a very rare in-

stance, of a high tone of morals being sustained among a *town* population; but, in that case, much of the superiority is attributable to the extreme care which, for many years, has been taken in the immense schools established by Mr. WOOD, at his sole expense, before the Act of 1833 came into operation; where sound religious principles have been constantly instilled; and where the children and young persons were, for a long time, very greatly indebted to the pastoral supervision of the Rev. G. S. BULL, now of St. Matthew's, Birmingham.

The working classes of Belper, taking them generally, are in a low state; many of them are stocking weavers, who have little or nothing to do; but yet there is not that distress which is so conspicuous in some towns. The workhouse is a handsome structure, and looks to the eyes of a stranger more like a gentleman's seat than a place for the destitute poor; but the internal arrangements are on the same miserable scale as in similar places in other towns. I could not help thinking, my Lord, that if the thousands of pounds which have been expended on this building, had been laid out in procuring comforts for the inmates, it would have been more to the credit of the managers of the poor-rates; this, however, would not have suited their object.

There is not a great number of cripples here, and the accidents are fewer than one might suppose; there are, however, some serious ones occasionally. I have not been able to learn how the Messrs. STRUTT behave to their work-people on such occasions. I hope they are considerate. I intend, my Lord, to proceed on my journey to Matlock Baths to-morrow, or next day, as the weather may permit, and will write again from thence in a few days.

I am, &c.

> " Beyond all sorrow which the wanderer knows,
>   Is that these little pent-up wretches feel;
> Where the air thick and close and stagnant grows,
>   And the long whirring of the incessant wheel
> Dizzies the head, and makes the senses reel:
> There, shut for ever from the gladdening sky,
> Vice premature and care's corroding seal
> Stamp on each sallow cheek their hateful die,
> Line the smooth open brow, and sink the saddened eye.''
>
> *A Voice from the Factories, p.* 16.

LETTER XXVIII.

Matlock Baths, December 6, 1841.

My Lord:

I arrived in this place on Saturday, to pursue my inquiries into the condition of the factory workers. With this view, I waited upon several persons connected with the mills. They were all very shy; being, as in most places, afraid of saying any thing concerning their employment. I found some intelligent individuals, however, who were independent of the Messrs. ARKWRIGHT, the great mill proprietors here, and at the same time are men well acquainted with the factories: their information, I think, may be relied upon as being correct.

After hearing a favourable report of the Messrs.

ARKWRIGHT, previously to leaving home, I have been greatly disappointed at finding things so different, in reality. I had been led to believe that the descendants of the great Sir RICHARD ARKWRIGHT (a name illustrious not only in England, but throughout the civilized world) were patterns for the manufacturers to copy after, in respect to kindness and humanity to their work-people ; but I now find I was labouring under a mistake. I had heard of their work-people keeping cows, and having pasture land, and had fondly hoped that the old state of things was existing here, as in the happier times, to which we now so often look back with regret. Your Lordship, therefore, may imagine my astonishment, on hearing from good authority the following particulars :—

" The scale of wages at Matlock is very low. The hands generally begin as boys, at 2s. per week, and get advanced by 3d. or 6d. a-year, mostly, if not in every case, the first week in the year, and at no other periods. In process of time the men get 10s. per week, and the women 6s. ; beyond which they never rise, except in the case of overlookers, who get about 12s. or 13s. I was credibly informed, by more than one person, that the Messrs. ARKWRIGHT pay the hands in all their three mills, consisting of about 1000 persons, including overlookers, workmen, women, and children, with 250l. per week ; averaging only about 5s. per head. One man was pointed out to me who had married when he was earning only 5s. 6d. per week. Another had done the same thing when his wages were 6s. 3d., and many of them had married when they could realize 7s. per week. When they get to 10s., they think they are well to do in the world. They do not shift about from place to place, as many of the factory people of large towns are in the habit of doing; but often spend their whole lives in these mills, and bring families into the world with no better prospects than their own. Of course, they see and know little beyond the beautiful and romantic hills by which they are surrounded.

" The hours of labour are twelve per day, or seventy-two per week; if they wish to have a quarter of a day on Saturday evening, which is customary in the trade, they are obliged to allow a quarter of a day's wages; and if they clean the machinery at meal-times, which they generally do, they are paid over-time for it; so that a balance has to be struck on the pay day, the over-time added, and lost time deducted; their wages, as above-mentioned, being understood as referring to seventy-two hours' work per week. Several of the men work six days and a half, or seventy-eight hours, per week, so there cannot be much time left for themselves."

I find that these long hours are attended with the same evils as at other factories, making cripples, keeping the work-people in a state of ignorance, and inducing immoral habits. I have been to visit one of their cripples, who is now living in Cromford. He is a sadly deformed young man, and tells his pitiful tale as follows :—

" My name is JOHN REED, I went to work in the

P

cotton factory of Messrs. ARKWRIGHT, at Matlock
Baths, at the age of nine years. I was then a fine,
strong, healthy lad, and straight in every limb. I
had in the first instance 2*s.* per week, for *seventy-
two* hours' work, or one farthing and one-third of a
farthing per hour. I continued to work in this factory for ten years, getting gradually advanced in
wages about 3*d.* or 6*d.* per annum, till I had 6*s.* 3*d.*
per week; which were the highest wages I ever had.
I never worked in any other factory than the one in
which I commenced. I gradually became a cripple,
till at the age of nineteen I was unable to stand at
the machine, and was obliged to give it up. My
lost time in sickness and lameness was about three
months. My over-time, viz., over and above seventy-
two hours per week, amounts in all to about six
months. The total amount of my earnings was
about 130*l.*, and for this sum I have been made a
miserable cripple, as you see, and cast off by those
who reaped the benefit of my labour, without a single
penny to bless myself with."

Here is a young man, who was evidently intended
by nature for a stout-made man, crippled in the
prime of life, and all his earthly prospects blasted for
ever! Such a cripple I have seldom met with. He
cannot stand without a stick in one hand, and leaning on a chair with the other; his legs are twisted
in all manner of forms. His body, from the forehead to the knees, forms a curve, similar to the letter
C. He dares not go from home, if he could; people
stare at him so. He is now learning to make chil-

dren's first shoes, and hopes ultimately to be able to get a living in this manner. He is a little more than twenty years of age, and lives at Cromford, about one mile from Matlock Baths; and it is well worth any one's while, who may visit Matlock, to go and see him.

The Messrs. ARKWRIGHT are said to be very good to those who have had the misfortune to lose their arms, hands, &c., by machinery. I was told an instance, of a man who has been receiving 5s. per week for a long time, who had been crippled in this way. They have also been " a father to the fatherless, and a husband to the widow," in cases where any of their men have been killed by machinery. But when any one has been *crippled by inches* with long hours, and constantly standing, as is the case of JOHN REED, *they have* (strange to say) *cast them off penniless, as if they were not as responsible for the one as the other.*

The females working in these factories are of the same class as in large towns, many of them working in an advanced state of pregnancy. I was informed, that there are at this time, eight single women in these mills known to be in the family way, and that they continue to work in this state till the last day. I was also shown a young woman of the name of M—— A——, who was working in the factory of Messrs. ARKWRIGHT, opposite the "Rutland Arms," on the 29th of July last, being at that time far advanced in a state of pregnancy. On a sudden she was taken in labour, and delivered of a female child *in the mill.* The room in which this circumstance took place was pointed out to me, and I conversed with several people who had prepared her gruel, linen for the child, and other little necessaries, so that there can be no doubt of the truth. The child lived only a few days, and in a short time the young woman went to her work in the factory again, where she toils still.

My Lord, I have taken several walks in the neighbourhood of this beautiful and romantic place, and seen the splendid castle, and other buildings belonging to the ARKWRIGHTS, and could not avoid contrasting in my mind the present condition of this wealthy family, with the humble condition of its founder, in 1768, as detailed in the *History of Lancashire.* One might expect that those who have thus risen to such wealth and eminence, would have some compassion upon their poor cripples. If it is only that they need to have them pointed out, and that their attention has hitherto not been drawn to them, I would fain hope and trust this case of JOHN REED will yet come under their notice.

I am, &c.

LETTER XXIX.

Derby, December 15, 1841.

My Lord:

I arrived here on the 13th, and I now forward to your Lordship my observations on the factories of this town.

Derby is a place which does not entirely depend on the manufacturing interest, and consequently we do not find the same amount of misery and wretchedness as in towns wholly supported by manufactures; however, there is much here to deplore, and which is the result of early training in factories. Immorality is by no means in the background, but occupies a prominent feature in the picture. I have visited several low haunts of the factory people, in company with a friend, at all hours of the day; and on all occasions saw something disgusting, particularly about ten o'clock in the forenoon, when the girls and their paramours were assembling to arrange their plans of operation for the day, and their victims to deplore the foolishness of the preceding night. The whole scene in these places at that hour affords a subject for the moralist, or painter, such as my feeble powers are quite unable to do justice to.

The town of Derby, on any evening except Sunday, presents a sad appearance to the eye of a thoughtful observer. Scores of girls, who date their ruin to the factories, nightly perambulate the streets, in order to procure the means of a scanty subsistence.

These girls are easily distinguished from others of a
more modest and virtuous character, by their conduct, and the general tenor of their behaviour, as
well as by their showy dress, or shabby, dirty, and disgusting appearance, according to the particular stage
of their career at which they have arrived. Three
years is said to be the average term of their existence in this line of life; during which time they under-
go a sad variety of circumstances, all tending to sink
them lower and lower in the depths of wretchedness.
One expedient gives way to another, till at last the
poor deluded girl finds herself spurned by all; even
her associates in crime no longer look upon her as
formerly, but gradually fall off one by one.   Drinking,
which has occasionally afforded her a temporary oblivion, now becomes the sole object of her study; to
obtain drink, she is ready to sacrifice every feeling of
conscience that may yet remain.   And, if she can
but obtain the means to procure the maddening
draught, which is to stifle her remorse, she cares not
whether she gratifies her evil propensity by introducing some girl, younger and more inexperienced,
to similar practices ; by inducing some careless
youth to rob his employers ; or by theft or robbery
committed by herself or her paramour.   Thus she
goes on, till, finding herself the victim of disease, and
the object of scorn rather than pity, in some evil moment, inflamed with liquor, she does a deed which
imbitters the remainder of her days, or plunges head-
long into an awful eternity, to escape the horrors of
her unhappy situation.

I find, my Lord, fewer cripples in Derby than in most places. This may be accounted for by the circumstance, that Derby offers many chances to parents of employing their children to better advantage; and consequently, as soon as an indication of their deformity is manifested, another business is procured for them; but, where this cannot be done, the unhappy being becomes a confirmed cripple. I have met with a few cases, equally bad as those in other towns; I give the following as a specimen.

"JOHN PURDEY went to work in a silk mill, at twelve years of age; was then quite straight and active. He continued to work in the mills until he was obliged to give over; he was then twenty-seven years of age. He has received nothing from his masters as a compensation. He is now twenty-eight years old, and unable to do a day's work at anything." PURDEY is very much deformed, having the right knee *in*, and the left knee *out*, as is the case with R—— H——'s, of Bradford. He has a stout-made body, and stands four feet nine inches high.

Married women are employed here, as in other places, in the factories. Two had been brought home from their work poorly, a little before I arrived. I visited these women, and found one in a very feeble state, produced by long hours in a close confined mill, surrounded by noxious exhalations arising from the silk. The other was in a far advanced state of pregnancy.

With respect to the hours of labour, it is scarcely possible to speak accurately, many of the silk mills working only short time at present; but twelve seems to be the ordinary number.

I can see nothing in the silk mills, generally, that can induce me to believe that the silk manufacturers have any claims whatever to a separate legislative enactment for the regulation of their works ; but, on the contrary, every thing tends to convince me of the necessity of their being under the same laws as the cotton, woollen, worsted, and flax mills.

My Lord, I intend to return to London in a day or two. I find I have taken a severe cold, in consequence of being exposed to so much wet weather of late. I shall, on my recovery, take the liberty of sending to your Lordship a concluding letter, in which I shall make such general remarks as occur to me.

And am, &c.

" Yet in the British senate men rise up,
(The freeborn and the fathers of our land!)
And while these drink the dregs of sorrow's cup,
Deny the sufferings of the pining band.
With nice-drawn calculations at command,
They prove—rebut—explain—and reason long ;
Proud of each shallow argument, they stand
And prostitute their utmost powers of tongue,
Feebly to justify this great and glaring wrong."

A Voice from the Factories, p. 19.

LETTER XXX.

London, January 18, 1842.

My Lord :

Since my return to London, I have devoted several days to looking over my notes and papers, from which I have drawn up a short report, which I beg to lay before your Lordship.

On looking at the factory districts generally, I find some things to approve, and many to condemn ; and as it may be proper to make a few remarks upon each of the most prominent features of the factory system, I shall begin with the manufacturers, they being the head, or prime movers in this great and important system.

I find, on looking over the list of firms which I have been able to analyze, and which I have reason to believe is a fair specimen of the whole, that *eight* out of every *ten* have begun business with little or nothing. If we look, for instance, at Leeds, we find that the manufacturers, almost to a man, have risen from an humble origin, although some of them now are supposed to possess from half a million to two millions sterling. It is not to be expected that men so circumstanced in early life, could have had a very liberal or sound education ; and many instances are on record of their ignorance on intellectual subjects. This want of general intellectual acquirements, has often been the grand cause of their success in life ; for *no body of well-educated men* could be found capable of conducting a system like theirs,—a system which compels them (carried on as it has ordinarily been) to sacrifice almost every good feeling of the heart.

It is clear that the ruling passion of most of them is the desire of riches, to obtain which they do not stick at trifles. I fancy their minds, if originally formed like those of other men, must have undergone a great and gradual change, as by a sort of rigid discipline, before they could be brought to enforce the arbitrary measures generally in use among mill-owners of the present day. Some of these measures I shall endeavour to explain, and first the fines. Fines are levied on various occasions. I have seen, early in the morning, at Stockport and other places, from fifty to a hundred men, women, and children, standing at the door of a factory, locked out for being *half a minute* too late. And, on making inquiry, I found they would *all be fined*, the men 3*d*., the women 2*d*., and the children 1*d*., and that it would take till ten or eleven o'clock in the forenoon to earn their fines. The above scale of fines for being late is moderate. At some places the men are fined 6*d*.; and at many places 4*d*.; many of these masters being in the constant habit of robbing the children and young people, without the slightest scruple, of a part of the meal-times which the Legislature has endeavoured to secure to them. Now, let us see, my Lord, how this system of fines will affect the master. The hands generally work by piece, so that their being out a few minutes longer, is very little injury to him; and by keeping, say ten of each, men, women, and children, a few minutes at the gate twice a-day, he would realize a profit of 3*l*. per week from this source alone; but I have reason to believe it is much greater in many factories.

Another source of profit to the manufacturers, in connexion with fines, arises from alleged bad work in spinning, weaving, &c.* In the spinning department the overlooker goes round, and examines the cops as they are taken from the spindles, and writes on a slip of paper his opinion (of course he has his instructions); for instance, he will write "good yarn, but soft cops," or, "fair cops, but indifferent yarn." This slip of paper is fastened to a cop on the top of the pile, for the inspection of the master, who calls out on seeing it,—"How is this? why don't you make better cops?" and, without waiting for a reply, continues "I shall fine you 6*d*.," which is accordingly booked against the spinner. I have conversed with some men whose fines amounted in all to 6*s*., and up-

---

* See Appendix (E).

wards, in a week; and a great number whose fines
were 3s. to 4s. per week. In the weaving department,
they generally throw the piece, however slightly injured, upon the weaver's hands, taking care to charge
1s. to 1s. 6d. more for it than the market. The poor
weaver has to lose considerably by selling it at an
under rate, or exchanging it for other goods. In
some towns, there are shops where they will take
the damaged goods in exchange for groceries, &c.
This will obtain for the manufacturer a large amount
per annum, the real loss being trifling, and, in some
cases, none at all. I have been informed that some
manufacturers maintain *their domestic establishments*
from the fines of their work-people.

In a moral point of view the general conduct of some
of the manufacturers towards their work-people is said
to be highly reprehensible; but this is a subject on
which I shall not dwell any further. I would fain
hope that the many serious charges which I have
heard alleged against the manufacturers, are exaggerated. Respecting some, however, they are but too
true.

Their love for machinery in preference to hand-
labour, is universally known and acknowledged, as
affording a greater scope for profit. There are, be it
always acknowledged, honourable—most honourable
—exceptions; but the majority of the manufacturers
do not trouble themselves about the number of hands
any new piece of machinery will throw out of employment; their only calculations being as to the amount
of money it will bring in to them.

If they were to take but half the care in improving
the condition of their work-people, which they take
in improving their machinery, they would not require
the Legislature to interfere with their doings.   If we
look at the condition of the croppers, flax-dressers,
wool-combers, hand-loom weavers, calico printers,
&c., previously to the introduction of machinery, we
shall find that all these were flourishing trades, the
earnings varying from 1*l*. to 2*l*. per week ; that the
husband could then support his family by his own
unassisted industry ; and that he was not then required to rise in the morning at the sound of the
bell ; but was comparatively an independent man.
As machinery became more general, the wages, as a
matter of course, became less, in consequence of a
number of hands having been thrown out of employment.   The husband then finding that his earnings
were insufficient to meet the family expenses, was
under the necessity of sending first the children, then
the wife, to work in the factories ; those places which
had monopolized his trade and calling.   These
women and children being made, with the assistance
of machinery, to do the work of men, the men were
cast off, or reduced in point of wages to a level with
the women.   We now find that men in the above
trades are working, for from 6*s*. to 10*s*. per week,
longer hours than they were working, a few years ago,
for *four times* the amount.   The introduction of
machinery has been the source of continual bickerings
between the master and workman, the one striving
to get his work done as cheap as possible, and the

other equally striving to uphold and protect his wages, and his living. From this cause riots have taken place, property and also lives have been sacrificed ; and yet, with all the exertions made by the workmen to protect themselves and their families from the consequences which they plainly saw would be the result of machinery superseding hand labour, the manufacturers have got over every difficulty, and now behold their victims powerless at their feet. To the unlimited introduction of machinery, therefore, may be attributed most, if not all, the distress which at present prevails in the manufacturing districts.

I would be the last person in the world desirous of depriving the manufacturers of any merit due to them for the skill and ingenuity they have displayed, or the ardour and perseverance with which they have prosecuted their several callings ; but when I see the havoc they have made in the physical energies of the country, whether as recorded in our blood-stained records, or as manifested in the deplorable and wretched condition of thousands of mutilated, decrepid, and emaciated beings, who now crawl over the counties of Yorkshire and Lancashire,—those counties which formerly supplied the army and navy with some of the bravest defenders of our country, whose hardy sons have planted the standard of England in every quarter of the globe,—I say, when I see these things, the conviction flashes across my mind, that we have purchased our manufacturing superiority at an enormous price, and that it would be better that our domestic system should have been maintained, rather than that we should have sacrificed the stability and strength of our population.

Let us now turn our attention to the condition of the people who have been thus deprived of their independence by this monopolizing system, and are now entirely at the mercy of their spoilers.

In proportion as the invention and improvement of machinery furnished employment to women and children in factories, the men became of less importance in the eyes of the manufacturers, and wherever it could be safely done, they have been displaced and cast off. And the women and children, being less able to maintain the wages than the men, and on that account more easily managed, have become general favourites; many of the manufacturers being unwilling to employ any men, except as overlookers. Thus the services of the men have been in a great measure dispensed with, and they, in turn, are now depending upon their wives and daughters for support. The injury thus inflicted upon the community, through these helpless beings, has long been made manifest to the public. In consequence of the long hours of labour, the females working in factories have not an opportunity of learning domestic duties and habits, or of qualifying themselves for the important situations they may hereafter be called upon to fill, as wives and mothers. Hence the domestic tie is broken; the husband not having those comforts at home, which he enjoyed in former years, and upon which he calculated when he married, seeks for plea-

sures of an improper kind in the public-house. His
time, without any fault of his own, hangs heavily
upon his hands. He becomes soured, discontented,
and often dangerous. The wives, also, finding themselves of more consideration in the estimation of their
masters, feel themselves equally entitled to gratify
their wishes, by indulging low vicious pursuits. And
thus the rites and ceremonies of the Church, particularly those of marriage and baptism, are in a
great measure disregarded, and the order of nature
almost inverted. The women, who in former days
enjoyed the privilege of superintending their domestic affairs, are now compelled to rise in a morning at
the sound of the factory bell, and toil through the
long wearisome day, immured in the mills, under
circumstances which give them claims to the special
care and protection of their husbands, but which they
seldom experience. The wretched offspring of these
people, brought into the world under such manifest
disadvantages, are weak, sickly, delicate beings, unable in most cases to bear up against the accumulation of ills which is before them; hence we find
that a vast number of these children die under the
age of three years. Should they be so strong, however, as to surmount the evils attending their infancy,
they are sent into the factories, as soon as the law
will permit, and there they have to encounter all the
hardships of factory life. Thus the evils are transmitted from generation to generation; every succeeding race becoming weaker, more depraved, and more
miserable than the preceding one.

I have received several letters since my arrival in London, from friends in the factory districts. One says, "in one factory in this town (Stockport) there are fourteen or fifteen overlookers, and several hundreds of young women; and it is melancholy to state, that each overlooker has, on an average, three females absent in consequence of sickness. There is one living next door to me (says this correspondent), who was brought home a few days ago, and who is not expected to live long; another of her class, belonging to the same factory, died of the same complaint [probably consumption] a few days ago." Another correspondent states, "I have a girl living with me at present, whom I allowed to come to our house, as she has neither father nor mother in this town (Bradford). She is about twenty years of age, and works at a *combing machine* in a worsted mill, from six o'clock in the morning until half-past seven o'clock at night, and has to lift a comb weighing about twenty-six pounds weight every minute. She has twenty minutes allowed for breakfast, forty minutes for dinner, and twenty minutes for drinking in the afternoon. For this work she gets 7s. per week. Four girls, and two boys, will turn off in a day between 300 and 400 pounds of combed wool, for the paltry sum of 1s. 2d. per day each, and some of them for even less than that." The same correspondent, in another letter, on the same subject, says: "Shame on a professedly Christian country like ours, which allows our infantile, and I may say, adult population, to be murdered in such a manner as I have endeavoured

Q

to describe. What would the Heathen world say to such work as this, if they could be made to comprehend it? I have just heard of a girl who dropped down dead beside the frame she was working at, a few days ago; her disease was called palpitation of the heart. Yes, it is always something; it is called anything but its right name, which is neither more nor less than *murder*."

In addition to the above evils is that of accidents. The accidents by machinery may be attributed to many causes, the chief of which are, the carelessness of the manufacturer, in not boxing-off his shafts and machines, and the work-people having to clean the machines while they are in motion; a practice which ought to be discontinued. I have shown in former letters, that a very great number of accidents take place in our manufacturing towns; and I may here say, that in the three months I have been from home, several accidents have come under my notice, the result of which is, that two young men have been *killed on the spot*; two other young men, and one young woman, *have died in a few days*, from injuries they had received. One woman has lost her *left arm*, another has lost her *right arm;* one man has lost *his leg*, another *his hand;* and many have lost *two* and *three fingers* each; all within my knowledge, in the short space of three months. This is what Dr. URE calls, the " bloodless strife of trade."*

---

* As these sheets are passing through the press, I perceive two more fatal accidents, of the most awful description, recorded in Lancashire newspapers of one and the same date,—namely,

The remedy I should recommend, is to make the manufacturer in some way *responsible for all cripples*,

---

Saturday, April 2. The first is the case of ALEXANDER PARKER, a workman employed at Messrs. NEWTON's silk manufactory, Heaton Norris, near Stockport. According to the report of the "Manchester and Salford Advertiser," this poor fellow, while engaged on the previous Tuesday in assisting another workman to arrange some machinery, lost his balance, and fell sideways amongst the wheels, by which his arm and leg were wrenched from his body, *in the presence of his wife*. He has left a family of six children to lament his untimely death. I have not been able to ascertain the verdict of the coroner's inquest. — The other fatal accident occurred on Thursday, March 31, in a cotton mill at Egerton, belonging to Messrs. HENRY and EDMUND ASHWORTH. In this case the sufferer was a young woman, about eighteen years of age, named MARY ROTHWELL. As a very incorrect account of her death appeared in the "Bolton Chronicle," I will endeavour to state the circumstances as I find them, after minute inquiry. MARY ROTHWELL was working at a roving-frame, at the end of which was an upright shaft, connected with other shafting by toothed-wheels. Above the frame at which she was employed, was a beam on which dust and flue were constantly collecting, which would occasionally, by falling, interfere with her work. Undoubtedly the proper time to clean the beam would have been when the machinery stopped. But the urgency, probably, was great, and thinking too much of her work, and too little of herself, she got upon her frame to reach the beam. The upright shaft had been only cased to the height of four feet from the ground, leaving all above unguarded. The poor girl happened to turn her back, for a moment, towards the shaft, when, in consequence of the shaft and wheels being left exposed, she was caught by her clothes, and drawn into the wheels, about the waist, and so crushed, that all was over in a moment. The guillotine could not have extinguished life more instantaneously. In addition to the crushing of her body, one arm was torn off. I cannot understand that the machinery which caused this calamitous event would have been *whether from accidents or otherwise,* made in his mill, unless he can clear himself from culpability and neglect. This would *prevent seventy-five per cent.* of the present number.

With respect to cripples from over-working, many erroneous opinions are afloat, even among the work-people themselves; the chief of which is, that some particular machines are more liable to make cripples than others. To a very limited extent this may be true; but my experience leads me to suppose, that, generally speaking, deformity is occasioned simply by *standing in one position,* a greater length of time than nature ever intended we should do. I am strengthened in my opinion, by the history of the cripples I have met with in different parts of the country, whether they have been brought up in the woollen, worsted, flax, cotton, or *silk* mills; nine out of every ten having been compelled to work from morning to night, without being allowed to *sit down* for a minute. In my letter from Ashton, there is a very bad case mentioned, of a young man who never

---

at all obstructed by more effectual boxing-off, which could have been done at a trifling expense; and this neglect is the more surprising, as a serious, though not a fatal accident, had pre-viously been caused by the same wheels. This poor girl was the second of seven children, was earning 8*s.* a week, and had been the main stay of her family. The Messrs. ASHWORTH, I regret to hear, have only paid the expenses caused by her funeral. It has been left to the work-people to raise a small subscription for the family among themselves. The verdict of the coroner's inquest, in MARY ROTHWELL's case, was "Accidental Death," as usual; no deodand was levied.

worked at any machine but the power-loom, at which he was obliged to stand constantly during the day. I have also observed that, so far from the ratio of cripples being in proportion to the weight of the work to be done, it is directly the contrary ; the woollen, which is the heaviest employment, furnishing the fewest cripples, and the silk, which is the lightest of all, the greatest number. I have also observed, that where *seats are provided*, and *extra hands kept*, so as to give the children time to rest occasionally (as in the worsted mill of Messrs. Wood and Walker, of Bradford), there *no cripples are made ;* and I have been assured that the work is in no respect injured, in consequence of this humane indulgence, but, in point of fact, is better attended to ; and yet, so far as I know, there are very few mills in the kingdom where seats for the children are provided, and no other where extra hands are kept.

Various remedies might be recommended for ameliorating the condition of the factory population, the first and most important of which is, a Bill to limit the hours of labour to *ten per day*. Without this vital measure, all other propositions are comparatively vain and useless. First recognise and establish this great principle, and other benefits will speedily follow.

It is now full five and twenty years since the late Sir Robert Peel himself, proposed *a Ten-Hours' Bill*, and on the 13th of June, 1815, a Committee of the House of Commons fixed upon *ten hours and a half*, as the daily period of labour for all between nine and eighteen. In the following year, the same, or a similar Bill, was referred to a Select Committee, on which occasion the same Sir ROBERT PEEL thus recorded his deliberate opinion of a state of things which, in many respects, might be advantageously compared with that which now exists :

" Such indiscriminate and unlimited employment of the poor, consisting of a great proportion of the inhabitants of trading districts, will be attended with effects to the rising generation so serious and alarming, that I cannot contemplate them without dismay ; and thus that great effort of British ingenuity, whereby the machinery of our manufactures has been brought to such perfection, instead of being a blessing to the nation, will be converted into the bitterest curse."

Another cotton manufacturer, Mr. WILLIAM RATHBONE GREG—bred up in the system, knowing it thoroughly, and the firm to which he belongs being the greatest cotton firm in England—writing upon this subject in the year 1831, says :

" At present the hours of work generally are about twelve of clear labour per day. This we would reduce to *ten hours;* and we again express our conviction, after regarding the subject in every possible point of view, that till this measure is adopted, all plans and exertions for ameliorating the moral and domestic condition of the manufacturing labourer, can only obtain a partial and temporary sphere of operation."

A third cotton manufacturer, Mr. JOHN FIELDEN,

of Todmorden, writes thus :—" We see, that to whatever hours we go, the French and Americans will go ;
and, if they cannot do it without having English
overseers to show them the way, they will have those
overseers ; and, more still, if bayonets even become
necessary, they will resort to bayonets, in order to
enslave their people to our state of slavery.   They
rival us at once, and Dr. URE tells us, that they have
become our victors in the shameful art of making
slaves.   But are we, therefore, to stride onward again
and out-Herod the monster that we have made, by
becoming more monstrous ? No, no : it must end
gently or violently ; and having first scourged our
own people, and then lent the means of scourging the
rest of the world, I think it is time that this ' bitterest curse' should be abated ; and, as it was we
who began the mischief, it is for us to begin the remedy, suffering patiently whatever loss may accrue
from it, as a very trifling part of the punishment that
we deserve.

" I have no idea that we shall suffer any loss
whatever ; but, if we were certain that we should,
still we are bound to listen to the dictates of humanity, and put all other considerations out of the
question ; and I am almost ashamed to have entered
upon the question of interest, in discussing the matter.

" I ask for what the work-people, and the good
men of all parties, have for many years been petition-
ing the Legislature to grant,—an *effective Ten-hour
Bill.*   I ask for what the late Sir R. PEEL asked the
House to grant in 1815 ; since which time the con-

sumption of cotton has increased from 6000 to 18,000
bags per week, and the labour of both children and
adults very much increased in intensity and depre-
ciated in value.   I ask for this, because it is all they
ask for.   For I think that our factory system will
not be what it ought to be, until the time of all be
reduced to *eight hours a-day*, with two hours for
training and instruction; such as I recommended to
the Regeneration Society in 1833.   A Ten-hour Bill
for *all*, then, I ask for; because I know that the adults
require it for their protection, equally with the children."

A fourth cotton manufacturer, *being the greatest
in all Scotland*, Mr. WILLIAM DUNN, of Duntocher,
told Mr. MACKINTOSH, the Factory Commissioner,
ten years ago, that he was of opinion that the Ten-
Hours' Bill, at that time before Parliament, would
benefit the masters, however it might operate upon
the work-people.

Two other extensive manufacturers, Mr. WILLIAM
WALKER and Mr. WILLIAM RAND, of Bradford, in
Yorkshire, in a letter to Sir JAMES GRAHAM, Bart.,
M.P., in answer to the objection, that, " if Parliament should interfere as they proposed, the English
manufacturers would be unable to compete with fo-
reigners," say : —

" We hold this argument to be a most fallacious
one.   Great Britain is, after all that can be said, the
great regulator of prices in most manufactured articles.   The foreign manufacturer would gladly get
better prices, if England were not perpetually lower-

ing the continental markets, in spite of their pro-
hibitory duties. Their tariffs, altered as they are
from time to time to meet emergencies, sufficiently
show in what dread they are of English goods. The
British manufacturer possesses many local and natural
advantages; but there is one which is too often lost
sight of, though it surpasses all others—he employs
*the most skilful and industrious people on the face of
the globe.* No race of people, of whom we have any
knowledge, will work with the steadiness and expert-
ness which so generally characterize the natives of
Great Britain. We may also offer the decisive fact,
on this head, that the cost of cotton goods in France
is thirty to forty per cent. more, than the cost of
similar goods in this country. This has been stated
by Dr. BOWRING, but other respectable authorities
have affirmed the difference to be much greater.
Next to Great Britain, France consumes more cotton
than any other nation. The same remarks apply in
a great degree to the United States of America,
which country, next to France, rivals Great Britain.
In America, we learn that wages are higher than in
England—that machinery costs double the price—
that fuel is much dearer—and the interest of money
greater. But if (passing over the question of *right*
and *justice*, which ought to be paramount) we must
argue this subject on the ground of political economy,
and are able to show that the limitation of labour in
factories to ten hours a-day would make no material
difference in *the cost of production*—the argument of
foreign competition must fall to the ground.

" Now it is universally admitted, that the term of twelve hours' labour cannot be maintained for any lengthened period. If it were constantly persisted in, the redundancy of goods in the market would be so great, that they would be sold at ruinous prices. All profit would be annihilated. It is also our conviction, that the daily hours of working in mills have not exceeded ten, *on an average,* for the last seven years. Moreover, the usual amount of orders could be executed with ten hours' daily labour, even without additions to the existing machinery. The markets would thereby be kept more regular, and, as a matter of course, employment and wages would not be subject to so many vicissitudes. There are persons who think that the cost of production would not be at all increased by a reduction of the hours of labour from twelve to ten. We are of a different opinion; but we are persuaded that the extent of its influence upon the *price of the manufactured article* would not exceed what is often effected by the fluctuations of a single market-day. It therefore cannot be right that a consideration so trivial as this, should delay the settlement of a great question, involving the highest interests of an immense population.

" The late king of Prussia having had his attention drawn to the fact, that the manufacturing districts under his dominion could not supply their contingents to the army, and that the agricultural districts had in part to make up the deficiency, made a law, bearing date March 9, 1839, which decrees that no young person under sixteen, employed ' in daily labour in any manufactory, or in the works attached to mines,' should be worked for a longer time than TEN HOURS in any one day. The regulations allow no child to be admitted to work before nine years of age, and are very stringent with regard to education."

Though I have already quoted from Mr. WILLIAM RATHBONE GREG's pamphlet, I cannot withhold another passage; it so perfectly expresses the views I humbly entertain :—

" It is no plaything we are about. Partial remedies will be of no avail. It is useless any longer to nibble at the evil,—it must be attacked in its strongholds,—must be uprooted from its source. We call upon every one to assist us in this great and important object. But although, from constitution and from principle, averse from feeling or acting as alarmists, we are certain, as far as reasoning from the past and the present *can* make us certain of the future, that unless some cordial, faithful, vigorous, and united effort is made on the part of the influential classes, to stem that torrent of suffering and corruption which is fast sweeping away the comfort and the morals of so large a portion of our poorer countrymen, and which, if not checked, will soon send them forth upon the world desperate, reckless, ruined men—ruined both in their feelings and in their fortunes;—unless some such effort is made, and *that* speedily, there are silent but mighty instruments at work, like an evil that walketh in darkness, which, ere long, will undermine the system of social union, and burst asunder the silken bonds of amity which unite men to their kind. But, even in this day of anxiety and suspense, we will not, for the honour of our common country, suffer our minds to be borne away with these melancholy anticipations. We will believe and trust that, notwithstanding despised sufferings, unheard complaints, unanswered entreaties, and neglected warnings, there is still a redeeming spirit in the feelings of the wealthy and the great, which will interfere, while interference may yet avail, and avert, by a wise, a vigorous, and an enlarged philanthropy, the calamities which threaten the peace, the prosperity, and the virtue of the country."

I have lately had the satisfaction of learning that in the West Riding of Yorkshire, *two hundred and ninety-three Mill-owners* have signed a petition calling upon Parliament to restrict the hours of labour for young persons engaged in factories, to *ten* per day. The question is evidently gaining supporters.

In addition to your Lordship's great exertions in the good cause of reformation in the factories, I scarcely need mention what has been done by those excellent men GOULD, SADLER, BULL, OASTLER, and others, who have sacrificed their private interests, and devoted their time and talents, and almost every thing valuable in life, to obtain that protection from the Legislature, for the people working in factories, which was denied them by their masters. After all these exertions, and forty years spent in legislating upon this question, it is melancholy to think how little has been done.

My Lord, I have endeavoured to describe to your Lordship, in these letters, those scenes, incidents, and occurrences, which I considered worthy of notice in my travels through the factory districts; and anything that I thought would bear upon the great object your Lordship has in view, the welfare of the factory labourers generally. I am fully aware of the imperfect manner in which this has been done, and that many inaccuracies of style, and some of grammar, will be perceptible in these papers. My chief object has been truth, to which I hope I have adhered closely, and if your Lordship will be kind enough to consider the many disadvantages under which I have laboured,—in many places being scarcely able to procure the materials for writing,— it will, I hope, induce your Lordship to overlook all imperfections.

I beg to subscribe myself,

My Lord,

Your Lordship's most humble

and most grateful servant,

WILLIAM DODD.

To the Lord Ashley, M. P.,
&c. &c. &c.

APPENDIX

(A).—*Page* 34.

MR. DRINKWATER'S REPORT ON FLAX MILLS.

Factory Commission, C. 1, *pages* 165 *and* 166.

THE opportunities that we have had of observing cotton mills have been so few, that it appears inexpedient to interfere with the information that will be communicated on that head from Lancashire ; but I shall always remain sceptical as to any tables or results which do not indicate a greater degree of ill-health in certain branches of the business carried on in *flax mills,* as they appear to be now necessarily conducted. The returns that may be procured from country mills of this description, will probably differ materially from those of town mills, as I am not yet in a condition to say how far a more perfect ventilation may be effectual to diminish the evils of these processes ; but, judging from what I have seen of them in LEEDS (and it is reasonable to suppose that we did not see them in their worst condition), it is difficult to exaggerate the abominable nature of the atmosphere which is inhaled in them.

The Central Board will, perhaps, wish that I should pursue the course I have adopted hitherto, of briefly detailing the various processes of manufacture, in order to

illustrate the evidence we have collected on them. In flax
spinning the processes are of the following nature :—The
flax, as imported, is delivered to the hand-hecklers, who
roughly separate the fibres by drawing the bunches through
heckles of spikes, fixed before them. This is a dusty process, but not now in so great a degree as when the whole
process of heckling was performed by the hand. These
hand-hecklers are invariably men or grown lads. After
hand-heckling, the flax is carried to the heckling machines,
and in these rooms the greatest number of children are
employed in this business: they are usually boys, but we
saw girls occasionally employed. The machines consist of
various sorts of cylinders, or rather polygonal prisms,
having heckles set on their edges, which revolve with
great rapidity; and the business of the *machine-minders*
is to fix the bunches on supports in front of these heckles,
and to move them from time to time from the coarser to
the finer heckles. The bunches, for the purpose of being
thus suspended, are screwed between two bars of iron,
which is the business of the *screwer* (generally a *younger
boy* than the machine-minder), and his labour appears to
me beyond comparison the most fatiguing that I have seen
children subjected to, independently of the noxious atmosphere, which is loaded with particles of flax incessantly
pulled off, and scattered by the whirling of the machines.
*The screwer seems not to have an instant's cessation from
labour;* bunch after bunch is thrown down before him to
fix and unfix, which he performs with astonishing rapidity.
If he does not perform his work properly, it mars the work
of the *machine-minder*, generally, as I have said, a bigger
boy; and the usual consequence of oppression of the weaker
seems to follow in this, as in every other case where the
labour of the workman is immediately dependent on that of
another. If the difference of age and strength were the
same between the machine-minder and the screwer, as
between the slubber and the piecener, I have little doubt

that the ill-treatment which is now almost exclusively the reproach of the slubber, would not be without a parallel.

The machine-minder is far from being idle; he has to move his flax when it has received its due proportion of heckling in one position, the arrival of which time is indicated by a bell; he has also to collect from between the rows of spikes, as they revolve, the tow or short fibres and refuse of the flax which they comb off. The boys soon become expert at this; but we found a great many among those whom we examined whose hands had been wounded, sometimes severely, before they became so. The tow is collected and carried to the card room, *which is still more abominable for dust than the heckling rooms.* Great part of this seems to arise from not having the cards sufficiently inclosed; but I apprehend it will never be possible, either in that manner, or by the use of ventilators such as are used by some, entirely to obviate the dust that attends this process. The ventilator that is used appears to be similar in principle to that introduced by Mr. STRUTT into the blowing room of cotton mills. A large tube is carried through the room with openings over the cards, and a rarefaction is produced at the extremity, where the tube leads into a waste room, by the revolution of a fan, so that a draught is produced directly from the cards through the tube. These ventilators are not by any means common.

After the tow has been carded it is ready for spinning, although the process, as in other trades, is seldom called spinning till the last stage. For the present object, however, the difference is immaterial. I believe that tow is invariably spun *dry*. The heckled flax or *line*, after being separated from the tow, is carried down to be sorted, according to its fibre, for various degrees of fineness. This is done by young men called line-sorters. It is then at the same stage as long wool when returned from the combers; and although the machinery is different, to suit the staple of the material, in a general point of view the process is the

R

same. Girls, termed line-spreaders, are employed to unite the bunches of line into one sliver, exactly like the breakers in the worsted trade, and thence it is roved and spun.

In spinning the line, it is necessary to pass the roving through a trough of [hot] water, which is placed at the back of the spindles; and the flies of the spindles, as they revolve rapidly with the yarn, throw off a continual sprinkling of water along the whole front of the frame. As another frame is placed at no great distance, the spinner is exposed to this small rain both before and behind, and there can be no doubt that it is sufficient to wet them thoroughly in a few hours, especially when the frames are placed too close to each other.

MR. STUART'S REPORT ON FLAX MILLS.

Factory Commission, A. 1, *pages* 10 *and* 22.

The nature of this work at the wet spinning frames requires that children of small stature, and of course young children in general, should be the workers at these frames. They constantly stand on a wet floor, and have *hot* water splashed on them in front, so that their clothes are drenched with it; and their hands must frequently be immersed in water, which we yesterday found at one of the mills we examined to be of the temperature of 110 degrees of Fahrenheit. The consequences are frequent colds, occasioned by passing from so warm a room, filled with steam, to the open air at all seasons, especially in winter evenings; hands much chapped and sore, here called "hacked," which it was in some cases painful to see, and considerable swellings of the feet and legs. Hoarseness is common among the people engaged in factory employment, but prevails, as we have observed, much more than in general among the children employed at the wet spinning frames.   *   *

In the course of this inquiry, so far as yet proceeded in, nothing has, I believe, so much surprised Sir DAVID BARRY and myself, who visited those mills, as to find such an obviously *unwholesome and horrid employment* carried on openly in this country by children, not only under the sanction, but sent or forced to it by their parents. The description of it given by Mr. HENDERSON, the manager, a very sensible person, and by Mr. BOYACK, the mill-owner, who corroborates Mr. HENDERSON's statement, requires no comment. I have no notion that even were those remedies adopted, the work could be carried on without great risk to health; *neither have I, I am bound to add, any notion that* Mr. BOYACK, *who is a most benevolent person, has ever, till now, been thoroughly aware of the mischievous nature of the wet spinning work to the health of those employed.*

Factory Commission, A. 1, *pages* 28, 29, *and* 30.

WILLIAM HENDERSON, forty-seven years old, solemnly sworn. Deposes that he is manager of Mr. WILLIAM BOYACK's four flax spinning mills, including those of which DAVID ROBERTSON is sub-manager, and which employ about 300 workers; that he has been nearly three years manager, and has been in the spinning trade since the year 1806; that the only wet frames in those mills are those four inspected on Saturday last, the 11th instant, and also this morning; that when the inspection took place on the 11th, the temperature of that apartment was seventy degrees of Fahrenheit, and this morning sixty-eight degrees, and of the hot water in the wet frames 140 degrees on the 11th, and 138 degrees this morning; that there was so much steam in going in at the door of that apartment this morning, that it was impossible to distinguish the persons in the apartment; that there was more steam than usual this morning, owing to its being a close, thickish morning; that there are sixteen female workers in that apartment, a male overseer, and a boy to oil and attend to the machinery; that the wet spinning in that apartment was commenced a few months ago; that he had previously seen wet spinning, in LEEDS and DUNFERMLINE, carried on in the same way, and without any further precautions being taken; that finer yarn can be made by the process of wet than dry spinning; that he recommended the process on coming here to Mr. BOYACK, who was then erecting new works; that, before proceeding, he explained to Mr. BOYACK that the process could only be carried on on a wet floor, with hot-water spray splashed on the workers, in a hot room or apartment, and by the workers dipping their fingers frequently in water of the temperature of from 120 to 140 degrees, but that Mr. BOYACK had seen the process elsewhere himself, and the work was set a going; that Mr. BOYACK gives the workers a thick linen petticoat to protect them from the wet, which, however, is such that *it gets through it;* that he views it as an unwholesome employment, and he thinks every possible precaution should be used to prevent its effect on the health of the workers; that he thinks the workers should be provided with aprons made of skins, waterproof, and with a sort of short boot of leather or India-rubber, to keep the feet dry; that at present the workers seem all to prefer to be barefooted; that no way occurs to him of preventing the hands of the workers from being occasionally dipped in the hot water, in order to take out the thread to put it into the roller; that he understands that the great heat of the room may be avoided by covering up the boxes containing the hot water, which boxes to be lifted up as wanted, when the workers must take up the thread; *that he has not heard of any precautions he has mentioned being adopted, or of any step being taken with that view in Scotland!* * * *

This witness further states on oath, that the apartment occupied by the wet spinners is about thirty-six feet square, and the spinners stand on a wooden floor about one inch and a half thick, laid in small divisions, that it may be lifted out, and *let the water pass below* to a floor of lead, from which the water and refuse are carried by pipes into a common sewer.

CATHERINE IRONS, eighteen years old, solemnly sworn. Deposes, that she has worked in the wet spinning apartment (above-mentioned) from the beginning; that *she stands on a wet floor;* that the wet spray of hot water is splashed on her waist so as always to keep her wet; and that every rove that comes forward, she has to put her hand into hot water; that she is very subject to colds since she worked in that apartment, and that she has hacked and swelled feet and hands; that the workers in that apartment generally complain of their health suffering, and some of them are often absent,—*seven of them this morning.*

MARY LIND, eleven years old, being solemnly sworn, and having heard CATHERINE IRONS' statement read over deposed to its correctness. Deposes that they cannot write.

APPENDIX (B.)—*Page* 157.

THE following Forms tend to explain the manner in which vast numbers of worthy and industrious families were induced to migrate from the Agricultural to the Manufacturing counties, in the years 1835 and 1836, to meet the demands of the mill-owners for additional hands. These Forms are a sort of invoice, or warranty, sent with the "live stock."

No. I.   *Descriptive List of every Person, comprised in the desirous of Migrating to any part of the Country where adequate*

No. of Family.	Name of each member of the family.	Age.	To what Parish belonging.	Condition. If adult, whether widow or widower. If child, whether orphan, deserted child, foundling, or bastard.	Whether he has pursued any and what calling, and for what period.	Character as a workman.
			Horham.			
			s. d. s. d. s. d.			
1	Spall, R. ...	45	11 0 12 0 13 0		Agricul-	Ex-
2	Patience, his wife..	46			tural	ceeding
3	Robert....	19	6 6 7 6 10 0		labourer.	good.
4	James	14	3 6 4 6 6 0	*Rent about 2s. 3d.*		
5	David	12	3 0 4 0 5 0	*Engaged to Robert*		
6	Emma	8		*Mann and Co.,*		
7	Jonathan..	4	Orphans.	*62, Church-street,*		
8	Pendal, G..	15	} 4 0 5 0 7 0	*Manchester.*		
9	William ..	13				
10	James	10	} 3 6 4 6 5 6			
1	Warner, W.	33	Horham.		Agricul-	Strong,
2	Susan, his wife	37			tural	and
3	Lydia	12			labourer.	very in-
4	Harriet ..	11				dustri-
5	Edward ..	9				ous.
6	William ..	7				
7	Susan	4				
1	Enolish, J.	32	Horham.		Agricul-	Beyond
2	Sophia, his wife	40			tural	the
3	Sophia	15			labourer.	com-
4	James	11				mon la-
5	Mary Ann	7				bourer,
6	Henry	5				and
7	Rebecca ..	2				very superior workman.

Families of Persons chargeable to the PARISH *of* HORHAM, *Subsistence may be obtained in return for their Labour.*

Moral Character.	Names and description of Persons, able, from their own knowledge to certify to the character of each person.	How long known.	Remarks.
Very good	James Jennings, farmer, Horham.	14 years	This is a good family, and if a contract can be obtained, they are willing to take on themselves the part of parents towards the three orphans of the name of Pendal, described beneath his family; these are strong and healthy children.
Good	George Greenard, farmer, Horham.	12 years	Exceeding healthy; a deserving family, and though apparently young, they are fine of their age; and the woman being a very active woman, will be able to add to the earnings of the family, if an opportunity is given.
Good	John Bolton, farmer, Horham.	16 years	What has been said of the foregoing family is applicable to this; better men and families there cannot be.

We are anxious, should a contract be obtained for the above families, that they may be able to go by the same conveyance all together.

We have numbers of small families, such as man and wife, willing, if you could engage them together, say man at 8*s.*, woman at 4*s.*

GEORGE GREENARD,
Guardian for Horham.

No of Family.	Name of each member of the family.	Age.	To what Parish belonging.	Condition. If adult, whether widow or widower. If child, whether orphan, deserted child, foundling, or bastard.	Whether he has pursued any and what calling, and for what period.	Character as a workman.
1	Hall, John	45	Laxfield.		Agricultural labourer.	Unexceptional.
2	Hannah, his wife	38				
3	James	16				
4	William ..	14				
5	John	12				
6	George ..	10				
7	Charles ..	7				
8	Mary	3				
1	Tennant, T.	50	Laxfield.		Labourer, and has been in trade.	Industrious.
2	Sophia, his wife	38				
3	Thomas ..	21				
4	Sophia....	19			*Engaged to Jno. Jas. Clegg, Heywood.*	
5	John	16				
6	Susan	14				
7	Caroline ..	12				
8	Mary Ann	4				
1	Wright, E.	34	Laxfield.		Widow.	Very good workwoman
2	James	18				
3	John	16				
4	William ..	14				
5	George ..	13	*Engaged to Mr. Haighes, Congleton.*			
6	Robert....	11				
7	Hannah ..	9				
8	Hatsell ..	7				

COUNTY OF SUFFOLK,

Laxfield.

Moral Character.	Names and description of Persons, able, from their own knowledge, to certify to the character of each person.	How long known.	Remarks.
Very good	Jephtha Smith, farmer, Laxfield.	15 years	They bear the best character possible for industry, &c.
Very good	John Wright, farmer, Laxfield.	20 years	
Good	Robert Scafe, farmer, Laxfield.	16 years	A healthy good family.

R. Green, Stationer, &c., Framlingham.

APPENDIX (C).—*Page* 158.

JOHN BALAAM'S NARRATIVE

OF HIS MIGRATING WITH HIS FAMILY FROM SUFFOLK INTO YORKSHIRE.

JOHN BALAAM, farmer's man. I came from Stowmarket, and belong to the parish of All Newton, Suffolk. Having a large family of children, I had occasion to apply for parish relief. JOHN MOOR, guardian of All Newton, and Mr. LAW, relieving-officer of Stow-up-land, were very much in favour of my coming into Lancashire. JOHN MOOR said, if I would come into the manufacturing districts, I might get a good living, save money, and have the pleasure of eating plum-pudding and roast beef. Tracts were circulated in our neighbourhood by Mr. LAW, stating that labourers were very much wanted in the manufacturing districts, and several families had gone into different parts. If they were badly clad, the masters bought them new clothing, and they liked them so well, that they advanced their wages ; they added, that working in the mill was such easy employment that the children had grown quite healthy and fat. Several farmers desired me to come, as the New Poor Law had taken the power out of their hands of granting relief, and had placed it in the hands of Commissioners and Guardians. In consequence of what I had heard stated, and had read in pamphlets, and the thought operating upon my mind that should I be without employment, and have no prospect of out-door relief, and having nothing but an Union poor-house before my eyes, that I should be separated from my wife and family, I made up my mind to come with my family into Lancashire, to better my condition, as I thought. Mr. MUGGERIDGE, of Manchester, was written to, and he sent an agreement for me to come into Yorkshire. I said, I preferred Lancashire ; but Mr. LAW said, I might do better in Yorkshire, and that mine was the best agreement that had been made of late. It is the following :—

To William Stead, of Temple Mill, Rishworth, Yorkshire.
John Balaam to have 12*s.* per year.

	Years.	1st year.		2nd year.		3rd year.	
		s.	*d.*	*s.*	*d.*	*s.*	*d.*
Mary Ann	24	5	6	6	6	7	6
Hannah	18	5	0	6	0	7	0
Susannah	16	4	6	5	6	6	6
Edward	14	3	0	4	0	5	0

Jemima, Eliza, Emma, and Charlotte, of the several ages of 10, 6, 3, and 1.

We sold the bulk of our furniture, and leaving Stow-market on the 5th day of May last, came by waggon to London, and then by PICKFORD's boat to Huddersfield. Slept in a warehouse on straw, and the next morning walked to Halifax; from thence went to Rishworth, by a cart. When we arrived at our destination, we were put into a house that had not been occupied for some time, and had nothing but bare walls. We purchased 3*s.* worth of straw for our beds. For three months Mr. STEAD stood by his agreement; and then he got it from me, and said I was not worth 12*s.* per week; so I agreed to work for 9*s.* Since then, at a moment's warning, he said he could not find me any employment. He has only found me one ten days' work this last fifteen weeks, and only paid me 1*s.* per day for it. Then he turned my daughters, MARY ANN and HANNAH, to piece work, and they have never averaged 4*s.* per week each, since. So the last fortnight, which ended on the 21st January, instead of receiving according to agreement 2*l.* 10*s.*, we only received 1*l.* 1*s.* 4*d.*, for ten human beings to subsist on for one whole fortnight. Being in this situation, I determined to go to Manchester. Accordingly I started on Monday the 23rd instant; so when I arrived there, I went to the office of Mr. M. MUGGERIDGE, agent, No. 15, Lever-street, Manchester. Mr. MUGGERIDGE was ill in bed, so could not be seen; but a young man of the name of THOMPSON was in the office, and he asked me, if my name was not BALAAM? To which I answered, "Yes."

I told him my story, and he said, "What! can you not get
on, now you are receiving 12s. per week, and your family
in the same proportion?" Then I told the young man
about Mr. STEAD not standing to the agreement; he said,
one tale was good till another was told; but, he added, he
would see Mr. STEAD, at market, on Tuesday the 24th
instant. He saw him accordingly, and desired him to go
up to the office. He promised to call, but could not spare
time then, but would call at some other time.

[This family was in a wretched condition. On Saturday
the 21st instant, the father, mother, and the oldest daughter,
did not taste victuals till night. The three that went to the
mill had ½d. worth of bread to their dinner, each half a cake
to subsist on till night; the other four youngest had only
a 1d. cake divided amongst them. The mother states that
they have not had half an ounce of butter since Christmas.
This family has often been without victuals these last two
months, and their clothing is fast wearing out, and no probability of getting new. All the family are so reduced that
they have not a change of linen. Their bed consists of the
3s. worth of straw they purchased, with not a single sheet
to cover them. One of the children has been without shoes
these several weeks. The mother states that they will
expend the 1l. 1s. 4d. in victuals by Monday night, the 30th
instant, and how they are to subsist the remaining five days
she does not know; that is, till Saturday the 4th February,
when they will draw some more money. But, rather than
see her family starve, she will go round the neighbourhood
and try the charitably disposed. They actually declare they
never was in such a wretched condition in all their lives.
When they were at Stowmarket, they were well to do, considering, having occasional relief under the Old Poor-law;
but might have been better, had not the Irish labourers
come into the neighbourhood during harvest-time. Mr.
STEAD has given them liberty to leave him, and get employment elsewhere, if they can. He does not wish to see

them starve on his premises. The mother thinks, that if their condition is not speedily changed for the better, the constitution of the family will be completely broken up. No manufacturer will employ them. But, notwithstanding their wretched condition, they state that they should not like to go back to their own country, for fear of having to go into the workhouse. The parish having been at the expense of bringing them here, they would be looked upon with disrespect.]   (Signed)   PHILIP PLATT,
Ripponden, January 29, 1837. `   JOHN MILLS.

WILLIAM BURLEIGH'S NARRATIVE

OF HIS MIGRATING WITH HIS FAMILY FROM SUFFOLK INTO YORKSHIRE, AS TAKEN BY A GENTLEMAN IN THE NEIGHBOURHOOD OF HUDDERSFIELD.

WILLIAM BURLEIGH says, "I came from Stradbrook, Suffolk, about the 21st of March, 1836; am a husbandman. I now drive Mr. WELLS's cart, at 8*s.* per week. I had 10*s.* per week at Stradbrook, and house and garden rent free. The house had four rooms : garden about nine rods. I grew as many vegetables as served my family. I had not much employment for my lads ; I had four of them. Martha, aged 22 years, Thomas, 20, William, 18, James, 17, George 15, Mary, 10, Eleanor, 5.—Wages for all, if well, 1*l.* 3*s.* per week.

"THOMAS and JAMES were in service, and well off. THOMAS hired at 6*l.* 10*s.* a-year; JAMES hired at 3*l.*; both of them to farmers. My daughters were all at home, when in Suffolk : I had not much for them to do. About twelve months ago, I was sent for to the Board at Stradbrook, and there found Dr. KAY ; and he looked at me well once from head to foot, and said, ' Well, BURLEIGH, you are just now the right age to go into Lancashire,' and that he understood that I was a man of good character. I said, ' I could not like to be sent away, I had done nothing that I ought to be

transported for.' Dr. KAY said to me, 'That I might go
out, and my case would be considered.' I was called again
into the room, and Dr. KAY said, 'That I was to have a fortnight to consider of it.' I told Dr. KAY, 'That I did not
know what he wanted to send me away for, as I had not
troubled the parish three months in my life.' Dr. KAY replied, 'That I and my family were just the sort to come
down into Lancashire.' When the fortnight was up, I
heard no more about it. A short time afterwards one of
the Guardians met with me, and said, 'BURLEIGH, I hope
you have made up your mind to go to Lancashire.' I answered him, 'No, sir, I should not like to go yet;' but he
over-persuaded me, until I gave consent. I told him, 'If
they could get me a berth, such as they told me of, I would
come and try.' They took my name and children's all down,
and their ages also; and sent them to Manchester, to Mr.
MUGGERIDGE. In about three weeks after, the contract
came down to the Board of Guardians, and they sent for me,
and read it to me. I did not like the terms of the contract;
but they promised that, if I would come, they had no doubt
that Mr. WELLS would advance my wages to 12s. per week,
and every lad 1s. per head more. I then answered them,
'Well, then, I'll go and try.' One of my daughters, twenty-
two years of age, was promised 1s. 6d. per week, and to live
in her master's house. On these conditions I agreed to
come to Mr. WELLS, of Sayland. I sold my furniture, except my beds : I brought them with me. The parish offi-
cers sent me and family by waggon to London, and put us
in a boat at PICKFORD'S Wharf, and we came thus to Huddersfield. Mr. WELLS sent a horse and cart to meet us,
and we got here that night. I have had my regular wages
of 8s. per week ever since.

"MARTHA went to Mr. WELLS's home, on the Monday
following, and stayed a week, and then came home poorly,
and was ill a week at home, and was then sent for by her
master ; she went back again, about a fortnight. Had for

her wages 1s. 6d. per week, and was then told to stay at home until she was sent for. She stayed at home several weeks, for which she had no pay, and then I asked Mr. WELLS to let her go into the mill; and he said, she might go and try to weave. But she had not been there more than a week, before he told her she had better go home, for she had done him more hurt than good. She was then sent home, and had no pay for what she had done. THOMAS has had 6s. per week for some time; he has now what he earns, which is about 7s. per week; WILLIAM 5s.; JAMES has not had as much as the contract since he came; he was eight weeks, and had no wages from his master. GEORGE has had his regular wages, 3s.; when ill his wages are deducted.

"Dr. KAY attended the Board regularly, and all the neighbouring Boards. He told me that the best beef was 4d. per pound, and flour 1s. 6d. per stone, and coals brought to the door for almost nothing; and clothes also. Only one of my children can read. I always attended the church.

"We had five pints of milk for 1d. in Suffolk. I never made any agreement with any one, but came under the direction of the Guardians of the Poor. I never saw any copy of agreement, but this paper; I never signed any contract with any one. Dr. KAY said, that in case I should become troublesome to the parish, I should be liable to be shoved into a workhouse, and my wife into another, and the children into another. The operatives did not like us at first, they mobbed us. The earnings of the whole family of nine persons is 31s. a week.

"A person of the name of MOTT, used to go to the workhouse, but I do not know where he came from. Rent of house, three rooms 2s. per week; paid to Mr. WELLS. The water frequently runs through the house. Half pay was only given to the children, during the first month.

"*Ripponden, December* 16, 1826."

[I have several accounts of other migrant families, but these will suffice as specimens.]

APPENDIX (D).—*Page* 173.

A TABLE, *showing the number of Persons employed at the six Cotton Factories belonging to the undermentioned firms, who were examined by* P. ASHTON, M.D., *and* JOHN GRAHAM, *Surgeon, in the month of March,* 1819.

This Table is compiled from their Report laid before a Committee of the House of Lords.

FIRMS ALL AT STOCKPORT.		AGE AT WHICH THEY BEGAN TO WORK IN THE FACTORIES.									EMPLOYED.	
		4 years.	5 years.	6 years.	7 years.	8 years.	9 years.	10 years.	10 to 20.	Above 20.	Males.	Females.
Garside and others ..	males	..	6	20	45	36	19	13	19	8	166	99
	fem.	..	3	11	22	14	17	12	17	3	..	..
Sam. Grimshaw and others ..	males	1	2	6	10	6	2	3	4	2	36	..
	fem.	..	2	4	4	10	1	5	8	..	..	34
Ratcliffe & others ..	males	1	3	8	6	9	12	8	13	7	67	..
	fem.	..	1	6	7	3	6	8	5	2	..	38
J. Lamb & others ..	males	..	8	8	7	11	6	4	8	2	54	..
	fem.	..	1	6	13	11	6	13	6	2	..	58
Mr. T. Garside	males	..	4	4	5	9	12	6	6	1	47	..
	fem.	1	1	7	8	11	18	10	19	1	..	76
Mr. A. Howard ..	males	1	3	6	10	9	7	11	9	3	59	..
	fem.	..	1	10	10	14	6	9	37	2	..	89
Total		4	35	96	147	143	112	102	151	33	429	394

It will be seen by the above Table, that three males, and one female, had been put to work at *four years of age;* and that 425, out of 823, had gone before nine years of age, which is the legal time at present.

The following Table will show the temperature of the Factories, and the Sickness of the Workers, in the preceding twelve months.

FIRM.	TEMPERATURE.		Males sick the previous 12 mon.	Time lost through sickness in 12 months.	Females sick the previous 12 mon.	Time lost through sickness in 12 months.
	Highest.	Lowest.		mo. w. d.		mo. w. d.
Garside and others ..	85°	58°	66	71 2 4½	55	54 3 2
S. Grimshaw and others	62	57	16	34 1 1	12	26 1 4
Ratcliffe and others ..	66	61	26	34 3 5	15	21 2 2
John Lamb and others	55	52	24	35 3 2	30	30 2 3
Mr. T. Garside	70	67	24	17 2 5½	38	40 1 0½
Mr. Appellis Howard..	76	68	26	23 0 2	54	44 2 4½
Mean temperature	69	60.5	182	217 2 2	204	218 1 4
Ditto in the open air	45					

The above Table shows that 182 males, and 204 females, had been off work through sickness the previous twelve months, and the time lost was 10,464 days, or about four weeks and a half each.

S

A Table showing the condition in which the above work-people were found, by P. ASHTON, M.D., *and* J. GRAHAM, *surgeon.*

Complaint.	Males.	Females.
Healthy	89	87
Sickly and delicate	142	172
Troubled with a cough	83	73
„ „ scrofula	15	12
Rheumatic affection	6	1
Bowel complaint	1	1
Difficulty of breathing	30	18
Asthma	5	1
Consumption	—	1
Pains in the head.................	7	18
„ „ back..................	1	—
„ „ breast	7	4
„ „ legs	1	3
Swelled legs	—	2
„ ankle-joints................	17	23
„ knee-joints	5	6
Both knees turned in	15	2
Right knee turned in	13	15
„ „ „ out	1	—
Left knee turned in	1	2
„ „ „ out	1	—
Lame of both legs	—	1
Stunted in growth	39	21
Bad eyes	3	1
Swelled neck glands	—	4
Lost one arm by machinery	1	1
„ a thumb by do.............	1	—
Lame arm by do.............	1	—
„ hand by do.............	1	—
„ hip by do.............	1	—
„ leg by do.............	—	1
Crooked thigh	1	—
Curved legs	1	—
Hernia	1	—
Distorted spine...................	—	1
Absent through sickness...........	3	1

The average age of these people at the time was eighteen years. And they had worked in the factories nine years and seventeen days each, on an average, and look at their condition!

APPENDIX (E).—*Page* 219.

A COPY OF THE RULES

To be observed by the work-people employed in the Cotton Factory belonging to Messrs. H——s, *of B—n.*

RULE 1.—Each person employed in this factory engages to serve Messrs. H——s, and to give notice to his or her over-looker, or the manager, previous to leaving his or her employment, such notice to be given on Friday preceding the usual *fortnight pay day;* but the masters have full power to discharge any person employed therein without notice, providing they are neglecting or spoiling their work, or conducting themselves improperly.

RULE 2.—All wages shall be due and be paid in the counting-house every *Saturday fortnight,* and any person leaving his or her employment without the required notice, shall *forfeit all wages due* at the time at which he or she left such employment.

RULE 3.—Any person not coming to work at the hour stated in the time list, shall for every offence forfeit and pay *three-pence,* and be further abated for the time they are absent.

RULE 4.—Every spinner shall attend the mill half an hour before the time of the engine starting on each Monday morning, for the purpose of preparing his wheels and putting them into proper working order before the engine starts, and in default of such attendance, shall forfeit and pay the sum of FIVE SHILLINGS.

RULE 5.—Any spinner's wheel or wheels standing either for want of piecers, or any other cause whatever, during the time of the steam-engine going, or not keeping them going at their proper and usual speed, *shall for every hour pay sixpence.*

Rule 6.—Each spinner to keep his or her wheels and wheel-house clean swept and flucked, and in default thereof, shall forfeit and pay the sum of *one shilling*.

Rule 7.—Any spinner discovered spinning with a crooked spindle in his wheel or wheels, shall forfeit and pay the sum of FIVE SHILLINGS.

Rule 8.—Any spinner, or young person employed, who shall damage, or in any way impair or render imperfect any of his sets of cops, whether the same be done wilfully or by the carelessness of such spinner, or any of his piecers, or other person, previous to being delivered to the proper warehouseman, shall forfeit and pay such sum of money as the masters fix, as *compensation* for the damage, spoil, injury, or imperfection, so committed ; and that such forfeiture shall be exacted from and paid by such spinner, or other persons, as in cases where the damage, spoil, injury, or imperfection, is discovered by the proprietors or overlookers before the yarn shall be sold or removed from the premises ; or in cases where such discovery and detection shall be made by any purchaser or purchasers thereof, whenever the same shall be complained of to Messrs. H——s.

Rule 9.—When any waste, rovings, utensils, or machinery of any kind, be misused, spoiled, lost, or carelessly misplaced, the person so misusing, spoiling, damaging, losing, or carelessly misplacing the same, shall forfeit *one shilling*, besides paying the value thereof if lost, spoiled, or damaged.

Rule 10.—Any person altering, in any way whatever, the wheels or other machinery on which he or she is employed, or permitting the same to be done without leave from a proprietor or overlooker, shall forfeit and pay TWO SHILLINGS AND SIXPENCE.

Rule 11.—Each person shall clean the necessary belonging to the room in which he or she is employed, when thereunto required by an overlooker ; and any one neglecting or refusing so to do, or wilfully dirting the same, or any part of the factory yard or adjoining premises, shall forfeit and pay TWO SHILLINGS AND SIXPENCE.

RULE 12.—Any person taking cotton or waste into the necessaries, shall forfeit TWO SHILLINGS AND SIXPENCE; and any one knowing of the same, and not giving information thereof, shall forfeit and pay the sum of FIVE SHILLINGS.

RULE 13.—Any person smoking tobacco, or having a pipe for that purpose, in any part of the factory or yard, or the adjoining premises, shall forfeit and pay FIVE SHILLINGS.

RULE 14.—Any person, excepting those especially appointed for that purpose, lighting the gas, shall forfeit and pay *one shilling*.

RULE 15.—Any person introducing a stranger into this factory, without leave from one of the proprietors, shall forfeit TWO SHILLINGS AND SIXPENCE; and any overlooker neglecting immediately to order such stranger out, shall forfeit FIVE SHILLINGS.

RULE 16.—Any person or persons neglecting thoroughly to clean the machinery under his or their care, *when required by an overlooker to do so*, and to the satisfaction of such overlooker, shall forfeit and pay TWO SHILLINGS AND SIXPENCE.

RULE 17.—Any person leaving the frame at which he or she ought to be employed, or in any way neglecting his or her employment, shall forfeit and pay *one shilling*.

RULE 18.—Any person taking tools out of the mechanic's or overlookers' rooms, except the mechanic or overlookers themselves, shall forfeit and pay FIVE SHILLINGS.

RULE 19.—When any window or windows shall be broken, the party breaking the same shall pay the damage; but if the said party cannot be identified, the charges of repairing the same shall be equally borne by *all persons* employed in the room in which such window or windows have been broken.

RULE 20.—Any workman coming into the factory, or any other part of these premises, drunk, shall forfeit and pay FIVE SHILLINGS.

RULE 21.—Any person destroying, defacing, or damaging *this paper*, shall forfeit and pay FIVE SHILLINGS.

RULE 22.—Any spinner or overlooker allowing the hands in their care, under eighteen years of age, to remain in the mill during meal hours, shall forfeit and pay TWENTY SHILLINGS.

RULE 23.—To avoid any misunderstanding or disputes, it is hereby determined that when a breach has been made, in any of the foregoing rules, and the party breaking the same cannot be identified, *double* the penalty hereby inflicted shall be taken from the persons employed in the part where the fault has been committed, whether it extends only to one room, one overlooker's department, or to the whole factory!

RULE 24.—That all fines, penalties, forfeitures, or sums of money hereby imposed upon, and directed to be paid by any persons employed, shall be deducted by the proprietors from the *wages* which, from time to time, become due and payable to such persons, that the proprietors shall have the power to remit or mitigate any of the fines, penalties, or forfeitures hereby imposed, according to their discretion, whenever they shall see cause for so doing; and that the payment of all or any of such fines, penalties, or forfeited sums of money, shall not debar the proprietors from proceeding against the offender or offenders, according to law, for the same offence, on account of which such penalties, fines, and forfeitures was inflicted.

———

I have obtained about one hundred tickets of fines, or, as they are generally called, " bate tickets," from which I have selected the following as a fair sample. These tickets were made out by the manufacturer, and given to the overlooker, by whom the fines are deducted out of the earnings of the workmen. The manufacturer who made out these tickets has six or seven mills, all under the same regulations. He pays up to the list of prices *as well* as any other master in his neighbourhood, but the reader will perceive that he gets a good share of them back in the shape of fines.

The first form of bate tickets to which I wish to draw the reader's attention is, for winding up a bad thread, or piecing, of which the following are verbatim specimens :—

" Tell T—— A—— I have bated him *a* 1*s.* for a roving piecing. Here is a beautiful sample! He had better *to* keep them out."

" Tell W—— C—— I have bated him 2*s.* for roving piecings. Here they are. How beautiful for an old spinner !"

It is but justice to the spinners to say, that in this mill in 1835, there were at work 33,696 spindles, and to work these it took 52 spinners, and 208 piecers ; but since that time, the machinery has been undergoing some " improvements," so that at present there are 33,040 spindles at work, and it only takes 26 spinners, and 102 piecers, to attend them. Thus, in 1835, the average number of spindles to each spinner was 648, and to each piecer 162 ; but at present the average number of spindles to each spinner is 1270, and to each piecer 324. And yet with all the additional work and care requisite, if one single bad thread is put up, they are fined, as the above tickets show.

The following fines are for taking the cops off the spindles before they were as heavy as the master wished.

" Tell A—— G—— I have bated him *a* 1*s.* for small cops. They are *only* a pound less than the last ! "

Fines for bad-shaped cops :—

" Tell J—— L—— I have bated him 2*s.* 6*d.* for small bad bottomed cops ; they are only pieces."

" Tell A—— G—— I have bated him 2*s.* 6*d.* for snicks at the bottom of the cops. He had better not attempt to cheat old snickey again. If I catch him, he will not do it a third time."

This mill is what is called a fine mill, and the spinners have no power to alter their mules. The master can put in what quality of cotton he thinks proper; but, no matter for this, if the work does not please, the spinner must suffer for all, as will be seen by the following tickets :—

" Tell O—— B—— I have bated him 5*s.* for rough, *rotten*, snickey, bad yarn; it's none spun."

" J—— L——'s setts are rough, snickey, bad stuff, and bad piecing. *I shall only pay for weft.*"

The fine in this case, by paying for weft instead of warp, amounted to 6*s.* 6*d.*

" J—— M——'s setts run

$$\left.\begin{array}{l} 9..4\ 172 \\ 8..4\ 172 \\ \hline 9..4\ 174 \\ 8..4\ 173 \end{array}\right\} \begin{array}{l} \text{Can he not spin 167 or 8? If} \\ \text{he cannot, I can; and will} \\ \text{pay for it. It's very poor} \\ \text{stuff."} \end{array}$$

The fine in this case, by paying the spinners for No. 167 or 8, instead of 172 or 173, amounted to 3*s.* $5\frac{1}{2}d.$

" Here is a sample of O—— B——'s stuff—runs

204	206
205	206

Very sneck, rough, rubbish. I shall only pay for 200 weft."

The fine in this case amounted to 12*s.* 3*d.*

" Tell J—— O—— I have bated him 5*s.* and shall pay for weft only, for snickey, rough, bad yarn, particularly at the bottom of the cops; here are samples."

Fine, 5*s.* Wefting, 5*s.* $10\frac{1}{2}d. = 10s.\ 10\frac{1}{2}d.$ in this case.

The spinners are paid once a fortnight, and the reader may imagine what their feelings must be, when they are bated 6*s.* to 12*s.* at one time, for what they cannot always prevent.

Besides these, there are other fines which do not require tickets, the men being sent for into the counting-house.

A NARRATIVE OF THE
EXPERIENCE AND SUFFERINGS
OF WILLIAM DODD

A

NARRATIVE

OF THE

EXPERIENCE AND SUFFERINGS

OF

WILLIAM DODD,

A FACTORY CRIPPLE.

WRITTEN BY HIMSELF.

GIVING AN ACCOUNT OF THE HARDSHIPS AND SUFFERINGS
HE ENDURED IN EARLY LIFE, UNDER WHAT DIFFICULTIES HE
ACQUIRED HIS EDUCATION, THE EFFECTS OF FACTORY LABOUR
ON HIS MIND AND PERSON, THE UNSUCCESSFUL EFFORTS MADE
BY HIM TO OBTAIN A LIVELIHOOD IN SOME OTHER LINE OF
LIFE, THE COMPARISON HE DRAWS BETWEEN AGRICULTURAL
AND MANUFACTURING LABOURERS, AND OTHER MATTERS
RELATING TO THE WORKING CLASSES.

SECOND EDITION.

LONDON:
PUBLISHED BY L. & G. SEELEY, 169, FLEET STREET,
AND HATCHARD & SON, 187, PICCADILLY.
1841.

PRICE ONE SHILLING.

TO

LORD ASHLEY, M.P.

My Lord,

The sympathy you were pleased to express for me, after seeing a brief outline of my sufferings, and witnessing the effects of the factory system on my person, and believing that a more extensive circulation of my narrative may, under Providence, be the means of assisting the strenuous exertions your Lordship is making on behalf of that oppressed class of work-people to which I belong, I have been induced to prepare for the press an enlarged and corrected account, to be issued in a separate form; and beg, as a token of gratitude, to dedicate these, my humble endeavours, to you, who are so thoroughly conversant with the momentous subject to which my remarks refer.

And am,

My Lord,

Your Lordship's,

Much obliged,

Humble Servant,

WILLIAM DODD.

23, *Little Gray's Inn Lane,*
June 18, 1841.

A NARRATIVE, &c.

———

DEAR READER,—I wish it to be distinctly
and clearly understood, that, in laying before you the
following sheets, I am not actuated by any motive of
ill-feeling to any party with whom I have formerly
been connected; on the contrary, I have a personal
respect for some of my former masters, and am convinced that, had they been in any other line of life,
they would have shone forth as ornaments to the age
in which they lived; but having witnessed the efforts
of some writers (who can know nothing of the
factories by experience) to mislead the minds of the
public upon a subject of so much importance, I feel
it to be my duty to give to the world a fair and im-
partial account of the working of the factory system,
as I have found it in twenty-five years' experience.

I cannot, at this distance of time, take upon myself
to say what were the predisposing circumstances by
which my parents were induced to send their children
to the factories, especially as I was very young at the
time my eldest sister first went, and cannot be
supposed then to have known much of their affairs.
I shall, therefore, confine myself, in the following
narrative, to such facts as may serve to show the

effects of the system upon my mind, person, and condition.

Of four children in our family, I was the only boy; and we were all at different periods, as we could meet with employers, sent to work in the factories. My eldest sister was ten years of age before she went; consequently, she was, in a manner, out of harm's way, her bones having become firmer and stronger than ours, and capable of withstanding the hardships to which she was exposed much better than we could: but her services soon became more valuable in another line of industry. My second sister went at the age of seven years, and, like myself, has been made a cripple for life, and doomed to end her days in the factories or workhouse. My youngest sister also went early, but was obliged to be taken away, like many more, the work being too hard for her although she afterwards stood a very hard service.

I was born on the 18th of June, 1804; and in the latter part of 1809, being then turned of five years of age, I was put to work at card-making, and about a year after I was sent, with my sisters, to the factories. I was then a fine, strong, healthy, hardy boy, straight in every limb, and remarkably stout and active. It was predicted by many of our acquaintance, that I should be the very model of my father, who was the picture of robust health and strength, and, in his time, had been the don of the village, and had carried off the prize at almost every manly sport.

A circumstance occurred between my fifth and sixth year, which places the fact of my being strong and active beyond a doubt. I was then about getting my first boy's dress of trousers and jacket, and, being stout, I had long felt ashamed of my petticoats, and

was very glad when I heard that a friend had offered
to supply my parents with the necessary articles of
dress for me, giving them a sufficient length of time
for payment. This friend lived at the distance of
three-quarters of a mile from our house; and I well
remember going with my eldest sister for my clothes.
There was a great quantity of ready-made dresses,
one of which was being selected and tried on, the
tailor thought it was rather too little; but I thought
it would do very well, especially as it had got a watch-
pocket in it; and not liking the idea of losing what I
had got, or of having again to wear the petticoats,
I ran out of the shop, and did not stop till I had got
home, my sister calling after, but not being able to
overtake me. I was put into the factories soon after,
and have never been able to perform this feat of
running three-quarters of a mile since.

From six to fourteen years of age, I went through a
series of uninterrupted, unmitigated suffering, such
as very rarely falls to the lot of mortals so early in
life, except to those situated as I was, and such as I
could not have withstood, had I not been strong, and
of a good constitution.

My first place in the factories was that of piecer, or
the lowest situation; but as the term conveys only a
vague idea of the duties to be performed, it will be
necessary here to give such explanation as may
enable those unacquainted with the business to form
a just conception of what those duties are, and to
judge of the inadequacy of the remuneration or
reward for their performance, and the cruelty of the
punishments inflicted for the neglect of those duties.
The duties of a piecer in the cotton, worsted, and
woollen mills, differ considerably, but their rewards

and punishments are very much alike. What I shall
have to say in the following pages, must be understood to relate to the woollen mills only, which is, on
all hands, allowed to be the best for the piecer. It is in
this situation of piecer that the greatest number of
cripples are made from over-exertion.

The duties of the piecer will not be clearly understood by the reader, unless he is previously made
acquainted with the machine for spinning woollen
yarn, called a *Billy*. I must, therefore, crave his
patience till I make this matter as clear as I am able.
A billy, then, is a machine somewhat similar in form
to the letter H, one side being stationary, and the
other moveable, and capable of being pushed close in
under the stationary part, almost like the drawer of
a side table; the moveable part, or carriage, runs
backwards and forwards, by means of six iron wheels,
upon three iron rails, as a carriage on a railroad. In
this carriage are the spindles, from 70 to 100 in
number, all turned by one wheel, which is in the care
of the spinner. When the spinner brings the carriage
close up under the fixed part of the machine, he is
able, by a contrivance for that purpose, to obtain a
certain length of carding for each spindle, say 10 or 12
inches, which he draws back, and spins into yarn;
this done, he winds the yarn round the spindles,
brings the carriage close up as before, and again
obtains a fresh supply of cardings. The side of the
billy appropriated to the piecers is composed of a
number of boards set in a slanting direction the
whole length, somewhat like the face of a writing-
desk; over these boards are put cloths made of coarse
wrapper, in the form of a jack-towel, only not so long,
and much wider. These cloths move on two rollers,

one at the top, and one at the bottom of the slanting board; and by this means the cardings, which are laid in parallel lines thereon, are conveyed, as they are wanted, to the points of the spindles. On the top of the cardings, and immediately over the upper roller, runs the billy-roller—the dreaded instrument of punishment for the children. This roller is very easily taken out and put in its place, and is at the full command of the spinner, and, being of great length, it is scarcely possible for the piecer to get out of the way, should the spinner think proper to give him a knock. On these coarse canvas cloths the piecer pieces the ends of the cardings, and prepares them for the spinner.

The cardings are strips of wool 27 inches long, and of equal thickness throughout (generally about as thick as a lady's finger), except about 2 inches at each end, which are smaller, in order that when two ends are laid one over the other, and rubbed together with the piecer's flat hand, the piecing may not be thicker than any other part of the carding.

These cardings are taken up by the piecer in his left hand, about 20 at a time. He holds them in nearly the same manner as a joiner would hold a bunch of ornamental shavings for a parlour fire-place, about 4 inches from one end, the other end hanging down; these he takes, with his right hand, one at a time, for the purpose of piecing, and, laying the ends of the cardings about 2 inches over each other, he rubs them together on the canvas cloth with his flat hand. He is obliged to be very expert, in order to keep the spinner well supplied. A good piecer will supply from 30 to 40 spindles with cardings; but this depends, in a great measure, upon the quality of the work to be done, and also whether it is intended for the warp or the weft of the cloth to be made.

The cloths upon which the piecer rubs, or pieces, the ends of the cardings, as above stated, are made of coarse wrappering. The number of cardings a piecer has through his fingers in a day is very great; each piecing requires three or four rubs, over a space of three or four inches; and the continual friction of the hand in rubbing the piecing upon the coarse wrapper wears off the skin, and causes the fingers to bleed. I have had my fingers in this state for weeks together, healing up in the night, and breaking out again in little holes as soon as I commenced work on the following morning.

Another source of pain in the hands of piecers, is their continually swelling from cold in the winter season; and this is an evil which, like the other, cannot altogether be prevented. In a future page, I shall have to describe the process of oiling the wool; at present, it will be enough to say, that the oil gets rubbed into the cloths upon which the cardings are pieced, and, as a matter of course, the cloths get black, greasy, and cold. With continually passing over these comfortless things, the hands get cold, and swell very much; and as there is but little, and in many places no fire allowed, it is next to impossible for them to keep their hands warm; add to this the clothes they have upon their backs, are generally as greasy and comfortless as those upon which they piece, and stick to their arms, legs, and thighs, more like a wet sack than anything intended for warmth and comfort.

The position in which the piecer stands to his work is with his right foot forward, and his right side facing the frame: the motion he makes in going along in front of the frame, for the purpose of piecing, is neither forwards nor backwards, but in a sidling direction, constantly keeping his right side towards the frame. In this position he continues during the day, with his hands, feet, and eyes constantly in motion. It will be easily seen, that the chief weight of his body rests upon his right knee, which is almost always the first joint to give way. The number of cripples with the right knee in, greatly exceed those with the left knee in; a great many have both knees in—such as my own—from this cause.

Another evil resulting from the position in which the piecer stands, is what is termed "splay-foot", which may be explained thus: in a well-formed foot, there is a finely formed arch of bones immediately under the instep and ankle joint. The continual pressure of the body on this arch, before it is sufficiently strong to bear such pressure (as in the case of boys and girls in the factories), causes it to give way; the bones fall gradually down, the foot then becomes broad and flat, and the owner drags it after him with the broad side first. A great many factory cripples are in this state; this is very often attended with weak ankle and knee joints. I have a brother-in-law exactly thus, who has tried every thing likely to do him good, but without success.

The spinner and the piecer are intimately connected together: the spinner works by the piece, being paid by the stone for the yarn spun; the piecer is hired by the week, and paid according to his abilities. The piecers are the servants of the spinners, and both are under an overlooker, and liable to be dismissed at a week's notice. Being thus circumstanced, it is clearly the advantage of the spinner to have good able

piecers, who ought, in return, to be well paid. At my
first starting in the works, I had 1*s.* per week, and got
gradually advanced till I was 14 years old, at which
time I had 3*s.* 6*d.* per week. The average wages are
about 2*s.* 6*d.*; and thus, for a sum of money varying
from one farthing to one halfpenny per hour, a sum
not more than half sufficient to find me in necessaries,
I was compelled, under fear of the strap and the
billy-roller (the smart of which I had often been made
to feel—with the force of the latter, I have been
struck almost motionless on the factory floor!) to
keep in active employ, although my hands were
frequently swollen, and the blood was dripping from
my fingers' ends. I was also compelled to listen to, and
be witness of almost every species of immorality,
debauchery, and wickedness; and finally, to be
deprived of the power of those faculties nature had
so bountifully supplied me with.

In order to induce the piecer to do his work quick
and well, the spinner has recourse to many expedients,
such as offering rewards of a penny or two-pence for
a good week's work—inducing them to sing, which,
like the music in the army, has a very powerful effect,
and keeps them awake and active longer than any
other thing; and, as a last resource, when nothing else
will do, he takes the strap, or the billy-roller, which
are laid on most unmercifully, accompanied by a
round volley of oaths; and I pity the poor wretch who
has to submit to the infliction of either.

On one occasion, I remember being thrashed with
the billy-roller till my back, arms, and legs were
covered with ridges as thick as my finger. This was
more than I could bear, and, seeing a favourable
opportunity, I slipped out, and stole off home, along

some by-ways, so as not to be seen. Mother stripped me, and was shocked at my appearance. The spinner, not meeting with any other to suit him, had the assurance to come and beg that mother would let me go again, and promised not to strike me with the billy-roller any more. He kept his promise, but instead of using the roller, he used his fist.

Another ignorant brute of a spinner whom I pieced for, had a great inclination to use his hand as an instrument of punishment. One time, when I was sleepy and tired, and did not keep my ends right, he struck me a blow on the side of the head, which made me reel about, and it was some time before I recovered myself. It was a great mercy I was not taken in by the machinery. For a long time after, I cherished a sort of revenge, and could not look upon the brute without remembering the blow, and used to say within myself, only let me get to be a man, and then I will pay you with interest. I am glad, however, to hear that he has since learned to read, and has become a worthy member of society. Should he see this, he may rest assured he has my forgiveness.

A piecer, it will be seen, is an important person in the factories, inasmuch as it is impossible to do without them. Formerly, boys and girls were sent to work in the factories as piecers, at the early age of five or six years—as in my own case—but now, owing to the introduction of some wise laws for the regulation of factories, they cannot employ any as piecers before they have attained the age of 9 years; at which age their bones are comparatively strong, generally speaking, and more able to endure the hardships to which they will be exposed.

They now enjoy many privileges that we had not,

such as attending schools, limited hours of labour, &c.; but still it is far from being a desirable place for a child. Formerly, it was nothing but work till we could work no longer. I have frequently worked at the frame till I could scarcely get home, and in this state have been stopped by people in the streets who noticed me shuffling along, and advised me to work no more in the factories: but I was not my own master. Thus year after year passed away, my afflictions and deformities increasing. I could not associate with any body; on the contrary, I sought every opportunity to rest myself, and to shrink into any corner to screen myself from the prying eye of the curious and scornful! During the day, I frequently counted the clock, and calculated how many hours I had still to remain at work; my evenings were spent in preparing for the following day—in rubbing my knees, ankles, elbows, and wrists with oil, &c., and wrapping them in warm flannel! (for everything was tried to benefit me, except the right one—*that of taking me from the work;*) after which, with a *look at*, rather than *eating* my supper (the bad smells of the factory having generally taken my appetite away), I went to bed, to cry myself to sleep, and pray that the Lord would take me to himself before morning.

Even Sunday—that day of rest to the weary and oppressed—shone no Sabbath day for me; for, although I was no longer urged on and kept in motion by the fear of the strap and the billy-roller, yet the leisure thus afforded to think and reflect upon my situation, only made me the more miserable!— If Sunday was bad, Monday morning was still worse—it was horrible! Even now, it makes me tremble, to think upon the sufferings of those mornings! My joints were then like so many rusty hinges, that had laid by for years. I had to get up an hour earlier, and, with the broom under one arm as a crutch, and a stick in my hand, walk over the house till I had got my joints into working order! and then, this day of the week was generally the most painful of the seven.

I frequently pressed my parent to get me something else to do, as I was anxious to leave the factories, and to get some work more tolerable. I got two engagements. At one place, they kept me a week, and the other only about a quarter of an hour. This latter circumstance is still fresh in my memory. I was engaged to be an errand boy to an ironmonger. This engagement was made without him seeing me; and, when he did see me, on account of my deformity, he expressed his fears I should not be able to do his work, but said I might try. On this morning, I had been drilling myself longer than usual on my crutch, and the hopes of getting from the factories had made me tolerably active! So, I set to work, to take down the shop-shutters, as he directed me. There was one step up, from the street into the shop; and, having got one of the shutters down, and on my shoulder, I was about to make this step—but it proved too much for me, and I fell beneath the load! My master seeing this, told me I was of no service to him, gave me three-pence, and dismissed me!

Judge what my feelings must have been at this time; after fancying myself on the point of leaving for ever a place wherein I had suffered so much, and then to see all my hopes dashed to the ground, and I sent back to what appeared to me the most hateful place on earth—the factories!

I have above alluded to the bad smells of the factories, which any one, who has ever been in or near a factory, must have noticed; and I shall here endeavour to explain what is the cause of those smells. If we examine a pile or fibre of wool through a microscope, we find it has a very uneven appearance, being notched or indented along its surface, somewhat similar to the teeth of a saw. It is this unevenness of surface, that causes the fibres to unite closely and firmly together in the formation of cloths, hats, &c.; but although it is ultimately an advantage, it presents an obstacle to the manufacturer, which he is obliged to overcome in the following manner:—

When the wool is sorted into the different qualities, it is sent in bags of 10 or 12 stones, of 16 lbs. each, to be teased, which may be considered the first process in the manufacture! the workman then spreads a layer of wool on the factory floor, and over this wool he sprinkles, by means of a can of a peculiar construction, a quantity of whale oil (generally in the proportion of one quart per stone), exactly in the same manner as a gardener watering his plants. Upon this he spreads another layer of wool, oiling it as before, and so on, till the whole is done. This oiling process overcomes in part the ruffness of the fibres, and enables them to slide more easily among each other in carding and spinning. It will be easily seen, that the oil will be pretty equally distributed among the wool, in the act of teasing, where it remains till the wool is formed into cloth: the cloth is then sent to the fulling mill, to have the oil washed and cleaned out by means of urine, fuller's-earth, and water.

Now, as it is impossible for any one to handle a soot bag without getting begrimed with the soot, so it is equally clear, that wool thus all but saturated with oil, will soil not only the hands, face, and clothes of the work-people, but the machines, walls, and floor of the factory (I have seen it dripping through the floors), or anything which comes in contact with it, and also emits a very unpleasant odour.

Another source of the offensive smell arises from the quantity of oil used in oiling the machinery. People who are at all acquainted with machinery, well know, that shafts, wheels, and spirdl es, in short anything, even a common wheel-barrow, that revolves upon its axis, requires to be kept clean and well oiled, in order that it may revolve smoothly and silently, and to prevent the undue friction or wearing of the brass step or collar in which it moves. For spindles and other light machinery oiling is sufficient; but for heavy pieces, such as upright, horizontal, and cylinder shafts, oil alone would not do, unless it was constantly dripping upon the part; and as that would be very expensive, the following cheap substitute is applied.

The fat of horses, dogs, pigs, and many other animals, which die a natural death, or are killed with some incurable disease upon them, is sold to the manufacturers, and kept for the purpose of greasing the heavy machinery. It may be imagined what sort of an effluvia will arise from the application of this fat to shafts almost on fire. I have frequently been sent to order this article, and have had to apply it to a shaft very much heated, and as one piece melted away, another was laid on till it got cooled, and all the time the smoke was arising almost sufficient to suffocate me.

One great cause of ill health to the operatives in factories, is the dust and lime which is continually flying about. A large quantity of skin-wool and cow's-hair are used in the manufacture of coarse rugs, carpets, &c. This is obtained from the skins of the animals after they are killed, by means of a strong solution of lime-water. This lime thus gets intermixed with the wool and hair, and in this state it is sold to the manufacturer; it is then put through the teaser, in order to shake out the lime and dust; and, as the teaser goes at an immense speed, the work-people, the machine, and all around, are covered with the lime; and consequently, every inspiration of air in such an atmosphere, must carry with it and lodge upon the lungs a portion of these pernicious ingredients: the result is, difficulty of breathing, asthma, &c.

On finding myself settled for life in the factories, as it was then pretty evident I should not be able to do anything else, I began to think of getting a step higher in the works. It will be necessary to observe, that hitherto I had only been a piecer; so I put myself forward as well as I was able, and master soon noticed me, and gave me a higher place, where the labour was not so very distressing, but the care and responsibility was greater; and although I was a complete cripple, I now began to feel a little more comfortable.

A great many are made cripples by over-exertion. Among those who have been brought up from infancy with me in the factories, and whom death has spared, few have escaped without some injury. My brother-in-law and myself have been crippled by this cause, but in different ways; my sister partly by over-exertion and partly by machinery. On going home to breakfast one morning, I was much surprised at seeing several of the neighbours and two doctors in our house. On inquiring the cause, I found that my second sister had nearly lost her hand in the machinery. She had been working all night, and, fatigued and sleepy, had not been so watchful as she otherwise would have been; and consequently, her right hand became entangled in the machine which she was attending. Four iron teeth of a wheel, three-quarters of an inch broad, and one-quarter of an inch thick, had been forced through her hand, from the back part, among the leaders, &c.; and the fifth iron tooth fell upon the thumb, and crushed it to atoms. It was thought, for some time, that she would lose her hand. But it was saved; and, as you may be sure, it is stiff and contracted, and is but a very feeble apology for a hand. This accident might have been prevented, if the wheels above referred to had been boxed off, which they might have been for a couple of shillings; and the very next week after this accident, a man had two fingers taken off his hand, by the very same wheels—and still they are not boxed off!

The gentlemen she was working for at the time had immense wealth, most of which, I have reason to believe, was got by the factories. They paid the doctor, and gave her ten shillings!—which was about three farthings per day for the time she was off work. To this sum was added seven shillings more, sub-scribed by the work-people! I need not say, that she has been a cripple ever since, and can do very little towards getting a living.

After the wool has been oiled, as before described, it is then put through the first teaser,* from which it

---

* The first teaser is a machine for breaking up the fleece wool, and consists of a very strong, firmly made cylinder, about 5 feet

is carried to the second teaser,* where it is prepared for the carding-engine. I had once a very narrow escape from death by this machine, when about 16 years of age, in the following manner:—

After finishing one sort of wool, it is usual to clean all the loose wool from the top and sides of the machine, previous to beginning another sort. This I was doing in the usual way, with a broom, and, as use begets habits of carelessness in boys, I had not used that degree of care requisite in such places. The consequence was, that the cylinder of the machine caught hold of the broom, and, if I had not had the presence of mind to let go my hold, I must have been dragged in with it. The broom was torn in a thousand

---

diameter, and 3 feet broad. Into the surface of this cylinder are firmly screwed a large quantity of iron spikes, about the size of a man's finger, in diagonal lines, about 2 or 3 inches apart from each other: in front of this cylinder are 2 rollers, called feeding rollers, about 8 inches in diameter, also filled with teeth of a different description. These rollers work into each other in such a manner as to hold the fleece of wool firmly between them, and as they revolve but slowly, they present the wool gradually to the teeth of the cylinder, which performs 400 or 500 revolutions per minute. The momentum of this cylinder in motion is very great, and the wool or anything which comes in its way is torn in pieces, and thrown out behind. When it is going at full speed, the machine, the floor, and everything around, are in a constant shake. It is called among the work-people the Devil, from its tearing off the arms, &c., of the workmen. I have known 3 arms torn off and 2 lives lost in consequence, in my time; and I must allow, that I have felt timid, when working at the very same machine that had a little while before been so employed.

* The second teaser is a more complicated machine than the first: it consists of a large cylinder and a number of rollers filled with teeth made of iron or steel, of the size and shape of a cock's spur, and thence called "cock-spurs". This teaser opens the wool more equally, and prepares it for the carding-engine: its capabilities of doing mischief to the work-people is nearly equal to that of the first teaser.

pieces—a great number of the iron teeth were broken out and scattered in all directions—and, by the care of a kind Providence, I came off with a few slight wounds, from these teeth having stuck into me in several places.

The wool is then handed forward from the second teaser to the carding-engine*, where it is prepared for the piecer; it was in this sort of engine my sister had her right hand so dreadfully lacerated.

When about 15 years of age, a circumstance occurred to me which does not often fall to the lot of factory children, and which had a great influence on my future life. I happened one day to find an old board laying useless in a corner of the factory. On this board, with a piece of chalk, I was scrawling out, as well as I was able, the initials of my name, instead of attending to my work, as I ought to have been doing. Having formed the letters W. D., I was laying down the board, and turning to my work, when, judge of my surprise, at perceiving one of my masters looking over my shoulder. Of course, I expected a scolding; but the half smile upon his countenance suddenly dispelled my fears. He kindly asked me several questions about my writing and reading, and, after gently chiding me for taking improper opportunities, he gave me two-pence to purchase paper, pens, and ink—which sum he continued weekly for several years, always inspecting

---

* The carding-engine may be briefly described as composed of 3 cylinders, from 4 to 5 feet diameter, 3 other cylinders, from 2 to 3 feet diameter, and from 20 to 30 rollers of different dimensions, all covered with cards. The wool is spread very equally upon cloths which carry it to the first cylinder, by which it is taken forward to the second, and so on till it comes out at the other end, in cardings ready for the piecer.

my humble endeavours, and suggesting any improvements which he thought necessary. He also (with the approbation of his brother, the other partner in the firm), allowed me to leave work an hour earlier than the other work-people every evening for a whole winter, in order that I might improve myself; and thus an opportunity was afforded me, which, with a few presents of books, &c. from both masters, were the means, under Providence, of laying the foundation of what I now consider a tolerable education.

This kindness on the part of my masters will never be erased from my memory. It is as fresh to me now as if it had occurred but yesterday.

With this encouragement, and impelled by the activity of my own mind, and an irresistible thirst after knowledge, I set myself earnestly to the acquisition of such branches of education as I thought might better my condition in after-life; and, although I had still my work to attend, I soon had the happiness to find myself in possession of a tolerable share of mathematics, geography, history, and several branches of natural and experimental philosophy.

So long as I was pursuing these studies, the thoughts of my unhappy condition were in some measure assuaged. But, in proportion as the truths of science were unfolded to my wondering sight, and the mists of ignorance chased from my mind, so the horrors of my situation became daily more and more apparent, and made me, if possible, still more fretful and unhappy! It was evident to me, that I was intended for a nobler purpose than to be a factory slave! and I longed for an opportunity to burst the trammels by which I was kept in bondage!

Being desirous of turning my newly-acquired

learning to some account, I engaged with a tailor, a neighbour of ours, to keep his books, draw out his bills, &c., in the evenings; by which means, I earned part of my clothing, and also got an insight into the trade, which was of service to me afterwards.

I became acquainted with a young man, who was very kind in lending me books, and explaining any difficulty I might be labouring under in my studies. I shall never forget his kindness—he was to me like a brother. And now that I began to derive pleasure from the perusal of books (and, in fact, it was the only source of pleasure I had) I did not omit any opportunity of gratifying it, particularly on the Sabbath day. It was customary for me, in the summer months, to take a book, and a crust of bread in my pocket, on a Sunday morning, and go to a very retired and secluded wood, about two miles from the town of Kendal, in which I lived, and there I spent the day alone, on the banks of a rivulet that ran through the wood. I have sat for hours together absorbed in study, unperceived by mortal eye, with nothing to disturb me, but the numerous little songsters that kept up a continual concert, as if to make the place still more enchanting to my imagination. These were seasons of real pleasure to me: they were also attended with some advantages in other respects.

I had for many years enjoyed but a delicate state of health owing to constant confinement, the smells of the factory, &c.; but these Sunday excursions got me a better appetite for my victuals, and I became more healthy and strong. I also derived considerable pleasure and improvement from the study of nature, in watching the habits of birds, bees, ants, butterflies, and, in short, any natural curiosity that came in my way; and when the evenings began to close in around me, and compelled me to return to the habitations of men, I felt a reluctance to leave my quiet and solitary retreat.

On some occasions, when I have been returning from my retreat in the wood on a Sunday evening, I have stood upon an eminence at a distance, and watched the gaily-attired inhabitants taking their evening walk in the fields and meadows around the town, and could not help contrasting their situation with mine. They were happy in themselves, anxious to see and be seen, and deriving pleasure from mutual friendship and intercourse: I, with the seeds of misery implanted in my nature, surrounded by circumstances calculated to make me truly unhappy—shrinking from the face of men to a lonely wood, to brood over my sorrows in secret and in silence. They were enjoying the fruits of their industry, but the reward of mine was—misery, wretchedness, and disease.

On one occasion, I was tempted to have recourse to a little of what the world calls policy, in order to gratify my appetite for reading, and which I knew at the time to be wrong. It was usual for us to stop the mill on the Saturday evening at five o'clock; then, after cleaning myself, I had a few hours to call my own, which were generally spent in my favourite occupation. One fine Saturday evening in June, I took a walk to the ruins of an old castle which overlooks the town of Kendal, and which was to me a very agreeable retreat from the noise and bustle of the factory, having previously laid out the only twopence I had in the loan of a book, which I had got snugly in my pocket, and was calculating on the pleasure it would afford me during the week. It chanced, however, to be one of those thinly-printed volumes with large margins; and seating myself on the above-mentioned ruins, I did not rise till I had finished it: when I did, the grey of the evening was fast closing in around me. But I had exhausted my whole week's stock of amusement. What was to be done? I could not think of borrowing two-pence for another volume, because I had no means of paying it back again. At last I hit upon a plan, which, after a little hesitation, I carried into effect. I took the volume back to the librarian, and requested him to change it for another, telling him it did not suit me. He, being a good-natured sort of man, did so, little thinking that I had read it through. I felt ashamed, and for a long time after could scarcely look in the man's face, but I made it up to him in another way, when I had it in my power.

But having completed my second seven years of servitude (somewhat earlier, indeed, than it is usual for work-men to have finished their first), I got advanced to 9s. per week, and began to think myself well-to-do in the world, and could, by following a rigid course of economy, spare a shilling or two occasionally for the purchase of such books as I took a fancy to. I kept an account of every item of expenditure, and regularly balanced up once a month: and, though it may surprise many, my expenses for board, lodging, and washing, over a space of three years, averaged exactly 7s. per week: so that I had 2s. a week left for clothes and books; and being a member of the Mechanics' Institute, I became acquainted with the librarian, who engaged me to assist him in giving out books two evenings in the week, which added a little to my resources.

When I came to that period of life when men generally think of taking a partner, and settling in some way in the world, I was again beset by insurmountable obstacles. I saw my more fortunate fellow workmen getting married, and settling around me—I saw them comfortable and happy in their families, and I almost envied them their happiness. But no remedy was at hand: to have married a factory girl, would only have involved both myself and her in greater troubles, I being a cripple; and it would have been something remarkable, if I could have met with one able to make a shirt. How could it be expected from those who had been so wretchedly treated?—who were sent into this world to be the comfort and solace of man, and who, had their faculties been allowed to develope under a more genial sun, might have been the pride and ornament of the age in which they lived. But how different is the sad reality! They have been kept as slaves at one toilsome task, till every fine feeling of their nature is blunted. Ignorant of everything calculated to elevate and raise them to that high station originally intended for them by their Creator, is it to be wondered at, if we find them sunk, degraded, and almost lost to every sense of shame?* and for me to have looked for a partner in another class of society, situated as I then was, would have been ridiculous in the extreme.

To turn my thoughts from my pitiful situation, I attended lectures on various subjects, repeated the

---

* I have seen some young women brought to work in the factories, who had been nurses in respectable families, and who seemed to be shocked, on their introduction, with what they heard and saw; but a very short time in such a school made them as bad as the rest.

simple experiments at home, made some curious models and drawings of machines, and could thus contrive to pass away my leisure time pleasantly. Besides, one of my sisters dying, left a son; and her husband being unable to provide for him, it was a source of pleasure and gratification for me to attend to his wants and improvement.

Although I was not, at this time, constantly employed within the mills, but had to attend to the packing department in the warehouse, and any other place about the works where I might be required, yet still the effects of former years of factory toil were on me—still my life was one of suffering, although not to so great a degree; and having it now in my power to procure comforts which before were unknown to me, I lived something more like a Christian than I had formerly been enabled to do.

Thinking I might stand in need of assistance at some future period of my life, as I had all along been obliged to prop myself up, and was evidently working above my strength, I joined. the Society of Odd Fellows, which is the best of this description that I am acquainted with: but it is not without its faults. In this Society I was soon put into office; and, having an active and persevering mind, I put myself forward, and was elected as the Secretary of the Lodge to which I belonged. On that occasion, I well remember. I had to address, for the first time in my life, a large body of men. I felt rather timid; but having practised in my room for a full hour, I delivered my maiden speech, which still remains fixed on my memory, as follows:

"Mr. Chairman and Gentlemen,—I now stand before you as a candidate for the important office of

Secretary—an office which, I am well aware, requires not only talent and abilities, but also great care and attention—(hear, hear); and although I can say nothing in favour of my humble abilities, having received no other education than what I have been able to scrape together after my day's work was done, still I trust that the interest I feel for the good and welfare of this Society, will stimulate me to use every exertion in my power in the discharge of the several duties of this office, should I be thought worthy of holding it. As I am convinced that you will act in this, as in all other matters, solely for the good of the Society, so I can assure you, that I shall be satisfied with your decision, whether it be for or against me."

There were five candidates for the office; and this was the state of the poll, as taken from the minute-book:—

William Dodd	64
W. S.	4
J. D.	4
J. B.	4
J. M.	4
	80

The other candidates thought I should have the lead, but each expressed a wish to be second. The result proved they were all second. These four members were tradesmen's sons, who had received a good education—I a factory cripple, who had never cost my parents a shilling for my learning. I was elected a second time to this office, and had, in 12 months, about 300*l.* of the Society's money through my fingers. I then received a vote of thanks, and was elected to a higher office. In the year 1835, I was elected to represent the district, a body of 700 men, in the annual meeting of the Society held that year at Derby; and in 1836 I was again thought worthy of a seat in that important meeting held in London. I shall have to speak of this Society again.

An easy clerk's situation being now vacant, I was advised by some friends to avail myself of the opportunity, and thus free myself totally from the factories, especially as I had several influential friends to forward my views. I mentioned the subject to my masters, and, after considering it, they made such advantageous offers, as induced me to remain with them. This step I shall have reason to regret as long as I live.

In 1834, the present law for the regulation of factories was about being put in force. I, being appointed timekeeper for the works, had to take the children before the doctor to be examined, as certificates were required from him, that they were of proper age to be admitted into the factory. I cannot describe my feelings as I went on those occasions, accompanied by about a score of little stunted figures, some of whom had been working in the factories for years, and whose parents had been in vain trying to get them something else to do; but I well remember, that I had great difficulty in convincing the doctor of their being of the age required, although I had no doubt of it myself, as I was well acquainted with their parents at the time of the children's birth; but their appearance was so much against them, that I fancied on some occasions, from certain expressions that the doctor made use of, that he thought I was deceiving him. Had he known my inmost thoughts, he would not for a moment have suspected me.

One of the most trying circumstances that occurred to me in all my factory experience, happened in the winter of 1834–5. I had then a youth, of about 17 years of age, placed under me, for the purpose of learning some of the higher branches of the business. I had been giving him directions what to do one day, and had gone up into the room above, for the purpose of superintending some other part of the works, when suddenly one branch of the machinery stopped, and, on turning round to inquire the cause, I was met by several persons, nearly out of breath, who said to me, "Tom has got into the gig, and is killed". I ran down in haste, but it was too true; he was strangled. A great many bones were broken, and several ghastly wounds were inflicted on various parts of his person!

After his mangled body was extracted from the machinery, by unscrewing and taking the machine in pieces, it was laid in a recess on the ground-floor, the same in which the accident occurred, to await a coroner's inquest, the works being all stopped, and the hands dismissed. One by one they gradually went home, and left me alone for some time. The reader may more easily imagine, than I can describe my feelings on this occasion, as I paced, with folded arms, the flags of this dreary place. It was a cold, wet night. I had a flickering light burning beside me, just sufficient to cast a sombre and gloomy appearance over the three water-wheels and the heavy machinery by which I was surrounded. Not a sound broke upon my ear, except the wind and rain without, and the water trickling through the wheels within, with the mangled remains of that youth, whom I had carefully instructed in his business, and looked upon almost like a son, laying bleeding beside me.

This boy's death occurred partly through his own carelessness, as he had no business at the place; but the same thing might have happened to people who had business there; and consequently, it shows the necessity of boxing up all parts of machines, and the gearing by which such machines are propelled, where there is the least appearance of danger. Had this precaution been adopted in every mill, such calamities could not have happened: and, in many thousands of cases, limbs and lives which have been lost would have been preserved.

If anything was wanted to make me disgusted with the system, this and other circumstances would have supplied the deficiency; for while I and hundreds of work-people were toiling and sweating day after day for the bare necessaries of life—struggling, as it were, against wind and tide, and still hoping that some favourable turn would afford a resting-place for our wearied and emaciated frames—the manufacturers were amassing immense wealth, and thus converting what ought to have been a national blessing into a national curse—"adding field to field, and house to house", and rolling about in their carriages, surrounded by every luxury that this world can give, and looking upon us poor factory slaves as if we had been a different race of beings, created only to be worked to death for their gain.

As there is (*sic*) various reports respecting the wages of factory labourers, I here subjoin a table of the money received by me from 1810 to the close of my factory experience:—

Age		Weekly Wages						Yearly Amount		
		s.	d.	s.	d.	s.	d.	£	s.	d.
6 to	7*	1	0 ..	1	3 ..	1	6	2	5	0
7	8			1	6 ..	1	9	4	4	6
8	9					2	3	5	17	0
9	10					2	6	6	10	0
10	11					2	6	6	10	0
11	12					2	8	6	18	8
12	13					2	10	7	7	4
13	14					3	0	7	16	0
14	15					3	6	9	2	0
15	16					4	0	10	8	0
16	17					5	0	13	0	0
17	18					6	0	15	12	0
18	19					7	0	18	4	0
19	20					8	0	20	16	0
20	21					9	0	23	8	0
21	22					10	0	26	0	0
22	23					11	0	28	12	0
23	24					11	0	28	12	0
24	25					12	0	31	4	0
25	26					12	0	31	4	0
26	27					13	6	35	2	0
27	28					13	6	35	2	0
28	29					15	0	39	0	0
29	30					15	0	39	0	0
30	31					17	0	44	4	0
31	32					17	0	44	4	0
Done up								540	2	6
* Part of this year was occupied in card making.		Overtime -						9	17	6
								550	0	0

Average about 8s. 3d.

It cannot, with truth or justice, be said that I was an idle workman, or an indifferent hand at my business. I have documents from my master to prove that I was not idle; and the fact of my having been

selected from a number of workmen to attend improved and expensive machinery for finishing cloths,
with which machinery I was doing as much work as
six men by hand, and where I was obliged to lock
myself in the room alone, and not allow any one to
enter but my master, and sometimes an assistant,
(in this manner I have worked for many years),
affords a sufficient proof that I thoroughly understood my business. Besides, the latter part of my time
I was a confidential servant, and in this capacity had
to receive and pay money, occasionally attending the
post office and bank with letters, bills, &c., and have
had frequently upwards of 1,000l. passing through
my hands in a week. At this time I was receiving 3s.
or 4s. a week more than many strong, able-bodied
men, which would not have been the case, if I had
not been considered worthy of it. This will at once
prove that I was receiving as much, or more, than
the generality of workmen; and that this table is by
no means to be considered an under rate of wages. It
is, at least, 70l. or 80l. more than my brother-in-law
has received in the same time.

From the first day I went into the factories, till the
time that I left, my lost time, in sickness, holidays,
&c., amounted to about four months. This lost time I
have worked up at least three times over. When we
were busy, I have worked as many as 18 hours per
day; and yet all I have received, whether as wages,
over-time, perquisites, &c., does not amount, as the
preceding table will show, to more than 550l.; and for
this paltry sum I have sacrificed my health, strength,
constitution, nay, almost life itself; while those who
have been reaping the benefit of my labours, have
been laying by their thousands yearly and every year,

and are now wallowing in riches, but nothing awaits me except the workhouse.

Let us see, on the other hand, what would have been the result, had I been brought up to a trade—say a carpenter and joiner, for instance. In that case I should have contracted a considerable debt before I began to receive any benefit—say 50*l*., for apprentice fee, tools, and clothes, the master finding, as is usual, meat and lodging: then, at 21 years of age, it is reasonable to suppose I should have been a free man, with a good robust form and constitution; and supposing I had earned 1*l*. per week for 20 years, 15*s*. per week for 10 years, and 12*s*. per week for 9 years more, (which, I think, is a reasonable estimate), this would have brought me to 60 years of age, beyond which no man, in my opinion, ought to work. At this rate, I should have earned, as a journeyman, 1,710*l*. 16*s*.; then, deducting 160*l*. 16*s*. for the repayment of apprentice fee, tools, and any other incidental expenses, it would leave 1,550*l*., which is 1,000*l*. more than I have earned in the factories; and, instead of being subject to daily and excruciating pains, I might have passed through life in comparative comfort, might with confidence have encountered the expenses of a wife and family, enjoyed the evening of my days surrounded by a smiling offspring, and sunk into the grave at peace with myself and all the world. But how different is the picture of my sad fate!

The way in which the bones in the legs become distorted, I mentioned in a former page: I shall here say a few words upon the shapes they assume. The most common is that of in-kneed cripples, generally the right knee, sometimes the left, frequently both, as my own. In this case, when standing in the easiest

position, the feet are about 14 inches apart, the knees
and thighs are then pressing close together, so that
the legs form a sort of arch for the support of the
body. On taking a side view of a person standing so,
he appears in the act of kneeling, about half way
down; the outsides of the feet or abutments of the
arch are flat and burst open the shoes, the centre of
gravity crossing the thigh and leg bones. Another
shape is that furnished by an acquaintance of mine,
of the name of Hutton, near Bradford, in Yorkshire,
whom I met with in London, a short time ago, and
who was put into the factories about the same time
as myself, perfectly straight and strong. This man's
legs are both turned one way—the right knee in, and
the left knee out; so that the legs and thighs are
parallel throughout, but forming an angle of about
60 degrees. He is almost frightful to look upon. A
brother of his, who was also straight on entering, is
still worse. His legs are curved *both outwards*, so that
a person may run a wheel-barrow between them.
These are some of the most common shapes, but there
are others equally bad.

One evil arising from the bending and curving of
the legs is the state of the blood-vessels; for if the
bones go wrong, the blood-vessels must go wrong also.
Nature has provided a beautiful contrivance for
propelling the blood to every part of the human
frame. This is done, in a well-formed person, with
perfect ease, without any appearance of difficulty
whatever. But it is not so with us factory cripples.
Our blood lodges, as it were, in little pools, in crannies
and corners; and the apparatus for forcing it along,
instead of being stronger, as in our case required, it is
actually weaker, in consequence of our weak state of

body. Thus, our very life (for life depends upon the circulation of the blood), at best, is only like the half-extinguished flame of a gas-burner, when there is water in the pipes—it jumps and flickers for a little while, and then pops out. But in order to keep it even in this state, we are obliged to have recourse to friction daily, and every day.

One serious evil resulting from this imperfect circulation of the blood, is the drying up of the marrow in the bones. The bones then decay, as in my arm; amputation is resorted to, or life is lost.

A variety of shapes is also visible in the curvature of the spine of factory cripples.

With respect to cripples who have been made so by over-exertion, it is usual for manufacturers to throw the blame entirely upon the parents of such children. How they can divest themselves of all blame, appears to me parodoxical. I cannot look upon them in any other light than as accessaries to the mischief, especially when it is considered that the several cases of distortion of the spine, contraction and other deformities of the limbs, &c., did not take place all in a minute, but that they were coming gradually on for years, and immediately under the eye of the manufacturers, who, by a single word, might have dismissed them from the place, and thus have saved them from utter ruin.

There are a great variety of cripples made by machinery. The most common are those wanting arms and legs, or whose arms and legs have been crushed or torn, and rendered useless.

A fine young girl is now laying under the hands of the doctor, from an accident in the same mill as my sister had her hand torn in. She, poor girl, has had *her leg torn off, both her thigh-bones broken,* and also received several internal and external injuries. Accidents by machinery in the North are of weekly, nay, almost daily occurrence.

A list of physicians' cases would be too long for me to furnish here.

Looking over, in my mind's eye, those boys and girls who were employed in the factories when I commenced, and who, like me, have been kept close to it from their youth upwards, I find they are generally weak, stunted, and in many cases deformed in person, childish, and ignorant in mind, not having been accustomed to some of the most important duties of life (their whole faculties have been absorbed in the daily routine of factory labour), they make, as it is very natural to suppose, but "sorry" heads of families; and their children, as a matter of course, are compelled, by dire necessity, to pass through the same dull, tedious, miserable state of existence.

Spinners suffer considerably. Some of my former masters have died, with every symptom of premature old age upon them, at 45 to 50. The overlooker has no very enviable berth. He has to study the interest of the master, the men, and his own. His own is usually consulted by having a general shop, where the work-people can lay out their money, and by lending small sums, with the understanding to receive interest after the modest rate of 65 per centum per annum, which I have paid. Yet some of them deserve all they get: they are generally ill-paid for their harassing duties. The baneful influence of the system extends even to the manufacturers themselves. As an instance, I may mention the case of the kind master who encouraged me to read and write, and whom, from long service, I looked upon with as much respect and love as if he had been my father. On some occasions when I have been in the counting-house with him, and especially after an unsuccessful journey—when some other manufacturer has been selling goods cheaper than he was—I have fancied I could see the canker-worm, care, corroding and eating into his very existence. The last time I had an opportunity of seeing this gentleman was on the 19th of May, 1840, in St. Martin's-le-Grand. He was with another gentleman, who I took, in the distance, to be his brother. I was on my way to the hospital, with my arm in a sling— that arm I was so soon to lose. He was an exception to the general character of the manufacturers. He died shortly after; and it is my opinion, that had he not been connected with the factories, he might have protracted his existence to a later date.

About two or three years before I left the factories, my mother being then on her death-bed, I thought it was time to look about me for a partner; and being then in comfortable circumstances, on good terms with my master, and everything appearing fair, I almost forgot I was a cripple, and began to look about me for a steady servant girl, on whom I could depend. I had no difficulty in finding one to my mind, and occasionally accompanied her to church and other places. People began to pass remarks; and even my masters spoke of my being about to marry, and were divided in opinion. One said he thought I should not, considering the state I was in—the other said I might do very well. However, the girl was too wise to join her destinies with those of a factory cripple. She left the town, and refused to answer my letters, which was a sufficient reason for my discontinuing to write.

Then I got acquainted with another respectable girl. She also soon left the town, but continued to correspond with me for some time, without signing her name. She soon broke off.

So I thought that I would go to work in another way; and in order to afford a convincing proof that I really did wish to get married, I took a house, and had it well furnished. I then laid siege to a third, and made myself quite sure—there could be no mistake about the matter this time: and as I had heard that after a certain age women would take up with anything, I thought I would try one older than myself. So I paid my addresses to a respectable housekeeper, who had known me for years, and who, apparently, was pleased with my attentions. She would walk with me to church, to a place of amusement, to her relations to take tea, in the fields, or anywhere but to the trap that I had baited for her. So I began to think old birds were not to be caught with chaff. However, I did not like the idea of giving up to be laughed at, so I persevered, and pressed my suit more warmly, but soon found that she was only playing with me, like a cat with a mouse.

One evening, being almost driven to desperation, I went with a determination to have a final answer before we parted. I got half way to her place of residence, and was about to return, in consequence of the moon at that time shining out, and showing my figure before me. However, I went into a public-house, had a glass of ale, and, thus inspired, went on again. When I got there, I was kindly received, as usual; so I made my business known as well as I

could, and gave her to understand that I was
determined to have an answer. She patiently heard
all I had got to say; and I watched every muscle of
her countenance, as if my very existence had depended upon her answer. I saw a slight curl of the
upper lip—her eyes then began to descend, till they
settled the intensity of their gaze upon my knees.
At that moment, I wished the earth to open and
swallow me up. She, seeing me agitated, took compassion, and told me, what she might have told me at
first, she declined. Thus was I compelled either to
return and take a factory girl (any of whom would
have thought themselves highly honoured by the
offer), or live and die a bachelor. I chose the latter as
the most preferable.

I have done everything that laid in my power to
prevent the evils that have come upon me, and to
avert the consequences of those evils I could not
prevent, by endeavouring to transplant myself into a
more genial soil; but all my exertions have proved
fruitless. Wherever I turned for succour, wherever I
looked for sympathy or kindly feeling, I was met by
repulses, derision, and insult; and this because I was
a factory cripple, and aspired to associate with those
whom I considered in a more respectable sphere of
life. The best feelings of my heart were played with,
wounded, crushed, and trampled on; and ultimately,
I was driven back, like the daw in the fable, stripped
of every feather, to the miserable squad from which
I attempted to emigrate, there to encounter the
sneers and the buffets of my fellow slaves.

Having now resolved to lead a bachelor's life, for
the best of all reasons, not being able to avoid it, I
contrived many little helps to make myself as com-

fortable as I could. I got some self-acting cooking utensils, by means of which I was able to get a warm dinner at the expense of one farthing. So long as the fine warm weather lasted, this Robinson Crusoe sort of life did very well; but when winter came, and I had no fire to go to, and very often wet and cold, it was too much for me to bear. Besides, I had not been able to forget my fair teaser; and giving way under the difficulty, I tried to drown my cares in drink. This only made bad worse, and got me into errors, besides wasting my money; so I resolved to give up my house, sell my furniture, and go to lodgings: and thus terminated my fruitless endeavour to get married.

I now turned my attention again to getting totally away from the factories; and getting acquainted with Mr. Hill, schoolmaster of the British and Foreign School in Kendal, and being informed by that genᵗle-man of the advantages held out to young men by the Society in the Borough Road to become teachers, I was inclined to think it might suit me to come and be instructed. This gentleman kindly undertook to apply for me, describing minutely my person. He received for answer, they were sorry to inform him, that in consequence of being a cripple, I could not be admitted. I applied to other schools in the same way, and received the same answer. My masters, partly to encourage me, established a night school for the piecers, and I attended two evenings in the week, and thus drilled myself into teaching. I had a twelve-month's practice in this way. We could scarcely keep the piecers awake, they were so done up. Sometimes they would fall off the form on to the floor, quite overcome with sleep.

Being weary of the factories, and having prepared

myself, as well as I was able, I opened a school in the early part of the year 1837, for the instruction of youth in reading, writing, and arithmetic; in hopes by this means to avert the impending danger that had so long threatened me. But I had not been in it long before the school-room was wanted by the proprietor, and, not meeting with another to suit me, I came up to London to the annual meeting of Odd Fellows, as before mentioned.

While in London, I thought I would try to procure a situation as clerk, and was encouraged in this idea by a distant relation, a licensed victualler, who kindly offered to take me into his bar till I succeeded in my wish. I accepted the offer. A few months after, an opportunity presented itself. It being necessary to write to my old masters for a character, I did so, and received the following answer:—

"Kendal, 10 mo., 6th, 1837.
"William Dodd, to whom we direct this, was in our employ for many years, and during that time was a trustworthy servant. We can give him a good character for sobriety and industry. He was in our employ as a warehouseman and packer, with some attention to the books.
"ISAAC AND WILLIAM WILSON."
"P.S.—W. D. left our situation about nine months ago."

The gentleman I was with, as barman, took a liking to me, and wanted to retain me in his service; but it being a line of life unsuitable for me, I was anxious to leave it as soon as possible, but not having any friend in London but him, I did not like to leave contrary to his wish. In his house I remained nearly 12 months, when I was taken ill, and had to go to Gravesend for the benefit of my health; and after five weeks' absence I again returned, and was in his service seven months longer. He then sold off part of his business, and had no more occasion for my services, but kindly allowed me to stay with him a few weeks; and as nobody would give me any work to do, I resolved to go into the west and south of England to seek employment. But very little employment was then to be met with for able-bodied men; as for cripples it was out of the question. Thus I travelled some hundreds of miles, sometimes riding a little, but generally walking: I also crossed over to the Isle of Wight, and visited all the places likely to afford me any employment, and could have got work if I had been a tailor or shoemaker, but not being either, and no chance of anything else turning up, I retraced my steps to London, having paid the last two-pence I had in the world to the boatman at Portsmouth.

While I was in the public line in London, I had to deal with all sorts of people, from the lowest to the highest. I heard all sorts of coarse brutal expressions; but in all that time, I never heard anything more vulgar, brutal, or wicked, than I was accustomed to hear from the master-manúfacturers, in my younger days—from men too who had received a liberal education, and who were called to fill the highest office in the town, and who, from their superior station in life, ought to have set an example worthy of imitating. The men eagerly followed the example set them by the masters, and cursing, swearing, and low language became the order of the day. Respecting the moral conduct of the young, I can say but little;

any one may think for himself what will be the result
of 100 young people of both sexes working together
under such circumstances, going together in the
morning, associating with each other through the
day, and returning again in the evening with no
moral restraint upon their action, no pattern shewn
them worthy of imitating; and where acts of gross
indecency, low, vulgar, brutal language, singing
immoral songs, swearing, &c. are not only tolerated,
but in many instances, actually countenanced and
encouraged. A person brought up from infancy to
maturity in such a school, and who can then retire
with clean hands, or a clear conscience, must possess
something more in his composition than human
nature can boast of—must be such an one as I never
yet met with, such an one as I am sure does not exist.*

In my travels through the country in search of
employment, I had frequent opportunity of witnessing the condition of the labourers in agricultural
districts, I conversed with many who received only
8s. or 9s. per week as wages, who were surrounded by
more real comforts than many of my class with several
shillings per week more. This may be accounted for
by the fact that 8s. in the hands of an agricultural
labourer, is at all times equal to 10s. or 11s. in the
hands of a manufacturing labourer: and this does not
arise from any carelessness or extravagance on the
part of the latter. For instance, an agricultural
labourer enjoys many privileges and advantages that
the other knows nothing of—such as an allowance of
potatoes, turnips, and other vegetables, and in many

---

* The scenes which I have witnessed, and it is with sorrow I say
have in some instances been participator in, are of such a nature,
as to be improper to lay before the public eye.

cases wood for the fire; his rent is also considerably lower; he also enjoys the blessings of breathing the pure air. Now, the manufacturing labourer cannot eat his machines or anything he may be making; and in consequence of inhaling the pernicious ingredients from the atmosphere in which he moves, and the nauseous smells by which he is surrounded, he cannot eat his food with a relish, and he is occasionally obliged to have recourse to medicine; and should he have any cripples in the family (which is generally the case), he must have a supply of flannel and linen bandages, oils, drugs, &c. constantly by him; and these little things form a considerable item in his expenditure. In all my experience, I do not remember ever to have been three months at one time free from bandages; and I have worked for weeks together with three or four of my joints thus secured.

The behaviour of agricultural labourers and their children is much superior to anything we meet with in manufacturing towns; and I have no doubt many of my readers will have noticed this in travelling through the country. This is easily accounted for. They are surrounded by circumstances so totally different, that there is no wonder at it. In the first place, the society around them is more polished and enlightened: in their daily toil they meet with so many instances of the wisdom and power of an all-wise being, that a love for his handiworks is sure to be impressed upon their mind;—the cheering influence of the sun, the refreshing breeze, the singing of birds, &c., all inspire this feeling. The manufacturing labourer knows nothing of these blessings by experience. He is placed in a mill or factory as a machine, for the performance of a quantity of labour—he hears nothing but the rumbling noise of the machinery, or the harsh voice of the overlooker—sees nothing but an endless variety of shafts, drums, straps, and wheels in motion; and though these may, at first, inspire him with a feeling of respect for, and admiration of, the inventive powers of his fellow-creatures, yet this feeling will vanish, when he reflects on their power to destroy or render useless for life that exalted piece of mechanism formed by and after the image of God!

I was forcibly struck with the kind behaviour of the agricultural labourers to me. The manner in which the family generally met together in the evening, brought to my mind the following beautiful description of a cottager's Saturday night, by Burns:—

"At length his lonely cot appears in view,
    Beneath the shelter of an aged tree;
Th' expectant *wee-things*, toddlin, stacher through
    To meet their Dad, wi' flichterin noise and glee.
His wee-bit ingle, blinkin bonnilie,
    His clean hearthstane, his thrifty *wifie's* smile,
The lisping infant prattling on his knee,
    Does a' his weary carking cares beguile,
And makes him quite forget his labour and his toil.

"Belyve the elder bairns come drapping in,
    At service out amang the farmers roun';
Some ca' the pleugh, some herd, some tentie rin
    A cannie errand to a neebor town;
Their eldest hope, their *Jenny*, woman grown,
    In youthfu' bloom, love sparklin in her ee,
Comes hame, perhaps, to show a braw new gown,
    Or deposite her sair-won penny fee,
To help her parents dear, if they in hardship be.

"Wi' joy unfeign'd brothers and sisters meet,
    And each for other's weelfare kindly spiers:

The social hours, swift-wing'd, unnotic'd fleet;
  Each tells the uncos that he sees or hears;
The parents, partial, ee their hopefu' years:
  Anticipation forward points the view:
The *Mother*, wi' her needle and her sheers,
  Gars auld claes look amaist as weel's the new;
The *Father* mixes a' wi' admonition due.

"Their master's and their mistress's command
  The younkers a' are warned to obey;
And mind their labours wi' an eydent hand,
  And ne'er, though out o' sight, to jauk or play;
'And, O! be sure to fear the LORD alway!
  And mind your *duty* duly morn and night!
Lest in temptation's path ye gang astray,
  Implore his counsel and assisting might:
They never sought in vain that sought the LORD aright'."

All who have been in a manufacturing town, will
recollect the disgusting scenes that are to be witnessed there on a Saturday night.

On Sunday I was much pleased at witnessing the
clean, decent, sober, and orderly appearance of the
inhabitants of the rural districts, and to see the
neighbouring gentry attending the church, preceded
or followed by their servants. This was so very
different from anything I had been accustomed to
before, that it made a lasting impression on my mind.

In a manufacturing town, some, from exhaustion,
prefer laying in bed—others are obliged to lay there
while the wife washes their clothes; some are strolling
about the streets or fields in their working dress, not
daring to go to church, for fear of falling asleep;
while those who wish to go, and would go if they
could, are compelled to labour two or three hours,
and getting heated, they must have a glass or two of
ale at a public-house to finish with.

The manufacturer and their families attend their place of worship, and wish to be considered patterns of religion and piety; but their pretences and their works are so widely different, that this cloak is easily seen through; for while they are attending meetings for the abolition of slavery, and the propagation of the Scriptures in foreign parts, they are compelling their servants, under fear of losing their situations, to be slaves, and to break the sacred commands of God, at home, even in defiance of the threats of the better sort of the inhabitants, and the public press; and this, too, without fee or reward.

From Portsmouth I came to London. My spirits getting heavier, and my bundle lighter at every stage, and not being able to meet with employment, I suffered considerably from want, visiting any place where I could get a mouthful to eat, and sometimes obliged to walk the streets by night, not being able to pay for a lodging—occasionally resting myself by sitting on the benches in Covent Garden Market, or stretching my weary limbs in the recesses of Westminster Bridge. When in this latter place, I was awoke one morning about two o'clock by the policeman on duty, and obliged to move on, cold, tired, and hungry, I dragged myself along, not knowing or caring where I went, with the dark lowering sky above, and the angry foaming billows beneath; and heaven only knows what would have been the consequence at that critical moment, had I not been sustained by that power which had protected me through all my difficulties.

Soon after this, there was a gentleman wanting a man to improve himself as a tailor and draper; and thinking, from the little knowledge I had acquired in the business at Kendal, and the lameness of my knees, that it would be a suitable situation for me, I applied, and was engaged for three years. For the first twelve months I got on very well; and being desirous to gather a connexion of my own against the time I should begin for myself, I took in little jobs on my own account, which privilege my master allowed me. This brought me in a little money, and was paving the way to a business in future; but I did not then consider that I was over-exerting myself, as I had my own work to do, after my day's work for my master was over, and when I ought to have been in bed.

In the spring of 1840, I began to feel some painful symptoms in my right wrist, arising from the general weakness of my joints, brought on in the factories. At first I was not alarmed at it, as I had occasionally felt similar painful sensations in all my joints for years previous to leaving the factories, and which had always gone off, by taking rest for a day or two, rubbing them with liniment, and wrapping them in warm flannel. But, this time, it resisted all my endeavours to restore strength, the swelling and pain increased; and although I had the advice of some of the most eminent medical practitioners, it was all to no purpose; and, having been off work for a length of time, and my resources failing, I was under the necessity of entering St. Thomas's Hospital, where I remained for upwards of six months; and where every care and attention was paid me, and every expedient tried, that skill and experience could suggest, but with no better success than before. The wrist at this time measured twelve inches round,—and I was worn down to a mere skeleton, not being able to sleep night nor day, except for very short periods, and generally starting up from pain.

It now became pretty evident to all who saw me, that I must, very soon, lose either my hand or my life. A consultation was held by the surgeons of the hospital, who came to the conclusion, that amputation was absolutely necessary; and the result proved their decision to be correct. They gave me a reasonable time to think the matter over—and I decided upon taking their advice.

On the 18th of July, I underwent the operation. The hand being taken off a little below the elbow, in order to clear the affected part of the bone; and thus, another plan to raise myself above want, and keep myself from the workhouse, was frustrated and dashed to the ground! On dissection, the bones of the fore-arm presented a very curious appearance—something similar to an empty honeycomb, the marrow also having totally disappeared; thus accounting at once for the weakness and pain I had occasionally felt in this arm for years, and which, without doubt, may be clearly traced to the same cause as the rest of my sufferings—viz. the factory system.

By the blessing of God, and under the care and attendance of the surgeons and nurses of the hospital, to whom I would ever hope to be thankful, I was restored to tolerable health, and was discharged on the 24th of November, 1840.

It will be necessary here to observe, that in consequence of not being able to meet with employment, I had not paid my contribution-money to the Society of Odd Fellows, and hoping for better days, I did not (as I ought to have done) make my case known; and according to the rules, that I had assisted to make at the annual meeting, I ceased to be a member; however, it is but justice to say, that the members in London behaved very kindly to me.

Having applied to my late master for a certificate of character, I received the following:—

"The bearer, William Dodd, has been in my employ for twelve months, during which time he conducted himself in a sober, honest, and industrious manner; and I should have taken him again into my service, but for the misfortune of losing his hand, which renders him totally unfit for my business. Given by me this 26th day of November, 1840.

"JOHN KIRBY.

"No. 2, Oldham Place, Bagnige Wells Road, London."

Figure for yourself, dear reader, my deplorable situation at that time—just leaving the hospital, after a residence of six months within its walls, having lost the best part of my right arm!—a cripple in my limbs!—without a home!—without friends!—and with only 8s. in money!—in a strange place, and nearly 300 miles from the place to which I belong!— and, in this condition, to brave the horrors of a severe winter! and provide myself a living in an unthinking and unfeeling world! But I put my trust in the Lord, and He has not forsaken me—He has provided me a shelter from the blast, and a crust to satisfy the cravings of nature.

In reading the history of some eastern nations, we find accounts of children having been tied in open baskets to the tops of trees, and there left exposed, an offering to their Gods, till the birds had eaten their flesh from their bones; and of others having been thrown into the Ganges, and there having found a watery grave—and eagerly, in our exalted ideas of civilization, denounce them as barbarians who could be guilty of such cruelties! But how much better would if have been for me, if I had had the good fortune to have been so sacrificed in my infancy, rather than have been put to daily torture for upwards of a quarter of a century, and *with the certainty of my miseries still continuing, till my feeble frame sinks beneath its load!*

Think not, dear reader, that I have here drawn an exaggerated picture of a factory life:—it would be well for me if it could be proved that I am wrong—if, instead of being a miserable cripple, scarcely the shadow of a man, it could be proved that I am straight, strong, and hardy as when I entered the factories. But as I feel convinced that this is not possible, it may be well here to say, that I am prepared to prove myself right; and that I shall not hesitate (if required) to wait upon any individual or party, for the purpose of discussing, explaining, illustrating, or proving any of the preceding statements; and further, that I do not shrink from any investigation, but court inquiry.

I would draw the attention of every person who can feel for the miseries of his fellow creatures, to this important subject; and after convincing him of the reality, and the great extent of country over which these evils prevail, ask the following question:—

Is it consistent with the character of this enlightened, Christian country, which has furnished such a proof of her benevolence and charity, in granting 20 millions of money for the abolition of slavery abroad, that we, who have exerted every means in our power in the production of the wealth of the nation, and have therein sacrificed everything valuable in life, that we, worn-out, cast-off cripples of the manufacturers, should be left to perish and die of want at home?—Forbid it, Heaven.

And to you, my fellow sufferers, I would say a word in conclusion. We read in the Scriptures, that God formed man of the dust of the earth, after his own image, breathed into him the breath of life, and endowed him with wonderful powers and faculties; and though these powers and faculties have, in our frames, been injured, rendered nearly useless, and, in many instances, almost destroyed, by our cruel task-masters, yet there still remains that vital principal, over which these earthly tyrants have no power, excepting so far as their evil example extends. It will therefore be our interest to endeavour, by every means in our power, to secure to ourselves this only source of happiness that is left us: and this can only be done by attending to the precepts of the Scriptures. Let us, then, duly appreciate the value of those blessings we do and may enjoy:—let us look abroad and examine the works of our Creator, and we shall soon learn to admire his wisdom, and tremble at his power. We shall learn to despise the riches and pageantry of this perishing scene of things, and fix our hopes on those which are permament and worth our care—to tread with patience the rugged paths of virtue, which will at length conduct us to the happy mansions of eternal repose.

23, *Little Gray's Inn Lane,*
    June 18, 1841.

For Product Safety Concerns and Information please contact our EU
representative GPSR@taylorandfrancis.com
Taylor & Francis Verlag GmbH, Kaufingerstraße 24, 80331 München, Germany

www.ingramcontent.com/pod-product-compliance
Ingram Content Group UK Ltd.
Pitfield, Milton Keynes, MK11 3LW, UK
UKHW021824240425
457818UK00006B/64

* 9 780367 177843 *